D1445132

F
548.52    Sullivan, Frank.
.D35
S84       Legend
1989

$17.95                              Cop. 1

| DATE | | | |
|------|--|--|--|
| 6/89 | | | |
| | | | |
| | | | |
| | | | |
| | | | |
| | | | |
| | | | |
| | | | |
| | | | |
| | | | |

6/89

CO.

# LEGEND

## The only inside story about Mayor Richard J. Daley

Frank Sullivan

Bonus Books, Inc., Chicago

93     92     91     90     89                           5     4     3     2

Library of Congress Catalog Card Number: 88-63356

International Standard Book Number: 0-933893-96-5

**Bonus Books, Inc.**
160 East Illinois Street
Chicago, Illinois 60611

*Typesetting by Point West Inc., Carol Stream, IL*

*Printed in the United States of America*

*Interview on pp. 14-16 is reprinted with permission from* We Don't Want Nobody
Nobody Sent *by Milton Rakove, Indiana University Press.*

*To Sally who shared the adventure*

# Contents

# Invitation

*1*

*"What I'm offering you is a view that most
people don't get; what I'm offering is a chance
to see the whole shooting match from the
inside."*

Mayor Frank Skeffington to his nephew in<br>*The Last Hurrah.*

In Edwin O'Connor's novel about political Boston, a 33
year old newspaper employee is given the opportunity
by the book's central figure, Frank Skeffington, to accompany him through a mayoral campaign. As a 37-year-old reporter
for the *Chicago Sun-Times,* I was invited by Mayor Richard J. Daley to
accompany him in a much longer and closer relationship.

The invitation—actually a series of invitations—came from the
Mayor beginning in the summer of 1967. By then I had spent three
years as my newspaper's City Hall reporter covering him and city government on a daily basis. First, I was asked by Daley if I would assist
him by handling media relations for the police, a position which I subsequently occupied for four years from March of 1968 until May of
1972. During this period, Chicago experienced devastating arsons and
lootings after the murder in Memphis of Dr. Martin Luther King, Jr.,
Mayor Daley's widely condemned and widely praised "shoot to kill"
order, the emotionally charged clashes involving the police and the
demonstrators at the 1968 Democratic National Convention, the fatal
shooting by police of the local leader of the Black Panthers, and almost continuing controversy involving the police, black militants,
members of radical movements and the media. The police conflicts
were accompanied by the federal government's most massive use of

governmental power to investigate and prosecute charges of police corruption.

After I expressed to the Mayor, late in 1971, my intention to resign
from the Police Department because of its leadership's unwillingness
to reform, he asked me to serve on his personal staff as an administrative assistant. During the year I did this, Daley and the 58 other elected
Democratic delegates from Chicago were barred from the 1972 national convention in Miami. In March of 1973, I was asked by the
Mayor to be his press secretary. I assumed this position for four years
at a time when many of the highest ranking elected officials of the
Democratic Party of Chicago were being indicted and convicted for
corruption. In the midst of this, Daley suffered a stroke and was absent from City Hall for four months. He returned to campaign and win
re-election to an unprecedented sixth four year term as mayor. The following year, I accompanied him on his return to national Democratic
politics at the Madison Square Garden convention where Jimmy
Carter was nominated. Then, as the year was about to end, it was my
sad duty to announce his death of a heart attack.

Throughout his career, Richard J. Daley distrusted and disliked
newsmen. Following the year of his first election as mayor in 1955, I
was the only reporter invited to enter his inner circle. In this capacity, I
worked with him closely for nine years which, he said, included the
most difficult ones of his life.

Daley, a politician for more than four decades, was a most private
man. Only one person was truly close to him. That was his wife,
Eleanor, with whom he had a life-long love affair. One of his strengths
as a politician was never to bare his soul, never to allow anyone, much
less a working reporter, to draw close. This also was destined to be one
of his weaknesses as far as history is concerned. Little in the form of
correspondence, memoranda or enlightening interviews, was left behind for historians. Until now, none of the books written about him
have come from people who knew him up close. Each has been authored by someone Daley kept at arm's length. But this book is based
on a nine-year adventure which he invited me to take and nine years of
notes about that adventure which I recorded almost every day.

I believe a reader should know about the attitudes a writer brings
to his subject. With this in mind, I note that the first time I had the opportunity to vote for Richard J. Daley in the Chicago Democratic may-

oral primary of February 1955, I voted for his opponent, the incumbent mayor, Martin H. Kennelly. The rationale for my vote was respect for Kennelly's record and a lack of admiration for the Democratic organization which opposed him and backed Daley. Two months later, however, I voted in the mayoral election for the primary's winner, Daley, over his Republican opponent, Robert Merriam, reasoning at the time, somewhat genetically, that a machine Democrat was still better than a Democrat turned Republican.

In 1959, I again voted for Daley. By 1963, however, as a newspaper reporter, I had increased experience with the Daley administration and concluded that a victory for his opponent, Benjamin S. Adamowski, would better serve the public interest. Needless to say, Daley won, but by a relatively narrow margin. My same reasoning applied in 1967 when, after two years covering Daley and City Hall, I was disturbed by the arrogance shown by his appointees toward the media, and decided a vote for Republican challenger, John Waner, was preferable.

In Daley's last two elections, 1971 and 1975, I voted for him. Much turmoil had happened during the years leading to these two votes on his behalf. A cynic also might note that in these two elections I was on the city's payroll. Like most of us, though, I prefer to think that my voting decisions were motivated by principle.

The gist of all this is that I had mixed opinions about Richard J. Daley throughout his years as mayor. I hope this has enabled me to achieve some degree of objectivity in writing about him. He was an important politician, probably the most powerful and controversial urban official in American history. He played a key role in many of our country's most turbulent political and social events. To me, he is most interesting, however, because of his personal qualities which enabled him to influence so many people.

Mayor Daley was loved and hated but, with both admirers and detractors, he became a legend. He offered me a priceless chance "to see the whole shooting match from the inside." In these pages, I hope to share with you that chance.

# Legend

2

Through all the years that Richard Daley spent in Chicago politics the legend grew that, somehow or other, if he smiled at you, good things would happen. Your brother, your sister, your mother, your father would all go on public payrolls, contracts would come your way, appointments would be received, fame and honor would flow in your direction. And Daley did everything possible to encourage that impression. Men, 50, 60 years old, mature professionals, were deeply concerned about how Daley felt about them. An illustration of this is a story Sidney Korshak told at a retirement luncheon for his brother, Marshall, who was stepping down as Director of Revenue for the City of Chicago. Sidney, whose reputation as a public speaker is subordinate to that of being the famous lawyer of Southern California and Las Vegas, and who was often described as a key man in organized crime, got up at the luncheon and said, "I love my brother more than anyone in the world. I talk to him several times a day from Beverly Hills, and every day my brother says to me, 'I passed Mayor Daley in the corridor this morning and he didn't smile at me, or I said hello to the Mayor in his office and he seemed rather distant, or Mayor Daley today was really friendly.' " Sidney then said, "I am so tired of getting that kind of phone call and hearing how my brother's day has been shaped by whether Mayor Daley at that moment likes him or doesn't like him. I'm so glad my brother is getting out of politics. Never again will I have to receive that kind of phone call."

# Kiss My Ass 3

*"If a man can't put his arms around his sons,
then what kind of world are we living in? If I
can't help my sons, then they can kiss my ass."*

I cringed when I heard him say it. I thought it was a public relations disaster—the worst public statement he had
ever made. That's what it was. But it also was, by far, his
most popular statement.

Daley made this remark when criticized by the media for arrang-
ing for his twenty-six year old son, John, to be the broker for and
thereby profit from $1 million of city insurance business given to him
on a no-bid basis. Daley's action was the ethical low point of his public
career. He had never used the Office of Mayor to enrich himself. But
in the 18th year of his 21 year administration, he decided to use it to
benefit financially one of his four sons.

When the insurance deal became public, Daley was deeply troubled. At one point he seriously considered preventing John from accepting the commissions. But in public, when criticized, he responded
defensively and justified the transaction.

At the time I was Daley's administrative assistant and only days
away from being his press secretary. I deplored what he said. He was
clearly justifying the use of his elected office to substantially benefit
one of his sons. This was against everything about government that I
believed in. But, to my surprise, most people loved what Daley said
about his son and admired him for it. Wherever I went, whether talk-

ing with taxi drivers in New York or waiters in San Francisco, people expressed solid agreement with him.

Daley's "kiss my ass" challenge provided an insight into Daley the politician. His use of it showed why he was a master. He talked to real people, not intellectuals or moralists. He cut through the distancing layers of political rhetoric which separate most elected officials from their constituents. Daley was the essence of all the people who live on the side streets of any great city and he spoke to these people directly. That is one of the reasons the people of Chicago elected him to six consecutive four year terms as mayor.

Once I saw and heard him inadvertently forget those people who live on all the side streets. It happened during his sixth and final campaign for mayor. The place was the auditorium of the Healy public school in his Bridgeport neighborhood on Chicago's near-Southwest Side. The enthusiastic audience consisted of his neighbors—many of them precinct captains and city job holders—and their families. They were among the people upon whom he was most politically dependent. They were his home base, the 11th Warders, and he was, before anything else, the Democratic committeeman of the 11th Ward. Newspapers and television routinely sneered and joked about these 11th Warders. They were the major part of Daley's patronage army which numbered in the tens of thousands. My predecessor as press secretary, Earl Bush, once insisted to me that Daley viewed himself not so much as mayor but as someone in charge of job placements for the 11th Ward. It was natural, therefore, that Daley should use this final mayoral campaign speech of his career to speak up for the people of the 11th Ward. "They are good people," he said. "They are simple people but good people." With these words his face remained impassive, as it usually was. I watched him from the side of the auditorium stage on which he spoke. His eyes indicated no mistake but he knew he had made one, a major one. He had talked down to his own people, the one thing in his political world he never wanted to do. He had called them "simple." By implication, he had separated himself from the people on his own side streets, the Mexicans, Lithuanians, Poles and Irish who sat before him in the auditorium. They, too, were impassive. Maybe they didn't hear. Maybe they were not offended, even a little bit. But that would be contrary to everything Daley believed about elective politics. That would be an assumption that voters are not smart, or that these voters were not smart. That might be the opinion of some political scientists. But Daley was not a political theorist. He was a political practitioner—the best urban America has ever seen—and he respected his constituency.

I never heard him speak about political theory either in public or in private. But he believed deeply in the elective processes. He believed that those who were elected represented the people and that, no matter where people lived or what they did, they were intelligent. That is the reason he had been so shocked three years prior to this speech at the Healy school, shocked by the 1972 Democratic National Convention in Miami when the delegates—most of them selected (not elected) in the undemocratic caucuses in private living rooms and church basements —voted not to seat him and the 58 other elected delegates from Chicago. He had been elected. Eight hundred thousand Chicago Democrats had arisen on that primary morning in March of 1972 and had voted for Daley and his running mates to represent them in Miami, but the other Miami delegates decided to seat the Reverend Jesse Jackson and his unelected associates. And the Chicago newspapers didn't care. In fact, they were happy. Daley got what he deserved, they said. But he never respected newspaper people anyway. No one elected them.

And so, on the stage of the Healy auditorium, he tried to make up for his "simple" mistake. He praised the people of the 11th Ward, hoping that, if he were extravagant enough and repetitive, they would forget that he had called them "simple."

Long ago, in some ways, he had left them psychologically. He had been invited to the White House by John F. Kennedy, who asked the Daleys to be the first overnight guests of his Presidency. Daley had long since ceased to be in awe of any man. Seven years before, in 1968, he had withstood the onslaught of national media criticism. He survived and won re-election in 1971. And his legend had grown. And now, in his final mayoral campaign in 1975, he was even more of a legend. But he was still someone from the side streets, a man who lived half a block from where he was born, in the parish where he received his First Communion. Others, when they became successful, could move away from the bungalows and clapboard houses of Bridgeport and the 11th Ward. But they never wanted to be mayor and never wanted to keep being mayor.

And so, Daley continued on for several minutes, successfully mak-

ing up for putting down his key voters. There had never been a chance they would show annoyance. They were his people and, to a large degree, beneficiaries of his political muscle. He spoke for them.

And he had spoken for a much larger audience when he challenged his critics to kiss his ass. He spoke for Chicagoans and people far beyond the city who would use government to enrich their families, if they only had the chance.

This remark had been sad because it did not truly reflect his ethics —not at least as far as enriching himself was concerned. He had made money in politics but it came before he was mayor and in an earlier era of political ethics. (We always keep hoping that our era is more ethical than the past.) The money came after he had been the Democratic leader in the Illinois Senate, the man who performed a key legislative role in merging the various private transportation companies in Chicago into a single public authority. After this, he was able to purchase a house on six acres of lakefront land in southwest Michigan to be used in the summers and on occasional weekends.

But when he became mayor, he was offered more money, much more, way over a million dollars in the first month. He told me he never took it and I believe him. "They thought," he said to me, "that because I was an Irish Catholic, the Office of Mayor could be bought and I was determined to prove them wrong."

But when his four sons became adults it was different. He was not enriching himself. He was helping them. Three of the four became lawyers and the fourth an insurance broker. Daley's major media critic, Mike Royko, thought it was sad but perhaps natural that a Daley son would seek to acquire his ward's insurance business. The father had seen generations of local politicians grow rich on insurance. Each of the city's 50 wards had its top politicians in the local insurance business. There was little competition to fear from non-political insurance brokers. Those non-politicians could not make implicit threats. But the political insurance men could. In each ward, tavern owners, real estate developers—anyone who did business—knew it was wise to buy insurance from the ward's Democratic power. This was a lesson not lost on Daley. And so, his son, John, opened an insurance office across from the Nativity of Our Lord Church at 37th Street and Union Avenue, just three blocks from the house at 3536 South Lowe Avenue where he lived with his parents. And soon a big opportunity came.

Joseph Gill, who had been the Democratic Cook County chairman immediately prior to Daley, died. Gill also had been the Democratic committeeman of the 46th Ward on the North Side and, as such, operated the ward's most lucrative insurance business. Because Gill had been an early friend of the Mayor, stepping aside in 1953 so he could become the Democratic chairman, the older man received some especially enriching insurance business from the city. Because, in Chicago, political fiefdoms and their accompanying wealth often are passed on to family heirs, the descendants of Joe Gill thought that, after his death, they would be in line to inherit the city insurance business. They were wrong. The Mayor knew a more deserving recipient, a young man who was just getting started in the business, his son.

And that is how the million dollars' worth of premiums ended up with John Daley and why the Mayor so colorfully, so succinctly, defended his action. His explanation cemented his bond with the electorate. Once more, he was able to confound his critics. After 1968 and the Democratic Convention, he had learned to withstand any kind of criticism. He had always been tough. After 1968, he was the toughest. In fact, there was only one other Chicago politician like him when it came to toughness and he knew it. She was his protege.

# His Protege

*4*

*"Don't worry about Janey. She can take care
of herself."*

His funeral took place three days before Christmas. To the Nativity of Our Lord Church in his frozen, snow-covered, Bridgeport neighborhood on the Southwest Side, came four men of special national prominence.

The first, Jimmy Carter, had been elected president of the United States just 50 days before. He had been nominated and elected without the need for help from Richard J. Daley. The second of the four was Senator Edward M. Kennedy, the brother of a man who once desperately needed and received Daley's political muscle in gaining the presidential nomination and election. Still another was the man who had engineered the Mayor being barred from the 1972 convention in Miami, yet later received Daley's backing in the election of that year, Senator George McGovern. Finally, there was a man who was in almost total contrast with Daley—a New York Republican inheritor of massive wealth and a media politician, the vice president of the United States, Nelson Rockefeller.

These four knelt together in the first pew on the right.

Immediately behind them were five empty pews separating the front row occupants from the other mourners who sat in designated portions of the church based on their rank. One area was for elected officials from across the country, another for those who were elected locally, and still others for appointed officials, and the rich and power-ful from the private sector. Directly across the center aisle, occupying the first six pews on the left, was the Mayor's family—his widow, their sons and daughters with their spouses and those grandchildren deemed old enough to attend.

The Mayor's casket rested on a bier in the center aisle in front of the altar just a few feet from the four national leaders. On the preced-ing day, the casket was opened for the thousands of bereaved and curi-ous to view as they filed by.

Now in the church there was a brief moment of silence as the or-gan stopped playing. The mourners were in their designated pews, but the clergy, including the Catholic Archbishop of Chicago, John Cardi-nal Cody, had not yet entered the altar. All the mourners were in place, that is, except one. During this moment of silence, with almost no movement in the church and every eye available to watch her, she walked down the center aisle escorted by a city employee who had been designated as an usher to direct her to an appointed pew halfway from the front of the church. She was the commissioner of consumer sales. The city's director of special events had assigned her to a seat with the other city department heads.

After genuflecting, preparatory to entering the pew, she hesitated and looked toward the front of the church. Then she strode forward down the aisle, past all of the mourners save the quartet in the first pew on the right. She then entered the second pew, kneeling alone be-hind the president-elect and the vice president of the United States, the brother of the assassinated president and the man who four years be-fore had been nominated for president. The woman now in the second pew was special. She was Jane Byrne.

Two years and 102 days after Richard J. Daley's funeral, with total opposition from the remnants of his political machine, Jane Byrne was elected mayor of Chicago. Shortly thereafter, a Washington, D.C., as-trologer who had never met her wrote that the new mayor's dominant quality was her opposition to authority, especially male authority, and that she gained immense satisfaction from the dominance and influ-ence she exercised over Richard J. Daley. This astrological observation coincided with the truth. But from Daley's viewpoint, Byrne was not dominant. She was his protege.

Jane Byrne grew up on the North Side of Chicago, the second oldest of six children. Her father, William Patrick Burke, was a vice-president of Inland Steel who later started his own steel warehouse business. According to a 1975 *Chicago Tribune* article based on an interview with Byrne, there was so little political discussion in the Burke family that she was not certain whether her parents always voted Democratic.

After graduating from St. Scholastica High School, she attended Barat College in Lake Forest, an expensive Catholic women's school conducted by the Religious of the Sacred Heart. Shortly after her graduation from Barat, she married William Byrne, a graduate of the University of Notre Dame who took flight training with the Marines. They were married in December of 1956. They had a daughter, Kathy. Everything went well until May 31, 1959, when Bill Byrne's Marine Reserve plane crashed near the Glenview Naval Air Station outside of Chicago and he was killed.

In the fall of the following year, Jane Byrne went to work as a volunteer in the Chicago presidential campaign office of John F. Kennedy. Few volunteers in political history have ever cloaked such a low level job with such an aura of importance.

After his election, the young widow retained her contacts with the new president's political associates. This led, three years later, early in November of 1963, to an invitation which, she maintained, came directly from the President. It was for her to be his guest at the Army-Air Force football game to be held in Chicago's Soldier Field. Byrne attended with her young daughter but, shortly before the game, there was an announcement that the President would not be there. Although the reason was not known at the time, Kennedy was detained in Washington because he had just learned that two allied leaders, the President of South Vietnam, Diem, and his brother, Nhu, had been murdered in Saigon.

Kennedy remained in Washington but, according to Byrne, key Kennedy aides, whom she had gotten to know well during the campaign, were at Soldier Field—Kenny O'Donnell, John Riley, and Pierre Salinger. Also in attendance was the Mayor of Chicago. Byrne later related that she and Daley chatted during the game. "He asked me why he always saw me at these political functions but I really was not involved," Byrne said. She then quoted the Mayor as having remarked "Why don't you come to see me?" So, according to Byrne, she did.

The 29 year old widow later related details of that first meeting at City Hall with the 61 year old Mayor. If her memory was accurate, it was the strangest conversation of Richard J. Daley's life.

"We didn't start off well at all," Byrne said. "I thought it was going to be a nice meeting. I was trying to study him a little bit, which you know everybody always did, but didn't get too far. I was trying to draw my conclusions from his face. Finally, he very arrogantly said, 'Why did you go to them?' I said, 'To whom?' He said, 'The Kennedys. Why did you go to them?' I said, 'Well, I wanted to help out.' He said, 'Did you not know of the Democratic Party in Chicago?' I said, 'Well, yes.' He said, 'Why didn't you come to us?' I said, 'It wasn't that kind of thing. You don't understand. Nobody was beating my door down to get me. You weren't and they weren't, and I was glad I was able to get involved.' He said, 'Do you know that we have the finest speakers' bureau? Do you know that we have the finest organization?' He said, 'You know, you wasted your time. You've lost two years.' It was like boom, boom, boom," according to Byrne. Continuing her recollections of that first meeting, "He said, 'Besides that, what did you get out of it?'

"Then I got mad," Byrne said. "I said, 'What do you mean, what did I get out of it?' He said, 'What did they do for you? We take care of our people. If somebody works hard for us, we're sure that they get something.' I said, 'I didn't want anything. Do you mean a job?' He said, 'Yes.' I said, 'They offered me a job in Washington, but I didn't want to go. I have a baby. I didn't want to go that far away. She has been uprooted twice.' He put his hand over his mouth and said, 'Oh.'

"But now I was insulted, when someone says what did you get out of it? I picked up my purse off the floor, and I said, 'I think I've come to the wrong place and I'm sorry I took up your time and I really do think that I am leaving.' He looked at me and said, 'What do you mean?' I said, 'I don't like what you asked me—what did I get out of it? Up until this moment with all the hurrah about this big bossism and you, I basically believed that I got the same thing out of it that you got out of it!' He said, 'What was that?' I said, 'I thought that what I got out of it was the first Catholic president of the United States. With all your political clout, I thought that deep down inside in your heart that was what you wanted. If you are going to sit here and talk to me about the spoils and who got what, then I really am not too interested in staying. And I want to say something else. You have been hitting that headquarters pretty much since I came in here. Why did I go there? What did they do? And they accomplished nothing? That was a very close vote in Illinois, and there was no doubt in anybody's mind that Cook County carried the presidency. But on such a small vote, maybe if we got five or six of those extra five thousand out there in the suburbs, maybe that was worthwhile. And that is really all I have to say, and thank you very much for your time.'

"He said, 'Sit down!'

"I sat down. Then he pushed his chair back and I guess my closing sentence was—'I guess it really didn't matter too much anyway what either of us has got out of it, did it?' He said, 'What does that mean?'

"I said, 'Well, it means he's dead anyway.' Well, at that, he said, 'Excuse me a minute.' His chair went back and he was down under his desk doing something and I thought to myself—What am I doing in this place? Those were my actual thoughts. He said, 'My shoelace is untied,' and he is saying this down low, and all of a sudden he comes up and his face is soaked and he is crying. We established an understanding at that moment. I said, 'I feel awful. I didn't mean to come in here and make you cry.' Then he turned his head, which he was common to do, then turned back in a few moments and said, 'Well, do you want to work with us? Do you want to come to us?' I said, 'Well, yes.'

"He said, 'What would you like?'

"I said, 'I don't know. You invited me; that's a silly question to ask me because you are the king-maker. From what I hear you can look at somebody and decide if they've got it or they haven't.'

"He said, 'Why don't you start coming here about once a month.' Then we went into what I was doing and he said, 'You've got to go and work for the Ward organization. You've got to.'

"I said, 'I'd be happy to.'

"He said, 'Will you ring doorbells?'

"I said, 'Sure.'

"He said, 'Will you put up signs?'

"I said, 'Yes.'

"He said, 'Well, you go there and you tell them that I suggested that you work there as a volunteer at the Ward organization.' Then he looked at me and he said, 'I could give you anything I wanted to. I could name you to any post. I could put you on committees and your name would get known throughout, but if you don't help out, no matter what I try to do, they'll get you down below. So go and work for your Ward organization.'

"So that's how I started. I kidded him about it later. The last time he ran, I said to him, 'I never got over the rudeness of you that day.' He said, 'I took a look at you that day and I said to myself—you need taking down and it didn't hurt you one bit.'"

That is how Jane Byrne recalled her initial conversation at City Hall with Mayor Daley late in 1963. It was a surprising Daley who, in the conversation, actually begged someone to come to him. It was a Daley engaging in traces of male-female repartee, at least that's the way Jane Byrne remembered it. For those of us who knew Daley and Byrne, her recollection tells far more about herself than it does about her mentor.

Byrne continued her recollections. "And he grew to understand, I guess, that I was okay as far as thinking and had some brains and could be trusted. From there I went on to become commissioner of consumer sales. I was active in the 1967 campaign. From 1968 on there was a tremendous amount of shifting sands on the national scene with the assassination of Robert Kennedy. Even before he got killed, well I never gave up those other friends, and I would oftentimes get some information out there. Up until Bobby was killed, there was still the belief that the Kennedys would come back, so we kept the foot-soldiers we had in order so that whatever was going on, I would be able to tell him [Daley]. That doesn't mean in any way that he didn't have a direct line of communication right to Bobby, but the underlying stuff about who did what, what Mayor Blank might be doing in Philadelphia and who was with us and here and there I would get from others. It was a good way to hear, that helped him and he liked those people. He was very smart that way. I would walk in and his hands would go up and he would say to me—'What are you picking up?' That would mean what did you hear out there."

Later in the same interview, Byrne talked about Daley's attitude toward women in politics and said that "I do not think that the Mayor was acting as some people say because of my 'in.' It was started before

my 'in.' And she spoke of working with one of the Mayor's sons, John, in the 1967 mayoral campaign. She also told in these 1978 recollections about working with the Mayor's wife. She quoted Mrs. Daley as saying, "Janie, after this campaign is over, you and I are going to all the Ward organizations and line up all the women." I was to learn several years before this pleasant recollection of teamwork that Richard J. Daley's wife detested Jane Byrne.

This long conversation with the Mayor led, Byrne said, to a job as an administrator with the federally funded Head Start Program. Then, after a couple of years, according to the *Tribune* interview, she was named by the Mayor as Director of Personnel for the Chicago Committee on Urban Opportunity, a position in which she functioned as a recruiter and "informal liaison" between City Hall and Washington. The CCUO was the Daley-created city agency for dispensing federal war-on-poverty funds. Byrne saw Daley much more frequently after that.

She was ambitious and had some valuable contacts in the Capital. Nevertheless, according to the *Tribune,* she wondered if she should return to the teaching job she held in a Northwest Side Catholic elementary school prior to her long City Hall meeting with Daley. But, she said in recalling her early city government experiences, "There is that little thing about politics, it bites you, gets in your blood. I wasn't content, though. I must have asked the Mayor three times after my third year, if there was no other place I could go. I didn't want to stay there [with the war-on-poverty] any longer. I couldn't do any more in that job than I was already doing. And he did say, no, go back."

Byrne stayed with the war-on-poverty until the Mayor asked her to take an administrative post in the City's Department of Weights and Measures.

That is when, as a newspaper reporter, I first became aware of her. John J. King, a lawyer from the Hyde Park community on the South Side, was serving at that time as acting commissioner of the City's Department of Weights and Measures. Daley, however, had received reports that King, an honorable man, was ineffective and a poor administrator. Byrne was assigned by the Mayor to work in that department to straighten things out. In her reports to Daley, she described King as incompetent and worse. His career in the city government ended shortly thereafter and he moved to Fort Lauderdale where he was elected a judge of Broward County. It was then that the department's name was changed to Consumer Sales, and Jane Byrne took over. More and more she became a frequent visitor to the Mayor's office.

When I first met Byrne in 1967, my initial impression was that she had a very agile mind. A not uncomely woman in those days, she also could attract male attention with a somewhat mesmerizing style of conversation and not infrequent winks. Her second husband-to-be once described her as having "great legs and a cute little ass." I began to see her on a frequent basis after May of 1972 when I was named to be one of the Mayor's administrative assistants. She was not only bright but also unafraid of speaking to the media, a characteristic not possessed by many of the Mayor's commissioners. The Department of Consumer Sales provided her with an excellent opportunity to be aggressive on behalf of the public interest. And she made the most of it. She became a media favorite because she took action on behalf of consumers and was willing to speak out against dishonest merchants. During this time she was a definite asset to the Daley administration. By 1972, however, she was still not important enough politically to play any role in the local party's attempt to be seated at the Miami convention. She was neither an elected nor an appointed delegate. Her day was still to come.

It was in 1973 that I first learned another side of Jane Byrne. Irv Kupcinet had an item in his *Chicago Sun-Times* column which said Mayor Daley would be disturbed if he knew that one of his very close commissioners was dating a newsman. As the Mayor's press secretary, I concluded the item was aimed at Byrne and, stupidly, telephoned her to comment on how unfair Kup had been to print such an inaccurate piece which could hurt her reputation with the Mayor. (Daley definitely considered it to be disloyal for members of his administration to be close to newspeople.) Byrne neither affirmed nor denied the truth of Kup's item. His clear implication was that the newsman who had the close relationship with Byrne was Jay McMullen, the *Chicago Daily News* reporter at City Hall. In my conversation with her, I mentioned something about McMullen's well known reputation as a womanizer. Within moments after our conversation, I received a call from McMullen in the City Hall press room demanding to know why I had said something derogatory to Byrne about him. She had responded to my remarks by telephoning McMullen to relate our conversation.

During this same period, Mayor Daley was concerned that his comments, while meeting with the 60 persons who headed city departments and agencies, were being leaked to the press. To the day of his death, the Mayor was convinced that South Side politician Marshall Korshak, who had been a Daley department head, was the source for the newspaper reports resulting from these meetings. Nevertheless, after Korshak left city government, accounts of the private cabinet meetings continued in Jay McMullen's newspaper.

By early 1974, Byrne was viewed by inner circle employees at City Hall as being a special favorite of the Mayor. These same employees concluded that she also was close to the Mayor's wife and children. It surprised me to find this was not true.

I first learned of the disdain which Daley's family had for Byrne after the Mayor was hospitalized for a "mild stroke" in May of 1974. The Mayor's bodyguards advised me that Mrs. Daley had left strict orders that Byrne was not to gain admittance to the tenth floor of Rush-Presbyterian-St. Luke's Medical Center where the Mayor's room was located. When, a day or so after Daley's hospitalization, the Mayor's family learned that, somehow or other, Byrne had slipped through the police security and was on the tenth floor, there was much consternation. Family members conferred briefly and it was decided that Mrs. Patricia Thompson, one of the three Daley daughters, would greet Byrne who had been momentarily detained by the bodyguards in a tenth floor waiting room. The two women embraced and both cried openly about the Mayor and what had happened to him with his illness.

This tearful scene was followed within several days by Byrne calling a news conference at City Hall to denounce, except for Daley, all the leaders of the local Democratic Party.

The Mayor had not gained and maintained dominance over two generations of politicians by being unwary of potential challengers from within the party. Consequently, although bedridden from a "mild stroke" and awaiting surgery on a carotid artery, he was, as always, alert to signs of rivalry, even imagined rivalry. He had been in the hospital only five days when a story appeared in the *Chicago Tribune* quoting the Republican Illinois attorney general as boosting Democrat

Michael Howlett to be the successor to Daley in the mayoral election the following year. Then, four days later, the same *Tribune* political writer reported that the Democratic speaker of the Illinois House was "filling the Daley void." These paltry signs of other Democrats gaining public attention were all it took to stir Jane Byrne to action. While Daley was in the hospital, she called a press conference at City Hall and issued the following news release:

"I would be disloyal and unappreciative if I didn't speak out on a topic that has become in my mind an outrage and an insult to the greatest political leader and Mayor this city has ever had, Richard J. Daley, whom I have served as consumer sales commissioner for six years. The outrage is the shameless and callous manner in which little men of greed within the Democratic Party have embarked on a campaign which I think is designed to force the Mayor to retire by giving the public the mistaken notion that he has endorsed someone to succeed him—that he is physically incapable of continuing in the job and that age has impaired his ability to conduct the affairs of Chicago and the Democratic Party of Cook County. Nothing could be farther from the truth, and I have chosen this occasion to repudiate these calumnies and state the real facts to the people of Chicago and the Democrats of Cook County. I have talked personally with the Mayor several times in recent days and I have been assured by him personally that he plans to return to assume his full schedule of duties as Mayor and Cook County Democratic chairman.

"I deeply resent, as I am sure thousands of other loyal Democrats do, the self-serving manner in which other so-called Democratic leaders have fallen all over themselves running to their favorite political writer, columnist, radio or TV commentator to assure them that they are the favorite of the Mayor to succeed him. I am suspicious that many of these speculative stories have been deliberately planted by these would-be mayors and that the Mayor has absolutely no favorite to succeed himself. The time has not yet come for the Mayor to designate any such favorite because he plans to continue in office and run again for another term himself. My discussions with the Mayor were wide-ranging, pointing even as far in the future as the next Democratic National Convention in 1976. I can tell you the Mayor intends to play a major role in this convention to pick the party's next presidential candidate. He assured me there is nothing in his physical condition to force him to retire in the near future.

"I have been shocked at the ghoulishness of political vultures who have been circling over the scene attempting to exploit the Mayor's temporary incapacity. Where has loyalty gone? Whatever the Mayor's condition, and it is my belief that it is good, I reject and condemn the transparent maneuverings of this wolf-pack of ambitious men jumping on the back of the leader to whom they owe so much at a time of his temporary incapacity. I predict Mayor Daley will be back and that he will come back strong. I also predict that he will run again and be re-elected by the same overwhelming majority that he has in the past, no matter who the opposing candidates are."

When it came to political in-fighting, Richard J. Daley and Jane Byrne were kindred souls. Both were tough and both tolerated no rivals. When it came to any kind of challenge to their political power, the mentor and his protege were in complete agreement. As a result of Byrne's warning to would-be contenders, Daley, from his hospital bed, telephoned her with congratulations. What is more, he designated her to speak on his behalf at the mammoth Democratic Party of Cook County fundraising dinner to be held the next night.

Later Daley underwent surgery to clear his left carotid artery. For the next three months he recuperated in his Michigan summer home. During the entire time of his illness and recuperation, both in the hospital and at Grand Beach, Byrne never saw him.

Upon his return to City Hall that fall, Daley created for her the new position of co-chairman of the Democratic Party of Cook County. State law, which carefully prescribes the rules for political parties, made no provision for a county co-chairman. Nevertheless, Democratic officials and the media did not question Byrne's appointment. Daley, moreover, created a private office for the new co-chairman just a few feet down the hall from his party office in the Bismarck Hotel.

During his sixth and final mayoral campaign in January and February of 1975, Byrne voiced objection to a television commercial for the Mayor's opponent, Alderman William Singer. In it, Singer claimed he had managed Senator Robert Kennedy's presidential campaign in Chicago in 1968. By this time, Bobby Kennedy had been dead almost seven years. There was a serious question as to how popular he had been in Chicago when alive. There was no question that there was little nostalgia about him seven years after his death. Nevertheless, Jane Byrne was greatly disturbed by Singer's claim of a relationship with Kennedy. She telephoned Kenny O'Donnell in Massachusetts and later reported that O'Donnell denied Singer had any significant role in the Kennedy campaign. Byrne made much of this in her campaign speeches on behalf of the Mayor and egged on Daley to do the same. The reaction of most listeners was, "Who cares?"

Byrne, however, was able to get Daley so inflamed that one day, before the primary, he actually went to the point of demanding that I contact NBC-TV in Chicago to insist that the station remove the offending Singer commercials. While walking with me in the Loop after an ethnic rally, he told me to contact Lee Schulman, the general manager of Channel 5, and insist that the Singer commercial be yanked off the air. I told Daley that this would be unwise. His opponents had long sought to portray him as intolerant of opposing views, I said, and a move to silence his opponent's commercials would be picked up by the national as well as local media, with much criticism directed at him. Daley stopped walking and turned toward me: "If you don't have the guts to do it," he snarled, "I'll do it, myself." I replied that I had the guts but I just didn't think it was in his interest. No more was said that night. The next day Daley did not raise the subject. I never contacted NBC, but Jane Byrne had come close to bringing it about.

On the night of Daley's primary victory over Singer, the Mayor went to the Chicago Room of the LaSalle Hotel to meet with the media. Accompanying him on the platform before the cameras were his wife and family, along with Jane Byrne and her daughter. Five weeks later, on April 1, the scene was to be partially repeated after Daley's victory over Republican John Hoellen in the mayoral election, but Byrne and her daughter were not permitted to accompany the Daley family onto the stage. Mrs. Daley had directed that the mayoral body-guards prevent any participation by the Byrne women.

Four months later, in July, there was more evidence of Mrs. Daley's strong dislike for Jane Byrne. The occasion was the U.S. Conference of Mayors in Boston. It was the custom of Daley at such meetings to invite those aides who traveled with him to be his guests for a dinner at a popular restaurant. The place chosen for this particular event in Boston was Jimmy's on the waterfront. My wife and I were seated moments ahead of the rest of the party and were joined at our long

family-style table by Mrs. Daley and one of her daughters, Ellie. Jane
Byrne came and sat with the four of us. When this happened, Mrs. Daley turned to her daughter and whispered, "Let's get out of here." The
Daley women then moved away. Meanwhile, the Mayor and the other
members of his party had sat at an adjoining table. During the course
of the evening, Byrne would write notes and pass them to other guests
for relay to the Mayor who sat behind her several seats away. Here was
a dinner party consisting of 20 people sitting at two tables, with the 41
year old co-chairman of the Democratic Party of Cook County slipping notes to and winking at the 73 year old party chairman throughout the course of the evening. A casual observer might have thought
that the co-chairman was flirting. She wasn't. She was showing everyone, however, that a special relationship existed between her and the
Mayor.

When the U.S. Conference of Mayors concluded the following
day, Mrs. Daley gave strict orders to the bodyguards that no one was to
know which return flight to Chicago she and the Mayor would take,
nor should anyone be told the time of their departure from the hotel.
She was determined, the bodyguards later said, that Jane Byrne not be
on the same plane.

There is no question that in the final eight years of his administration, Jane Byrne was the closest person to Richard J. Daley in government. He admired her greatly. He saw some of his qualities in her. She
was tough. Shortly after his death and before she was elected mayor in
her own right, she was asked by Professor Milton Rakove: "Did Daley
have any weaknesses as a mayor and a politician?" Byrne replied: "I
couldn't find any in him as the Mayor. I used to think that sometimes
from what he would say to me, and you have to understand that I was
for two and one-half years a co-chairperson of the Cook County Central Committee and we would talk about things. I used to think sometimes maybe he was a little too soft on some of the committeemen. . . .
I would think to myself, 'you know, why don't you cut him down a little bit, that would be my reaction.' And he'd say, 'Well, what can you
do?' "

On the day Richard Daley died, the person most frequently interviewed on television was Jane Byrne. Two days later, she attended his
funeral. The day after the funeral, Mrs. Daley invited to her home
eight men and women from the Mayor's administration. They were his

two secretaries, Kay Spear and Kay Quinlan, Fire Commissioner Robert J. Quinn, Police Superintendent James M. Rochford, Deputy Mayor Kenneth Sain, Administrative Assistant Thomas Donovan, Special Events Director Jack Reilly and me. The purpose was to thank us for our work with the Mayor. Jane Byrne was not invited.

She had long pledged that if Daley ever stopped being Mayor, she would leave city government within minutes. After Daley's death, however, she remained in her job as commissioner of consumer sales for 11 months until she was fired by the Mayor's successor, Michael A. Bilandic, for making accusations against him to federal authorities, accusations about illegally assisting taxi cab operators which never resulted in criminal charges.

On March 17, 1978, St. Patrick's Day, Jane Byrne married newsman Jay McMullen. The next day she announced that she was running against Bilandic for mayor in 1979. In winning that 1979 election, she used a tape recording of Daley's voice praising "Janey Burns." His family, which strongly supported Bilandic, objected to her campaign use of the Mayor's voice. Once in office, Jane Byrne became the greatest single detractor of Daley's reputation, repeatedly accusing him of financial mismanagement of the public school system.

There is intense irony in Daley's life. He was totally devoted to his wife and children. He cared deeply about their future happiness. Yet, within three years of his death, the woman who he had made his protege had become his family's greatest enemy. Jane Byrne was the supreme misjudgment of Richard J. Daley's life.

There were to be other misjudgments and one of them was his appointment of a man to lead his police. Another was an order he gave: shoot to kill.

# Seeing It All Close-Up    5

*"...he is a boss-mayor whose power seems to be dedicated to making Chicago a better place."*

—*Time* magazine

The primary responsibility of any municipal chief executive is the administration of effective and efficient public services ranging from public safety to housekeeping. Daley was a master of this kind of administration. His success was due to his extensive knowledge of city government, his expertise in municipal finance, his concern for details, the fact that a huge percentage of his city employees were personally cleared by him, and his complete hands-on style of supervision.

Each department head reported directly to him in one-on-one meetings. There were no bureaucratic buffers, no channeling of the dozens of department heads into any "deputy" mayor's office. The central portion of Daley's work day was this continuing flow of meetings in his fifth floor office at City Hall.

His personal supervision built the morale of his department heads and sparked their motivation. They had quick access to him at all times. This did not go unnoticed by their subordinates and it provided the department heads with a healthy aura of power.

By and large, Daley appointed effective men and women to lead the city's agencies. If a professional background were required, the appropriate appointee was selected. At his or her side, however, there always was a political appointee as top aide. This was a plus, not a minus. Local government must be sensitive to the needs of the public. Political astuteness, meaning the ability to understand the constituency's needs, is required at all times.

Daley's career can be judged at different levels. First, there was his effectiveness at getting elected to office. Then there was his political power, brought about by assembling a sizable team of elected cohorts in the Illinois state capital and in Washington.

There was his pragmatic astuteness in gaining political support for national leaders like Kennedy and Johnson, and there was his ability to create a positive business atmosphere in Chicago to attract corporations. The list is long. At no level, however, was Daley's achievement more important than in providing municipal services. Without a high score in this area, he could never have been elected six times.

Daley knew that quality municipal services were the essential ingredients to be mayor. This knowledge was shown in his political campaigns. In his instructions to me and everyone who played a role in his political advertising, Daley insisted on only one theme: the ads must remind the public of the services his administration was providing— efficient refuse removal, convenient and economical public transportation, good city colleges, highly competent fire protection, and rapid, effective police service. These were but a few of the municipal operations on which he knew his political power was based.

I spent four years as his appointee in the most crucial city department, the police. There I could see firsthand, as I never could by being a mayoral aide at City Hall, the strengths and weaknesses of Daley as an administrator. To write about him only from the perspective of his successes and failures in politics and public policy, would overlook the most integral part of being mayor—how his administration served or failed to serve the people of Chicago. By being his personal appointee as the spokesman for the Chicago Police and, thereby, able to take part in that department's highest councils, I was able to see "the whole shooting match from the inside."

What is remembered best about Daley and his police are two events which did not help his reputation. The two were his highly publicized "shoot to kill" order in the aftermath of the rioting following the assassination of Dr. King in Memphis, and the emotion-charged conflicts four months later between the police and demonstrators during the Democratic convention. I was deeply involved on both occasions. To tell the story of Daley as I knew him, it is essential to report about these events, not from the fifth floor of City Hall, but from the streets of the city where they had their impact.

In the March 15, 1963, issue of *Time* magazine, with Daley on the cover, the Mayor described himself as "the first of the new bosses... the first of the new leaders," and *Time* seemed to agree. Daley differed from his predecessors, the magazine wrote, "in that he is a boss-mayor whose power seems to be dedicated to making Chicago a better place."

He was mayor for 21 years partly because he conducted an administration which worked smoothly, staffed with professional téchnicians as well as political operatives. To head those city departments requiring specialized qualifications, such as public works, streets and sanitation, health, law, and finance, Daley, by and large, appointed top-notch professionals. But he had a serious weakness in one area— law enforcement appointees and candidates. More often than not, he made poor judgments in selecting them. For some unexplained reason, Daley, who generally rejected newspaper recommendations, seemed to make his law enforcement appointment decisions based on newspaper clippings. If the media ballyhooed a particular individual as being a great potential crime fighter, Daley sought him out. Because of the media's hype, he backed two losers for sheriff, Roswell Spencer and Minor Wilson, and for state's attorney, his biggest slating mistake, Edward Hanrahan.

A major exception to Daley's proclivity for poor law enforcement choices was his selection of Orlando W. Wilson to lead the Police Department in 1960. Without question, this was the most successful appointment during his more than two decades as Mayor. But in appointing a successor after seven years of Wilson, Daley again lapsed.

James B. Conlisk, Jr., had been the number two man in the Police Department under Wilson. Conlisk possessed almost every fine quality needed to make him an outstanding police superintendent. He was impeccably honest. He had an encyclopedic knowledge of police operations. He was devoted to police service. But he could not lead.

He made it clear to me at our first meeting, shortly after Daley named him police superintendent, that the days of Orlando Wilson, when the spotlight was on one man in the department, were over. From the moment he became superintendent, Conlisk said, the police were to become a team effort. There no longer was to be a focus on the top. That was his philosophy in the age of television. Because of it, this gentle, good man, along with Chicago and Mayor Daley had a most unhappy six years together. Ahead lay Daley's shoot to kill order and the 1968 Democratic National Convention.

# Shoot to Kill 6

*"I am not going to be the one who has to go before a federal grand jury."*

As Martin Luther King, Jr.'s death was being reported to a stunned nation, Chicago's Police Superintendent, James B. Conlisk, Jr., was dining with his wife in a Loop restaurant. His aide, Captain Patrick V. Needham, telephoned with the news of the murder. Conlisk, nevertheless, left the restaurant with his wife, as planned, to attend a stage performance of "The Man of La Mancha." It was the first of many questionable judgments Daley's top appointee was to make in 1968.

Several weeks before April 4, 1968, I had left my job as a *Chicago Sun-Times* reporter covering City Hall to become, at Daley's request, the press officer for the police. My North Side home was next to that of Commander James J. Riordan, who was in charge of the police district for downtown Chicago. When I saw the news of King's death on television, I immediately went to inform Riordan. He and I then left in his car for police headquarters at 11th Street and State. When we arrived, the department's number two man, Deputy Superintendent James M. Rochford, already was in his office. He had issued an order cancelling all days off for police personnel for the shift which was to begin at midnight and had telephoned Bloomington, Illinois, to the home of Richard T. Dunn, the commanding general of emergency operations of the Illinois Army National Guard. The police official advised Dunn of the strong possibility of violence on the streets of Chicago. Rochford was on that night, as he was to the conclusion of his police career in 1977, a man of action.

There were rumors of street disturbances on Thursday night immediately after King's murder but nothing materialized. The troubles began the next morning following the start of the school day when thousands of black students left their classrooms and took to the streets. The police radio was filled with reports of traffic being blocked and automobile and store windows being smashed as youths rampaged through the West Side. Conlisk, having had a peaceful evening at the theater the previous night, responded calmly and efficiently that morning in the communications center, personally assigning police throughout the city to meet with the growing mob problems.

The tempo of the disturbances accelerated almost minute by minute. It was shortly before noon that the first reports of looting began to reach police headquarters. By 2:00 p.m., the situation on the West Side was deteriorating so rapidly that Conlisk telephoned Mayor Daley and recommended that Lieutenant Governor Sam Shapiro be requested to activate the National Guard to supplement the police. (Governor Otto Kerner was vacationing in Florida at the time.)

At about 3:45 p.m., columns of smoke began to rise high above the West Side stores which had been set on fire by the mobs. It was an awesome scene. As I sat with Conlisk in his office on the fourth floor of police headquarters, I could see smoke billowing hundreds of feet in the air in the area of West Madison Street. The superintendent, however, sat calmly at his desk computing what his eventual pension would be if he remained superintendent until the date when he could first retire with maximum benefits. I was to conclude later that it is the police pension and the police passion to receive it that too often bind officers in a fraternity which refuses to expose official corruption in its ranks. Few want to be responsible for the termination of a fellow officer's pension.

On that Friday morning, all police reporting for duty had been told to take "aggressive action." Nevertheless, throughout the afternoon and evening, the arson, looting and gunfire continued. By sundown, Conlisk and Rochford began to hear anonymous reports that the police were not being aggressive in making arrests. If this were true

—and Conlisk and Rochford did not believe it to be so—how could the high command act to assure more arrests? Rochford, conferring with Conlisk in the deputy superintendent's sixth floor office, suggested that a teletype message be issued to all police districts calling upon personnel to engage in an aggressive arrest operation. Both men discussed whether there should be any reference to the use of deadly force. They decided against it. The police, they reasoned, knew the law and the department order allowing the use of deadly force only under specific conditions. The midst of a riot was not the time, Conlisk and Rochford concluded, to gamble with the potentially inflammatory effect that a new order on the use of firearms could have on their personnel. Their decision proved to be a wise one.

As a result of Conlisk's and Rochford's discussion, beginning Saturday morning, an order was broadcast on police radios every hour calling for police supervisors to insure that their personnel took "aggressive action against all law breakers." No mention of deadly force was made. The Mayor did not know about the discussion between Conlisk and Rochford. Unfortunately, Daley was later to come to his own conclusion about the police and the use of deadly force which would do great harm to his reputation.

The violence in Chicago and dozens of other cities continued through Friday night and into early Saturday morning. In Chicago, National Guard troops were deployed on the West Side. On Saturday morning, Conlisk met at City Hall with the Mayor and General Dunn. Following the meeting, Daley announced that a curfew was to take effect that night from 7 p.m. to 6 a.m. for all persons under 21. Taverns were ordered closed on the West Side, and the sale of gasoline in containers was banned in an effort to stop the arson.

On Saturday afternoon, at the Mayor's request, President Lyndon B. Johnson ordered the Army onto the streets of the city. Conlisk had requested the troops in case the rioting spread from the West Side to the South Side. The burning and looting of stores continued Saturday night but tapered off after midnight. Early Sunday morning Army units began to arrive from Fort Hood, Texas, and Fort Carson, Colorado. Some bivouacked at O'Hare Airport, others in Jackson Park and at the Glenview Naval Air Station. Some were assigned to patrols on the South Side.

Throughout the two days following King's murder, however, Daley had been dissatisfied with Conlisk's performance. The destruction of property on the West Side had been extensive. Nevertheless, the police were to be praised by much of the media and the public for their conduct, contrasted with the criticisms received by the Washington D.C. police for allegedly being ineffective in trying to quell the rioting in that city.

Neil F. Hartigan, later to be elected Lieutenant Governor and Attorney General of Illinois, was Daley's liaison with the police during the period immediately following King's murder. Early on, Hartigan advised me that Daley believed Conlisk had moved too slowly in stopping the spread of violence and destruction.

Sunday, Monday and Tuesday, the 7th, 8th and 9th of April, were relatively quiet. As a result, on Wednesday, April 10, the Army and the National Guard withdrew from the streets and the curfew was lifted. The trouble was over for the city but not for Conlisk.

The statistics for the rioting were formidable: 3120 arrests, of which 2411 involved male adults, 163 female adults and 546 juveniles; 908 were for burglary, 979 for disorderly conduct, 887 for curfew violations, 19 for arson, 308 for aggravated battery, aggravated assault, robbery, theft, unlawful use of weapons, criminal damage, reckless conduct, and 19 for other crimes. Nine civilians died in the rioting. Six of the deaths were from bullet wounds, the sources of which were never determined. Ninety police officers were injured. Two of them were shot by snipers. Forty-six civilians were wounded by gunfire, 20 of whom were hit by stray bullets and 26 were shot "by persons in the riot area." The insured losses from arson and looting totaled $14 million. The actual losses were much higher.

On Monday, April 15th, one week after the rioting had been halted, the superintendent was ordered by Daley to meet with him at City Hall. The Mayor said he was very displeased with the way the police reacted to the looting and burning. He advised Conlisk that a public statement would be made to that effect. Later that morning, the Mayor told a news conference that he had ordered Conlisk during the riot to issue a shoot to kill order. Daley was greatly distressed, he said, to learn that no such order had been issued. He said he told Conlisk to make sure that it was issued at this time.

Daley had done something he had never done before as mayor. He had publicly rebuked a city employee in the strongest terms. And the man he rebuked was his number one appointee.

The Superintendent returned to police headquarters a shaken man. When informed that, after he left City Hall, the Mayor had made his shoot to kill statement, Conlisk met with Captain Needham and me in the superintendent's office. Never, Conlisk said, had he received anything from Daley that could be interpreted as a shoot to kill order during the rioting. Now the superintendent's problem was how to issue one. "I am not going to be the one who has to go before a federal grand jury," Conlisk said, referring to how such an order might bring about wrongful police conduct.

The problem was how to draft an order which would comply with the Mayor's directive and, at the same time, not deviate from the department's order pertaining to the use of deadly force which was based on a state statute. Daley had talked in simple terms of shooting to kill arsonists and shooting to maim looters. The law made no such distinction. There was a series of conditions to be met and, if met, deadly force could be used by police officers. There was no such thing as "shooting to maim." The law said that if a police officer was justified in pulling the trigger, any resultant death was justified.

Conlisk, Needham and I agreed that there should be a teletype message to all police personnel which would simply restate the department's general order on the use of deadly force, the same order which had been issued by former Superintendent Orlando W. Wilson 11 months before. The message was sent. The next day, few news accounts pointed out that there was no change by Conlisk on the subject of deadly force and that, indeed, there was no new order. Most of the media maintained that Conlisk had now finally issued a shoot to kill order.

Daley had publicly chastised his top appointee and had done so five days after all supporting troops had left the city and the rioting had ended. Earl Bush, Daley's press secretary at the time, blamed the Mayor's statements on what Bush called the "Irish Neanderthals" who influenced Daley's action. These "Neanderthals," Bush said, were Fire Commissioner Robert J. Quinn, Special Events Director Jack Reilly and Sewer Commissioner Edward Quigley, who was the Democratic committeeman of a heavily damaged West Side ward. The three had repeatedly told the Mayor there would not have been block after block of gutted stores and burned out buildings if the police had moved aggressively with gunfire against looters and arsonists. Corporation Counsel Raymond F. Simon and Bush had sought unsuccessfully to dissuade Daley from any public rebuke of the superintendent. Bush, however, was also the subject of the Mayor's ire. The press secretary had been out of the country on vacation during the rioting and failed to cut his vacation short and return when he heard about it. Daley, greatly displeased, fired Bush on the same day he publicly denounced Conlisk. Several days later, when the Mayor calmed down, Bush was reinstated.

Daley's verbal attack on Conlisk caused the superintendent to be even more timid in his actions and almost totally subservient to the Mayor's wishes. This was to have harmful consequences on the police, the city and the Mayor in the months ahead.

The immediate effect of the shoot to kill order was the generation of strong antipathy by the national news media toward Daley. A 32 year political career, which was more liberal than conservative, was overshadowed by a three word phrase. The remnants of Daley's former reputation as a mayor who could make life better for the people of a big city, as the king-maker for John F. Kennedy, and the strong supporter of Lyndon Johnson's Great Society, was greatly harmed. In New York City, Mayor John Lindsay led a nationwide chorus of intellectuals in denouncing the Mayor's statement.

Just as shoot to kill earned Daley the enmity of the country's intellectuals, so, too, would it earn him the support of an even larger number of bigots who now viewed him as the new champion of "let's get tough with the blacks." Men and women, many of whom before the shoot to kill order had looked down on Daley as simply a big city, Irish-Catholic political boss, now wrote by the thousands to City Hall from all over the country expressing their support for the Mayor's position. Again, the political deeds of more than three decades were forgotten and replaced by the memory of those three words.

Shortly after the rioting, Daley appointed a commission headed by Federal District Court Judge Richard B. Austin to prepare a report on the events of early April and to make recommendations for the future. That report vindicated Conlisk and the police. With some exceptions, it stated, the police showed "a sound understanding of their role as law enforcement officers in the use of deadly force." The police conduct in the rioting deserved the "highest commendations and approval of all Chicagoans." Daley's chastisement of Conlisk was implicitly rebuked by the commission. But the report went almost unnoticed. It was issued in August of 1968 as the city prepared for the Democratic National Convention.

# The Night That Shaped an Image

# 7

*"All prisoner vans to the front of the Conrad Hilton."*

—Chicago police radio message, 8:26 p.m.,
Wednesday, Aug. 28, 1968.

The decades-long argument about what happened on the streets of Chicago during the 1968 Democratic National Convention is the result of conflicting perceptions. One side saw the events as a brutal and senseless action by Mayor Daley, using his police to repress protests by young Americans. The other side saw the events as efforts by a mixed age group led by radicals who, with the objective of a victory by the North Vietnamese over American forces, sought a confrontation with the police. The purpose: to convince the public of the alleged oppressive nature of our governmental system as it operated in this country and in foreign lands.

Because of these two totally different perceptions, the details of the Chicago conflict never can be reconciled. Chicago in 1968 was one of the rare moments in this century when two segments of the American population were in complete emotional opposition to each other. Mayor Daley emerged the hero of one and the villain of the other.

It was a time of terrible emotions—terrible because they tore away civilities. That, of course, is what the demonstrators wanted.

Their leadership called themselves the National Mobilization Committee to End the War in Vietnam, a name which only partially expressed its objective, for it sought to end the war with a North Vietnamese victory. Its type of tactics had been tested in other countries through the years with success, namely, seek to change a government policy by portraying the government as an oppressor, causing the government and its policy to be discredited in the eyes of the people. The leadership had every reason to believe these tactics would be successful in Chicago. So they came—the leaders of the National Mobilization Committee to End the War in Vietnam, including pacifist David Dellinger and former Communist Party official, Sydney Peck, with the support of about five thousand demonstrators and, most importantly, a huge segment of the national media. What happened here had an impact on history in general and on the life of Richard J. Daley in particular. This is how I saw it as Daley's police spokesman.

In May of 1968 the Chicago Police had begun their preparations for the Convention. During the almost four months which were to follow, the news media, local and national, worked to build a frenzied atmosphere which was to envelope the Democratic gathering. David Dellinger and those who had organized the National Mobilization Committee repeatedly stated that Chicago, during the convention, would be the scene of street demonstrations aimed at influencing the Democratic Party and the federal government to reverse their positions on United States involvement in Vietnam. The news media pounded away on the theme that Chicago was a powder keg about to explode in the last week of August. The Mayor and the police sought to diffuse the situation with no success.

Later, the media was to accuse Daley and the police of helping to create the conflicts on the streets by forecasting them. The opposite was true. Over and over, the Mayor at news conferences stated that he did not expect trouble. The police department turned down media requests to have the police demonstrate on television the use of mace and to discuss the possible acquisition of armored vehicles to be used in crowd control. A seller of armored vehicles once parked a sample of his wares outside police headquarters and local newsmen were pleased at the thought the police might make such purchases and, thereby, contribute to the psychological build-up in which the newsmen were engaged. No such purchase was contemplated.

Requests came to me from network-owned television stations to permit the filming of police target practice, to arrange for interviews with members of the police anti-sniper teams, and to set up demonstrations of any police training to combat rioting. All such requests were denied in an effort to discourage the build-up of tensions.

Much of the media worked to develop the thesis that the police planned to have a confrontation with the demonstrators. The truth was that confrontation was the National Mobilization Committee's goal and the police hoped to avoid it.

Everything connected with the police was given a sinister connotation. Helmets, for example, had been worn by the 900 police officers assigned to protect Dr. King during his marches in Chicago in the summer of 1966. In the summer of 1968, however, helmets became symbols of the alleged intent of the police, not to protect citizens and themselves, but to attack demonstrators.

A detrimental by-product of Daley's shoot to kill order was that Superintendent Conlisk rarely spoke publicly during this pre-convention period. When he did speak, however, it was to state that he did not expect trouble or rioting during the convention.

The build-up continued. Reporter Bill Plante of CBS-TV showed a film clip of the International Amphitheatre where the convention was to be held, as he put it, "in a ghetto area with only one access route." Henry De Zutter of the *Chicago Daily News* wrote how police were assigned to the Lincoln Park area to watch "the McCarthy people." Ron Kozial of the *Chicago Tribune* played up security arrangements at the convention hall. Television camera crews filmed demonstrators in Lincoln Park rehearsing methods to break police lines. William F. Buckley, Jr., contributed to the emotional build-up by reporting an alleged plan by radicals to contaminate the Chicago water supply. Police denials that there was such a plan received little coverage.

I recommended to Conlisk that he meet with newsmen to brief them on police plans for traffic and crowd control during the convention, but the superintendent, of course, never liked that part of his job which called for public exposure. Now, this natural reluctance to appear before television cameras was reinforced by the Mayor's public censure of the superintendent after the April rioting which Conlisk interpreted as an order to maintain a low profile.

One of the contributing factors to the conflicts between the police and newsmen during convention week was the disagreement over parking arrangements for television vans near the hotels. Foolishly, such arrangements were made the responsibility of the city's Department of Streets and Sanitation, not the police. Many of the parking requests from the television networks and stations, however, were forwarded by the newly appointed Streets Commissioner, James McDonough, to Colonel Jack Reilly, the Mayor's Director of Special Events. Reilly, who had a low regard for the news media, ignored the requests.

During the week before the convention, I learned from Conlisk that he had been told by the Mayor to notify television representatives that no arrangements could be made for parking their mobile vans near the entrances to the Loop hotels serving as headquarters for the presidential candidates and housing delegates. I immediately telephoned the Mayor's press secretary, Earl Bush. This was a policy position, I said, which obviously would result in the ill will of the television networks. Bush agreed. He and Corporation Counsel Raymond Simon suggested to Conlisk that a more conciliatory letter be forwarded to the television network representatives stating that, while no parking could be arranged on the streets or at hotel entrances, everything possible would be done to acquire parking spaces for the television mobile equipment in nearby parking lots and other off-street locations close to the hotels. (This still was a needlessly negative position by the city.) Conlisk agreed with the revised letter and it was sent by him to the network representatives.

Unfortunately, only the part of the letter stating that parking spaces could not be made available at the entrances to the hotels was made public by the media. Eric Sevareid set the tone for the television reaction by going on the air to denounce Daley for a lack of cooperation. Sevareid was right.

On Saturday, August 23, two days before the convention was to open, Daley, in response to this television criticism, arranged for a meeting in his office with vice presidents of the three networks in an effort to resolve the problem. The Mayor agreed to assist the newsmen, and assigned Streets Commissioner McDonough, Police Commander James J. Riordan and me to accompany the television representatives to the convention hotels to determine at which street locations their cameras could be placed. At the intersection of Balbo Drive and Michigan Avenue the newsmen sought permission to construct a television platform on the southwest sidewalk. The location was a poor one for filming anyone entering or leaving the Conrad Hilton Hotel entrance one-half block to the south, but a great location if there was going to be violence at the intersection. Commander Riordan denied the request on the grounds that the platform would unreasonably interfere with pedestrian traffic and contribute to vehicular congestion. He said television cameras could be set up on the public way at the hotel's entrance and on a hotel canopy near the intersection but that there would be no elevated platform at Balbo and Michigan. No city official knew then how important that intersection would become to the television networks four days later.

Although the day-to-day building of tensions by the news media had gone on for almost four months, nothing that had taken place prepared the Mayor or the police for the torrent of national media criticism which was to become intensified on Sunday, August 25, the day before the convention opened. The anti-Chicago, anti-police verbal assault began on NBC with Frank McGee's commentary followed by Chet Huntley and David Brinkley, and on CBS, by Walter Cronkite. The latter told his national television audience there was no other way to describe Chicago except as a "police state."

After midnight, on Sunday, having failed in their efforts to have the demonstrators comply with a city ordinance barring everyone from Lincoln Park after 11:00 p.m., the police began a drive to clear the park. City officials had refused the National Mobilization Committee's request for permission to remain in the park overnight. At no time, however, had Conlisk indicated to me that the police planned to clear the park. It is my opinion that he had no knowledge of this and that the decision was made by others. First Deputy Superintendent Rochford later said he did not know who gave the order. It was a needless and harmful one.

For months I had expected serious problems between newsmen and the police during the convention. As a reporter, I had been taken into custody by the police on March 17 of the preceding year while seeking to cross State Street during the St. Patrick's Day Parade which I was assigned by the *Sun-Times* to cover. (Only television reporters, I was told, could be in the street.) I was well aware of the unfortunate animosities which existed between the police and the media. I thought, however, that the major problem at the convention would be verbal disagreements between the authorities and the press, leading, possibly, to arrests. I never envisioned news personnel being physically attacked by police with night sticks. At about 12:30 a.m. Monday, I went home from police headquarters thinking, mistakenly, that there would be no further news until the convention opened at 10:00 a.m. The superintendent also left at that time for his home. At about 2:30 a.m. I was awakened by a telephone call from Sam Boyle, city editor of the *Philadelphia Bulletin*. He said one of his reporters, Claude Lewis, had been unjustly attacked by the police near Lincoln Park and was being treated at Henrotin Hospital. I apologized on behalf of the department and promised an investigation.

At 8:00 a.m. I took the "L" to work, reading en route a *Sun-Times* article citing police assaults on at least half a dozen other newsmen. As soon as I reached headquarters, I drafted a proposed order noting that there had been reports of unjustified attacks on news personnel and calling for an end to such assaults. I took the proposed order to Deputy Superintendent Rochford because experience convinced me he would act faster than Conlisk. The superintendent, moreover, had never impressed me as being sufficiently concerned about the rights and safety of newsmen. At any rate, I thought he would have to consult with Rochford or Captain Needham before acting, and the urgency of this situation did not allow for such procrastination.

Rochford agreed there should be an order. He made one change in the wording, however, adding a sentence which stated that the police should cooperate with newsmen "despite any personal feelings." I thought this injected an undesirable tone to the order, with the implication that the police might be reasonable in harboring personal antipathies to the newsmen. I so stated but Rochford wanted the addition and I felt it was important to issue the order even with this flaw so as to lessen the likelihood of assaults on news personnel. The order was issued.

That afternoon several hundred persons marched around police headquarters in what they described as a "free Tom Hayden" demonstration. The Students for a Democratic Society leader had been arrested earlier in Lincoln Park for a minor offense.

Monday evening I remained at headquarters until midnight and then, foolishly, went home, knowing that once again the police were going to clear Lincoln Park but not expecting that again newsmen would be attacked. They were.

When I arrived at work on Tuesday morning at 8:30 a.m. there had already been numerous calls from the media. I immediately began work on a statement which I hoped Conlisk would issue and, perhaps, even deliver on television, calling for peace between the police and the media. At about noon I received a call from Emmett Dedmon, editor of the *Sun-Times*. He said that eight top executives from the media wanted to meet with Conlisk as soon as possible. The Superintendent had left for lunch. I went to a downtown restaurant hoping to find him. It was crucial that there be a peaceful relationship with the news media and I felt that the Superintendent should be immediately advised of Dedmon's request. My efforts to find Conlisk were unsuccessful. After his lunch, at 2:00 p.m., he returned and agreed to meet with the news representatives. But he did not want to be later questioned on television about the meeting.

At 3:30 p.m. Conlisk met in his office with Dedmon, Ben Bradlee and Hal Bruno of *Newsweek,* Lloyd Wendt, editor of Chicago's *American,* Roy Fisher, editor of the *Chicago Daily News,* Tom Wolfsmith, representing the *Chicago Tribune,* Angus Corley, news director of the NBC–TV station in Chicago, and Bob Ferrante, his counterpart at the CBS–TV station. The newsmen demanded that steps be taken to end the attacks on reporters, cameramen and photographers. Corley was the most emotional. He charged that two of his employees were singled out for assaults because they were black. Dedmon acted as the leader of the group and remained calm.

The newsmen asked that specific police officers be assigned to the various trouble areas to make certain the rights of the media were not violated. Conlisk agreed. After leaving the office, Dedmon told waiting reporters that the meeting was satisfactory. I began to draft the order which could comply with the newsmen's request. Conlisk softened the proposed order, but, at 7:00 p.m. it was issued. That night there were no attacks on newsmen.

CBS Vice President Bill Leonard later wrote that, at this point, it looked like everyone would get through the convention week without a serious conflict. This, of course, was a view about Sunday and Monday nights not to be shared by those who drafted the Walker Report after the convention.

Wednesday, August 28, was to be the key day of the convention. In the evening, the Democratic candidate for president was to be nominated. In the afternoon the National Mobilization Committee was to hold a rally at the Grant Park Bandshell. I arrived there about 2:30 p.m. and, a short time later, some bottles and other objects were thrown in the crowd causing people to scatter in various directions. I ran back across the adjacent Columbus Drive and stood at the foot of a pedestrian bridge to view the proceedings. The rock and bottle tossing and consequent pedestrian scattering, with police moving in and making some arrests, were filmed and used in the movie *Medium Cool*. The incident appeared to be far more violent on film than it was.

From the pedestrian bridge, I saw National Guard troops being moved up from the parking lot south of Soldier Field to the south end of the bandshell area, and police reinforcements taking their positions north of the area. Dick Gregory and other speakers at the rally strongly denounced the police and the United States. I wished then, and today, that the networks had televised the rally so a national audience could have seen and heard the leaders of the group which sought a confrontation with the police. At the conclusion of the speeches, approximately 1,700 spectators moved off the grassy area and lined the sidewalk along Columbus Drive leading north to Balbo Drive. Handbills were passed out by the police warning that there was no permit to march to the International Amphitheatre six miles away and that anyone who violated the law would be arrested.

A police car with a public address system moved up and down Columbus Drive cautioning spectators not to line up with those persons on the sidewalk who were about to begin their march. A short distance away, at a street department equipment garage, I joined with Deputy Superintendent Rochford, Assistant Corporation Counsel Richard J. Elrod, and Sidney Peck, a former official of the Wisconsin State Communist Party. The three men were discussing a possible alternative to marching to the convention hall. Rochford and Elrod told Peck that the demonstrators would be permitted to march west across the Balbo Drive overpass to the Conrad Hilton Hotel if they would agree not to go to the International Amphitheater but, instead, hold a rally on the lawn across Michigan Avenue from the hotel. Peck said he was not authorized to accept such an offer. Only David Dellinger could do this, Peck said. Rochford and Elrod thereupon left with Peck to walk a couple of hundred yards to Dellinger who declined the city officials' offer.

The crowd then began to move out. To the east on the Balbo

Drive overpass a police line was standing. Newsmen as well as demonstrators were being prevented from continuing a half block west to Michigan Avenue. I assisted Larry Green, then a reporter for the *Chicago Daily News,* to get through the line, and was joined by columnist Gary Wills and Don Rose, a publicist and strategist for the National Mobilization Committee, both of whom I also assisted.

The police line on Balbo remained in position so the crowd was unable to move to Michigan Avenue at that point. Suddenly, to the north, marching south on Michigan amidst moving and parked cars, came hundreds of demonstrators, chanting and shouting. They had crossed over from Grant Park on an unguarded street two blocks north of Balbo Drive and were now charging south toward the intersection of Michigan and Balbo. The police and National Guard had failed to keep the demonstrators in Grant Park. They were now headed to the very spot where the television networks had sought to build a special platform for their cameras. The cameras were there anyway, even without the platform. Cameramen were standing atop a small canopy, which projected from the hotel near the corner, and mobile cameras were at numerous locations. Other stationary cameras were set up on the sidewalk one-half block to the south in front of the hotel's main entrance.

I ran down from the Balbo overpass to the intersection with Michigan Avenue. The police had hurriedly set up a line of men across Michigan just south of Balbo. Deputy Superintendent Rochford arrived at the scene. The size of the mob confronting the police increased to about a thousand. Officers then blocked Balbo to the west of Michigan. Rochford called for a police car with a public address system. He asked the mob to clear the intersection and said they could hold a rally on the lawn on the east side of Michigan Avenue across from the hotel. The chanting grew in volume, "Fuck LBJ—Fuck LBJ."

Then Reverend Ralph Abernathy's mule train from the Southern Christian Leadership Conference appeared on the scene coming north on Michigan Avenue toward the police line at Balbo from the rear. The mule train was allowed through and moved on.

I was standing in the middle of Michigan Avenue a few feet south of Balbo next to Rochford when the fighting began. From where I stood, it seemed that persons in the front line of the mob started to rush the police line. (I later learned from overhead film that the police facing east on Balbo had forced the mob into the police on Michigan Avenue.) There was a surge and the police strung across the avenue started scuffling with demonstrators who were coming forward. Prisoner vans were quickly moved into position behind the police line. I leaped onto a van tailgate for safety from the swinging police clubs. Arrested persons were being taken to the vans. They were struggling with the police, resisting arrest, and the police were hitting them with their batons. Then, the police moved north on Michigan through the intersection. It appeared as if the mob was being attacked from three sides and there was little room for it to escape, only north on Michigan. Police waving night sticks waded in and the scenes went out over television to much of the world with an impact which has never been matched. "The whole world is watching," chanted demonstrators and spectators.

The police wave moved on. I was disturbed. There seemed to be little room for the mob to flee. I walked to the sidewalk east of the hotel, spotted Jack Clarke of the Mayor's Department of Investigations. We both shook our heads slowly from side to side in disbelief at the spectacle we were witnessing and well aware of the anti-Chicago Police image being created.

Some members of the mob fled into a group of spectators standing behind wooden barricades erected by the police on the southwest corner of Balbo and Michigan in front of the hotel. Police officers pursued. There were sounds of breaking glass and cries of fear and pain, as windows in the hotel's Haymarket Lounge were smashed.

Objects were being thrown from hotel windows and members of the mob who had reached the lawn across the street from the hotel were now tossing rocks at the main entrance. Rochford gave an order that only police officers in uniform were to be on Michigan Avenue. The order was needlessly detrimental to newsmen. An ABC-TV crew standing on the sidewalk near the entrance was being pelted with various objects thrown from the windows above (later identified as McCarthy headquarters). I tried to move the TV crew out of the line of fire and into the entrance to the Hilton. A police lieutenant ordered them back into the unprotected areas of the sidewalk. He also tried to chase me off Michigan Avenue because, although a police official, I was in civilian clothes and Rochford's order permitted only uniformed police to remain.

Demonstrators had put stink bombs in the hotel lobby. Women guests in evening gowns were running with fright through the corridors. The demonstrators, who had broken through the windows at Balbo and Michigan, were arrested in the lobby. Through it all, the mob continued chanting, "The whole world is watching."

I ran north on Michigan Avenue as the police pursued the mob. Newsmen were being chased by Assistant Deputy Superintendent Merlin Nygren. I told Bob Jamieson, then of CBS, Jimmy Murray, a reporter for Chicago's *American,* and other newsmen to ignore Rochford's order and keep close to me so that the police would not interfere with them. I saw an ABC camera crew filming the burning of signs in a litter basket. I did not know what a congressional investigation would later learn: the television crew had started the fire to add to the drama.

I then went to the basement of the Hilton and, for a few moments, watched the television coverage of the events inside the convention hall. Out on the street again, I was advised that my office was looking for me—Mike Wallace of CBS had been taken into custody by police at the Amphitheatre. In the weeks before the convention I had stated several times to friends, half seriously, half in jest, that the animosity between police and the press was so intense that I anticipated Walter Cronkite being arrested during some convention altercation. Now, what I thought was probably the closest thing to that had happened. I returned to police headquarters at 11th and State Streets to learn that Wallace had already been released at the convention hall.

The confrontation at Balbo and Michigan lasted approximately 20 minutes. No event had a greater effect on Richard J. Daley's image. He was never near Balbo and Michigan that night but, through the medium of television, his image at the convention hall was mixed with scenes of the street fighting in the minds of tens of millions of people. Much of the world and most of its intellectuals would view Daley as a villain because of that night. Much more of the world would view him as a hero who had stood up against the forces of radicalism which, they believed, threatened the country. Largely forgotten would be Daley's public deeds during the decades preceding this fight between policemen and demonstrators. What the world thinks of Daley will forever be affected by what each of us thinks happened that night.

On the following day I awoke at about 7:00 a.m. I knew even before going to sleep the previous night that I wanted to go on television to speak out on behalf of the police. When I awoke, I began to formulate what I would say. At about 8:00 a.m., I received a phone call telling me that NBC's Hugh Downs had told his "Today" audience there was only one word that could be used to describe the Chicago Police and that word was "pigs." I told my wife I was going to try to go on television. She was worried about how the news industry might retaliate for my criticism. I left home determined not to read any news accounts about Balbo and Michigan. I had always tried to balance my views, to look for the good and the bad, and to accept the fact that human events are often complex. On this morning, however, I did not want to hear or read what was being said about police conduct because I knew that, although their conduct was subject to criticism, I did not want to be deterred from speaking in their defense. Some police conduct was wrong but the overall position of Daley and the police was right.

During my years as a reporter covering the Mayor, I had learned, by listening to him at press conferences, that sometimes there is no way to effectively qualify a public position with conditions. In some instances the public decides simply to be either for or against a policy. That was the way it was about Balbo and Michigan and the street conflicts of the 1968 Democratic National Convention. For months a propaganda battle had been waged against Daley, the police and Chicago by the national and, to a large degree, the local news media. Now there was an opportunity for us to win that psychological battle. This was no time to haggle or soul search over whether, in a more perfect world, things could have been done better.

So, I went to work that day not really knowing but guessing the hostility which the news media felt about the police because of the events of the preceding night. At 9:15 a.m. I went into Conlisk's office. He was with General Dunn, the commanding officer of the National Guard on the streets of Chicago. I asked the Superintendent for permission to call a press conference. "There are some things," I told him, "which I think have to be said and they should be said by someone who is not a police officer." Conlisk shrugged his shoulders, and said, "I don't have any objection."

I thanked him and proceeded to inform the media that there would be a press conference at 10:30 a.m. I then telephoned Daley's press secretary, Earl Bush, and told him there were things that had to be said in defense of the  city, the police and the Mayor, and that I was going to call a press conference to say them. He said he would check to see if the Mayor approved. I told Bush not to tell Daley. I was afraid the Mayor would order me not to do it, and I didn't want to hear that. "If I'm wrong, the Mayor can fire me," I told Bush. "O.K." he said, "but if you do it, you're on your own and this conversation never took place."

One of the problems of a political system in which one man is so dominant is that his friends, allies and employees, seldom, if ever, speak out, partially because of concern that the leader does not want them to speak and, partially, because it's easier to leave it all to him. During the months of propaganda against the police, no one in Chicago had spoken out in their defense except Daley. Conlisk and, because of him, the entire Police Department remained silent. Now, someone had to speak besides the Mayor.

At the conference I went on the offensive. No reporter on a news assignment should be interfered with by the police. That was the first principle I spelled out. There was no justification, I said, for policemen to be assaulting newsmen. There must be no equivocation on that point.

The news media, I continued, had been engaging in "colossal propaganda" against the City of Chicago, its mayor and its police. Eric Sevareid, Walter Cronkite, Chet Huntley, David Brinkley, Roger Mudd,—they did not like the fact that the Mayor of Chicago took seriously the need for security requirements.

I was critical of the television industry and its coverage of the police. "Someday," I concluded, "a mob may come into your town, may come down your streets, and you will want your police department to stand its ground the way the Chicago Police Department did."

After the news conference Bush informed me that the Mayor was going to meet with newsmen at his own news conference at about 12:30 p.m. Meanwhile, Bill Leonard, the CBS vice president who was in charge of that network's convention coverage, telephoned me and said Cronkite wanted to interview the Superintendent on camera at the Amphitheatre before the convention session that evening. I told him I would relay the invitation. I did, and Conlisk declined. CBS, it turned out, did not need him. The Mayor agreed to be interviewed by Cronkite at the Amphitheatre.

During that evening's news on NBC, David Brinkley read a statement from the network's news chief, Rueven Frank, denying my accusations of unfair television coverage. CBS news vice president Richard Salant also issued a similar statement which was read by Walter Cronkite. Both networks attacked me for making what they said were unjustified criticisms. At about 6:30 p.m. the Mayor was interviewed by Cronkite. It was one of Daley's finest moments. Cronkite in the years to come repeatedly apologized to Daley-haters for not taking the offensive against the Mayor.

On camera, the Mayor spoke about convention security in the perspective of the political assassinations which had shocked the nation in the preceding five years. He was a man displaying reasonableness and calm, a total contrast to the villain's image which the networks had sought to convey the previous evening.

Meanwhile, amidst all the violence on the streets, the Democrats had nominated their candidate for president of the United States, Senator Hubert H. Humphrey.

On the following day I received a telephone call from the Mayor thanking me for my news conference in defense of the police and him. "You were," he said, "true to the tradition of your Irish forbearers."

I was to later learn that Daley had ambiguous feelings about the police and what happened that August night so long ago at Balbo and Michigan.

# Convention Aftermath 8

*"...we fought those coppers all the time."*

A short time after the convention Daley invited me to join him for lunch at Democratic headquarters on the second floor of the Sherman House. We talked for more than an hour about the police department and the superintendent.

I told the Mayor that Conlisk was a good and honest man but that he was deathly afraid of television—a great handicap for the city's top police officer. Daley replied that the superintendent should only read prepared statements on camera and never answer newsmen's questions.

Our discussion continued. I told the Mayor that the police tactics were terrible at Balbo and Michigan. He was concerned, he said, about the obvious misuse of police batons and the lack of proper training in crowd control. He said he would order Conlisk to carry out such training immediately. After asking me to stay in close touch with him, our meeting ended.

In the days that followed the convention, the Mayor's Office received more than 100,000 letters, of which the ratio in favor of his policies, regarding permits for demonstrators and the police actions, was 20 to one. One result of the convention week, however, was the creation of a total breach between much of the local press and the Mayor. The exceptions were many of the older reporters, cameramen and photographers, along with much of the staff of the *Chicago Tribune* and its editor, Don Maxwell. In the period following the convention, Daley and Chicago had no defenders more staunch than they. This support was to continue until the day that Clayton Kirkpatrick became the *Tribune's* editor.

The aftermath of the convention as it affected the Chicago Police lasted for many months. Investigations were instigated by a committee of Congress, the FBI, the U.S. Attorney's Office, and the Federal Commission on the Causes of Violence which had been created by President Johnson following the murders of Dr. King and Senator Robert F. Kennedy. The man appointed to head the Commission's Chicago Study Team in probing the violence of convention week was a lawyer who had served as a member of the Mayor's committee to investigate the rioting after Dr. King's death—Dan Walker.

Those of us in local government and the media knew that his report would come down heavy on the police. On November 30th it was released to newsmen and the expression "police riot" was introduced.

The following morning I met with Mayoral Press Secretary Bush and Corporation Counsel Simon at City Hall to discuss suggestions for the Mayor's public response. Bush and Simon insisted that the body of the report should be praised as excellent. I said this was much too favorable an assessment but my view was the minority. Bush wrote a proposed mayoral statement. Daley told him to add strong words backing the police. I then advised Conlisk by telephone that the Mayor was about to issue a statement and that I would ask him whether he wanted the Superintendent to say something publicly. "Do you have to?" Conlisk asked. "Do you have to say anything?" He made it clear that he preferred to remain silent with no defense of the police.

After conferring with the Mayor, Bush said Conlisk could issue a statement the following day and phrase it according to how the reaction shaped up to the Mayor's remarks. The next morning I showed Conlisk a suggested statement I had written regarding the Walker Report. He said he did not want to make any public comment. Inquiring newsmen should be told, he said, that he was studying the report. Monday night NBC anchorman Floyd Kalber noted on his 10:00 p.m. news program that no one connected with the police department would comment on the report.

Tuesday morning I again recommended to Conlisk that it was in the best interest of the department for him to make a statement in support of the police. He said no. Deputy Superintendent Mulchrone, who was in the Superintendent's office, agreed with this negative decision.

I called Bush regarding Conlisk's position. "Does he want to wait until the Mayor orders him?" Bush asked. He added that he would advise Daley of the situation. I asked him not to and said I would attempt to persuade Conlisk to speak on behalf of his own men. When I returned to the superintendent's office, however, he exclaimed, "I never know what that man [Daley] wants me to do." He thereupon telephoned the Mayor and read my suggested statement criticizing the report and backing the police. Daley suggested that a sentence be added calling upon Walker to produce for the Superintendent any new evidence of wrongdoing by police personnel which he might have in his possession.

Bush later called me to say the Mayor was annoyed at the superintendent. "Isn't there anybody who can make a decision without coming to me?" Bush quoted the Mayor as saying.

Conlisk's written statement was handed out to the press but he refused to go along with my recommendation that he also read it for television and radio. The animosity from newsmen increased. I warned Conlisk he was going to be ripped to pieces by the news media for his refusal to make any statement in public about the Walker Report and the Democratic Convention. Conlisk was adamant. More harm than good would come from any television or radio appearance, he insisted.

The following day, December 4, there was an editorial attack on the lack-of-news situation at police headquarters, but it was directed, not at Conlisk, but at me. The *Chicago Daily News* editorially called upon the Mayor and the superintendent to replace me with someone who did not "view his role as that of a propagandist and white-washer for the Department." The editorial apparently was a delayed reaction to my August 29th post-convention news conference, and was triggered by the absence of any response from the department following the issuance of the Walker Report. I showed Conlisk the editorial. Neither then nor at any time thereafter did he comment on it.

In the months that followed, Daley spoke with me frequently about the inadequacies of the police department and its superintendent. The Mayor's strongest private comments came during a conversation on June 10, 1969.

He called me to his office and said he did not know how much longer Conlisk could remain as superintendent. His performance at a meeting on the previous day, the Mayor said, was something he had never before experienced. "Conlisk," Daley contended "had blown up" when the head of the city's youth programs made a mild criticism of the police.

The Mayor talked about the police for more than an hour. He spoke of former Police Commissioner Timothy J. O'Connor. Conlisk, Daley said, was just like O'Connor. The latter, the Mayor maintained, should have been fired after the mayoral election of 1955 because of his conduct in the Democratic primary. O'Connor, Daley continued, had sent "his biggest and strongest men into our ward" to help Martin Kennelly. "After the election I called O'Connor into my office to fire him but he appealed to me to let him keep his job. He had a sick wife," the Mayor said. "I told him you should have kept your coppers out of the primary." Then addressing me, the Mayor said: "I came from tough people. My father was an organizer for the sheet metal workers and we fought those coppers all the time."

Returning to his story about O'Connor, Daley said he had continued to chastise the former commissioner who finally exclaimed that he assumed the Mayor was going to fire him. "I didn't say that," the Mayor recalled, "but I warned him not to ever misuse the police again."

Daley said he told O'Connor to start checking on policemen who slept while they were supposed to be working. The commissioner was instructed to visit his own district on the far South Side and make a check. He did, Daley said, and found "half the policemen he checked were in bed when they were supposed to be working."

The Mayor then asked me what I thought of Commander Paul McLaughlin, a Daley neighbor, who had just been named by Conlisk to be commanding officer of the Central Police District. I replied that I really didn't know him very well. The Mayor said he had told McLaughlin never to take a "dirty dollar" from anyone. "I said," Daley continued, "if you ever need any money for your wife or family or anything, to come to me and I'd give it to you but not to take from anybody. I told him," Daley said, "not to let the people of our neighborhood down."

He went on and spoke of what he described as the lack of discipline and supervision within the department. "That was why," he said, "we had that disgrace over at Balbo and Michigan." The lack of discipline and supervision, the Mayor said, were ultimately Conlisk's fault.

"I know," Daley continued, "people think I fix the police and fix appointments but all I ever asked is that the superintendent and the fire commissioner appoint men who they would want to lead their sons. I had hoped that Conlisk would resign after the *Life* magazine article." He was referring to an article by Sandy Smith the previous December alleging that command corruption produced a lack of discipline which, in turn, led to police misconduct during the convention. In the article, Smith wrote about Conlisk, "He is never out with the men and he doesn't know how to handle the press."

Handling the press also was not one of Daley's finer skills.

# Daley vs. the Media— 9
# Round 1

*"There is nothing more immoral than a
newspaper man. You ought to know, Frank,
you were one of them."*

Daley once said to me that he admired Harry Truman
for being "the last president who got up in the morning and didn't check the newspapers to find out what
he was supposed to do that day."

The Mayor was a pre-television politician. He also may have been
the last major "non-media"-influenced elected official in the United
States. His elective career began in 1936, a decade before television
came to Chicago and to most of the nation. There was no "news media" when he was first elected to the Illinois House of Representatives,
only "the press." His view of the press in those days was dramatically
different from how the press and the media came to see themselves
throughout much of his career and how they view themselves today.

"The press" in the mid-1930s in Chicago was five daily newspapers, four of them owned and operated by men of vast wealth who
were strong opponents of President Franklin D. Roosevelt, the Democratic Party and Richard J. Daley's political philosophy. Two of the papers, the *American* and the *Herald and Examiner,* were owned by
William Randolph Hearst. The *Chicago Daily News* was controlled by
Colonel Frank Knox. Colonel Robert R. McCormick, the nation's
number one anti-New Dealer, was editor, publisher and owner of Illi-

nois' largest circulation daily, the *Chicago Tribune.* Only the *Chicago Times,* among the city's papers, was pro-Democratic.

The four anti-FDR publications were not examples of objective journalism in Daley's opinion. They were not independent newspapers fighting for truth, justice and the betterment of the citizenry. To Daley, they were tools used by their owners in their pursuit of political power. They sought to achieve this power without experiencing the hard and uncertain tasks of running for and holding elective political office. Let the Richard Daleys of the world struggle economically through law school, ring doorbells to promote candidates, work their way up the political party system, and put their reputations and futures on the line seeking the support of their constituents. This was the slow, cumbersome and uncertain way to political power. Moreover, the Richard Daleys had to reflect and serve the political views of their constituents. There was no need or desire for Hearst, Knox and McCormick to do the same. These were men who, as Daley saw it while a young politician, wanted to bypass the political process in their desire to use their newspapers to fight the New Deal in Washington and Springfield and shape the nation's foreign policy.

Daley's encounters in Springfield in the 1930s and 1940s were with reporters he viewed as the hired hatchet-men of the Chicago newspaper czars. A political writer like George Tagge of the *Tribune,* in Daley's opinion, was not a representative of what subsequent reporters were to term "the people's right to know," but an errand boy for Colonel McCormick, using threats of journalistic rewards and punishments to bring about his boss's political objectives.

Daley held the same opinion about most other newsmen. He considered it hypocritical that news personnel saw themselves as representatives of the people. He was determined, he once told me, never to let newsmen push him around.

Changes occurred rapidly in the newspaper business during Daley's 10 years in the Illinois General Assembly (1936–46). In the mid-1930s Hearst's two Chicago newspapers merged to become the *Herald American.* Colonel Knox became supportive of FDR's foreign policy and, in 1940, was appointed by the President as Secretary of the Navy. His newspaper, left under the stewardship of Chicagoan John O'Keefe, ceased its attacks on the White House and toned down its anti-Democratic domestic views. In 1941, Marshall Field III, heir to the

Chicago retail fortune and publisher of the left-leaning evening newspaper in New York City, began publishing the *Chicago Sun*. Its principal purpose was to challenge the isolationist and domestic Republican
positions of the *Tribune*. This goal was substantially blurred three days
after the *Sun* began publishing when the Japanese attacked Pearl Harbor, compelling Colonel McCormick to support the United States in its
struggles while still insisting the war was Roosevelt's doing. The *Chicago Times* during these years was led by news veteran Richard J. Fin-
negan who was a strong FDR supporter and backed Democrats like
Daley in Springfield.

After the war ended in 1945, Daley experienced even more reasons to bolster his dislike for the press. In 1946 he left his position as
minority leader of the Illinois Senate to make a try for an office which,
he thought, was more important, Sheriff of Cook County. Chicago
Democratic politicians have always considered Cook County elective
offices to be highly desirable, especially if becoming Mayor of Chicago
was the eventual goal.

Being sheriff was a dangerous political position. Those who held
it prior to Daley's 1946 campaign never moved on to higher office and
often retired with their reputations besmirched by either direct or implied involvement with organized crime. Nevertheless, the office controlled much political patronage and the opportunity to gain
substantial newspaper attention. But this attention was risky in that
newspaper coverage of a sheriff usually ended up negative. It is surprising, in retrospect, that Daley sought the office.

His Republican opponent was Elmer Michael Walsh. Daley's
Democratic colleagues were annoyed that Walsh used his middle name
in the campaign and on the ballot. The name "Elmer" alone, they believed, would have caused Irish voters to doubt the Republican's Catholicism, thereby adding to Daley's vote total.

Colonel McCormick and the *Tribune* were strong supporters of
Walsh. They warned editorially and in news columns that a victory for
Daley would be a victory for the Capone mob. At that time, Al Capone was dying from syphillis at his Palm Isle home in Florida. But his
heirs were a powerful factor in Chicago and Cook County politics.

Daley, who was not then, nor ever, mob-connected, was stunned
by the *Tribune's* accusations. They added to the reasons for his life-
long dislike of the press.

In November of 1946, Daley received the only elective defeat of his political career when the people of Cook County voted for Elmer Michael Walsh to be their sheriff. The defeat was a blessing. After four years, Walsh vanished from the political scene. Daley was spared what might have been the same fate. He later frequently quoted what his mother said to him at the time. "The Lord never closes a door that He doesn't open a window." Daley had been battered by the press but he would survive for his greatest triumph nine years later.

A window was opened in 1947 when the precinct captains of the 11th Ward elected Daley as the committeeman. He was now a member of the Cook County Democratic Central Committee.

In 1948, Adlai E. Stevenson was elected Governor of Illinois and, after his inauguration, appointed Daley to be the State's Director of Revenue. Meanwhile, Marshall Field purchased the *Chicago Times* and merged it with his sagging *Sun.* The *Sun,* deprived of much of its anti-McCormick thrust because of the war's diffusion of many foreign policy issues, had never been able to truly challenge the *Tribune* for circulation and advertising. The *Daily News,* following the death of Colonel Frank Knox, was sold to Miami publisher, John S. Knight, who exhibited reduced Republican partisanship in his Chicago acquisition.

After the war, Chicago television began. Almost a decade was to pass, however, before its local news coverage had substantial impact. Meanwhile, Daley served in the Stevenson state cabinet until the opportunity came for him to return to Chicago politics. It took place in 1949 with the death of the Clerk of Cook County, Michael J. Flynn. Daley was appointed by the Democratic-controlled Cook County Board to fill Flynn's unexpired term. In 1950, he was elected to a full four year term. Three years later, an opportunity opened for him to eventually become the mayor of Chicago. He was chosen by the Democratic machine to succeed Joseph Gill as chairman of the local Democratic Party. Daley was now in the position to block the incumbent mayor, the non-political, ex-moving company president and reformer, Martin H. Kennelly, who sought a third four year term in office.

As party chairman, Daley was easily elected again as County Clerk in 1954. Kennelly's second term as mayor was to expire in April of the following year. Late in 1954, the 50 Democratic ward committeemen were convened by their chairman, Daley. They voted 49 to one to endorse their chairman over incumbent Kennelly for mayor of Chicago in 1955. (The lonely negative vote was cast by County Assessor Frank Keenan.)

It was that mayoral campaign which hardened Daley's already negative opinion of the press. Three of the four daily newspapers—the *Tribune, Daily News* and *Sun-Times*—strongly opposed his candidacy, warning voters that a Daley win would mean victory for the mob. He would, they maintained, allow organized gambling and prostitution. The depth of the newspapers' antagonism embittered him.

Years later he said to me: "There is nothing more immoral than a newspaper man." Then he added, "You ought to know, Frank, you were one of them."

In the 1955 mayoral primary and in the general election, Daley was backed by the *American*. He never forgot the role that the paper's publisher, Stuart List, and the business manager, Don Walsh, played in bringing about the newspaper's support.

Daley was elected mayor that year with the help of another man— one who was to be of great assistance to him for the next 18 years— Earl Bush. When he met Daley, Bush was operating a small business which provided information about what was going on at City Hall and the County Building for neighborhood newspapers. Daley hired him for the campaign. Faced with a generally hostile downtown press, Bush fed a steady stream of pro-Daley stories to the community newspapers. His efforts were important in overcoming the downtown papers' depiction of Daley as a man who would make Chicago a wide-open town. After his victories over Kennelly in the primary and Robert Merriam in the election for mayor, Daley would never forget the importance of the neighborhood papers. They, in turn, supported him for the rest of his career.

In the late 1950s, during Daley's first four year term and after his re-election in 1959, the Chicago press continued its tradition of presenting the city to the world as a basically dirty-looking, crime-infested, politically corrupt city. Historically, the newspapers had seen no relationship between their economic success and that of the city. It was as if Chicago would always be strong economically and, therefore, newspapers attacks on every phase of city living could only make for good reading. There was, it was believed by the publishers and editors, no downside. Thus, on a January morning in 1960, when eight Chicago police officers were arrested in early morning raids in their homes and charged with burglaries, the newspapers were elated. It was one of the better stories of Chicago journalism. The burglars in blue for more than a year had been teamed with a 23 year old thief in breaking into and stealing from a long list of North Side businesses. The Summerdale police scandal, named after the police district where the eight officers were assigned, made front page headlines for months.

The police commissioner, Timothy J. O'Connor, was ousted and Daley began a national search for his successor. For weeks the papers wrote about police corruption. Then Daley found a new man to head the department—the Dean of the School of Criminology of the University of California, Orlando W. Wilson. Wilson was an absolute master at public relations. Moreover, his arrival in Chicago had a positive effect on its newspaper hierarchy. Confronted with the post-war decline in circulation brought about by the increasing inroads of television and the movement of a large segment of the city's population to the suburbs, the newspaper brass decided the time had come to stop knocking Chicago. It was no longer economically sound for the papers to continually deprecate the city in which they operated and, hopefully, made respectable profits. The result of this turnabout in editorial approach was newspaper support for Daley's new police superintendent. The papers praised Wilson and backed his reforms.

The new superintendent was a Norwegian-American Protestant fresh from the faculty life of pre-revolutionary Berkeley. No Irish-Catholic cop was he. Wilson was comfortable in board rooms and exclusive clubs, and, unlike any of his predecessors, he knew how to charm the city's top executives, especially in the newspaper business. It was a new day in Chicago journalism and Daley benefited from it. He might not be so bad after all, the press suggested. Wasn't he responsible for bringing in Wilson?

In the mayoral election of 1959, the three former anti-Daley newspapers had joined with the *American* to make unanimous the press endorsement of Daley for re-election. Now, with Wilson and police reforms, the Mayor was receiving good press—so good that by 1963 he was on the cover of *Time*. His relationship with the press, with the exception of a few months just before his death, was never better than it was in 1963.

In the early 1960s, something very different began to happen to the coverage of news in Chicago and, in varying degrees, throughout the country. A major factor in this change was the phenomenon of street demonstrations which, although not unknown in the history of American cities, began to develop with a new consistency and intensity in the 1960s. The impetus came from the desire of certain blacks to use public assemblies and, later, confrontations with authorities as tactics to right wrongs.

In Chicago the street demonstrations began as protests against the Superintendent of Schools, Benjamin C. Willis, who was accused of being an obstacle in efforts for more integration. One dramatic result of the frequent marches on the offices of the Chicago Board of Education and City Hall was the bringing together, in tense situations, of many newsmen and newswomen who had never previously covered police news, and many policemen who had never previously come in direct contact with news personnel. Added to this development of face-to-face confrontations between media representatives and policemen in highly emotional settings, was the fact that many of the reporters believed deeply in the principles of advocacy journalism. They did not agree with the friendly, and sometimes "kept," relationships which often existed between beat reporters and the police. The new breed of newsmen felt that exposures of police corruption did not go deep enough. They subscribed to the view, which was to become commonplace on college campuses and in the media, that there was a need for radical changes in police policy and operations. They believed they were the instruments to carry out these changes.

Combining with the street demonstrations and the philosophy of advocacy journalism to compound the problem in 1963 was the expansion of television news programs from 15 to 30 minutes as described by Theodore H. White in *The Making of the President, 1968*. Television began to demand news with action, and the easiest way to get it was with conflicts between marchers and policemen.

Throughout the five years prior to 1968 the division widened between the police personnel who were assigned to prevent disorders during demonstrations and the newsmen who worked through their reporting and personal conduct to bring about social and political change.

On June 10, 1965, demonstrators, including comedian Dick Gregory and Catholic nuns attired in habits, marched through the streets of the Loop seeking to bring about increased pressure for the removal of Schools Superintendent Willis. The actions of the nuns in defying police orders by obstructing traffic at Chicago's busiest intersection resulted in many arrests and genuinely shocked police officers who had never expected such conduct by members of religious orders.

The gulf between the police and other segments of the community was enlarged in the months that followed. In August, on the West Side, a fire department hook and ladder truck went out of control, striking a street sign which in turn fell, killing a black woman. Rioting ensued which caused Governor Otto Kerner to call out the National Guard.

After Martin Luther King brought his campaign to Chicago, far more serious rioting took place in July of 1966, with sniping, looting and widespread destruction on the West Side which again required the National Guard's assistance for police on the streets of Chicago. Throughout this period, tensions increased between the police and newsmen but never really broke into the open until one Saturday in April of 1968.

The flash point came 12 days after the Mayor's shoot to kill order. It was an event which was to have long range detrimental effects on the relationship between the Chicago Police and the men and women of the news media. The Chicago Peace Council had a permit for an anti-Vietnam War march to the Civic Center. Superintendent Conlisk, goaded by the Mayor's previous criticism, made one of his rare appearances on the streets to personally command the police detail assigned to assure a peaceful and orderly march.

At the Civic Center, the marchers, numbering about 10,000, were stopped by the police and advised that their permit did not entitle them to hold a rally in the Civic Center Plaza but simply to continue their march around the Plaza's edge. The march leaders disagreed. Many in the crowd began to defy the police and scuffling ensued. Before the afternoon was over, policemen were assaulted, arrests were made, marchers were chased through the streets by pursuing police, and newsmen were assaulted and arrested by the police.

Although Conlisk was there that day and saw what happened, no disciplinary action was taken by the department against the policemen who assaulted newsmen.

A WGN-TV film of the disorder, along with police department films, subsequently was shown to top personnel at police headquarters. One of the films showed two policemen take a demonstrator by the arms and legs and throw him into the fountain in the Civic Center's Plaza. A police captain was identifiable in the film as a witness. The incident was brought to the attention of Deputy Superintendent John Mulchrone who was responsible for the Internal Affairs Division which investigated allegations of police misconduct. He shrugged it off. No one in the Department was reprimanded. It was apparent that more serious conflicts were to come if steps were not taken to avert them.

Following the April 27th disorders, representatives of the Chicago Press Photographers Association requested a meeting with the Superintendent to seek to prevent attacks by the police like the one on *Sun-Times* photographer Jack Lenahan who had been pummeled by a group of officers in the middle of Randolph Street. I arranged for the meeting and invited the president of the Chicago Newspaper Guild to attend. Conlisk was cordial and acceded to the photographers' request that they be permitted to publicly display their Chicago Police press cards in clearly marked armbands to enable the police to know the professional newsmen at any given scene. Later, however, the city editors of the four metropolitan dailies vetoed the idea of armbands.

Subsequently, a group of citizens, headed by Dr. Edward Sparling, the former president of Roosevelt University, issued a report on the April 27th conflict. Its tone was so one-sided in criticism of the police that it had no effect in preventing the more serious altercations between police and press which were to come before the summer of 1968 ended.

# His Rules for Power                    *10*

*"Do you like hockey, Frank?"*

When we talk about the life of Richard J. Daley, too often we focus on the events in which he participated and neglect his qualities and characteristics. In the final analysis, however, it was Daley's personal traits which made him such a rare politician and governmental leader.

Strangely, although he was on the public scene for four decades and Mayor of Chicago for more than two, few of the younger politicians whose lives he touched seemed to have profited from the experience of knowing and observing him.

Mayor Daley was a master at gaining and maintaining influence over other people. He understood human frailties and strengths and constantly played on them. Some of this was learned through years of political competitiveness. Much of it seemed to be intuitive—characteristics he possessed even as a youth living in Bridgeport and working in the Stock Yards. He actually verbalized only a few suggestions that others might follow. But based on watching and listening to him closely and talking with him over a period of a dozen years, these are what I believe to have been the "rules" he followed in achieving so much political power.

First and foremost, Richard J. Daley was always devious. He rarely let people know exactly what he thought regarding specific human relationships. He never bared his soul to others. His only confidant was his wife, Eleanor.

He never allowed others to draw too close. In this regard, he was a General MacArthur-General deGaulle-type leader. He kept people at arm's length. He was determined that no one could legitimately boast he could deliver Daley on any specific subject. This was essential protection for a man who was daily besieged by favor seekers.

He made a practice of not disclosing his personal strategy, or even acknowledging that he had one. He never apologized for anything publicly. For 20 years he built a reputation based on leading others to think that in politics and local government he was omnipotent. To publicly acknowledge a mistake and apologize would conflict with this image. Would MacArthur apologize that he had ordered a landing on the wrong beach? Would deGaulle apologize for decisions he made on behalf of the Free French during World War II? These, of course, were men who dealt with issues on a global scale while Daley's arena was much more limited. Nevertheless, he followed the same principle. In the insurance scandal involving one of his sons, he never apologized although he knew, as he acknowledged privately to me, that he was wrong. He believed, and rightly so, that if you apologize for one mistake, your political opponents will want you to apologize for a second, a third and a fourth mistake. Apologies are not rare among politicians. But then, few are viewed as omnipotent. Many of Daley's associates and followers acted as if he were. And he was determined not to acknowledge that he wasn't.

Daley believed familiarity breeds familiarity. He prevented others from attaining or even seeking familiarity. Often men and women who work for or with a powerful politician want that politician to see them in a special light and sense their great importance. Daley kept those about him on edge, never certain about their status. This practice, he seemed to be saying, was far more effective in sustaining loyalty than providing the accolades fellow politicians and employees sought.

If Daley were expressing his rules to gain and maintain influence over others, they would include conduct not generally viewed as relating to the acquisition of power. He would say "be devoted to your wife and love and protect your children." He did say on more than one occasion that a husband who would betray his wife would also, most likely, betray Daley. Unlike most late 20th century politicians, he believed there was a relationship between marital fidelity and upholding a public trust. For this, he was often ridiculed by writers. But it was quintessential Daley.

Never go to taverns. That was an expressed rule. "Early on," he said to me more than once, "Sis and I decided that a person can only get into trouble by going to saloons. We decided that we would stay at home." It was not bad advice for a man to follow who was constantly in the public eye. Contemporary politicians who did not follow this rule lost favor with him. Even reports of employees having an alcoholic beverage at lunch could cause them to fall from the Mayor's favor.

Be courteous to all people at all times. Daley was that rarity of human beings who treated shoeshine boys the way he treated bank presidents. It was never an act with him. His conduct was based on a philosophy he once made clear during an exchange with him at a news conference. There had been reports that the federal government was going to provide funds for new housing for the inhabitants of Chicago's West Madison Street Skid Row. As a reporter, I asked the Mayor why we should be spending so much money on derelicts. Daley responded in a soft but firm voice with emotion: "These men are not derelicts. Some of them are pensioneers who live alone on Madison Street. Some are alcoholics. Others are just down on their luck. But don't ever call another human being a derelict."

I wished that I had never asked the question.

There were many elements about Daley which enabled him to win political victories by wide margins throughout most of his career. He said things which would cause sophisticated people to smile with bemusement. His remarks were often corny. But he was not speaking to people who were, by and large, sophisticated. He was talking to the people who lived on all the side streets of a huge twentieth century city. He repeatedly praised his parents. He praised fathers and mothers and families and what he called "good family men." He spoke almost ad nauseam with platitudes like "no man walks through life alone," and "never forget the people from whom you came." He praised "the good Lord," but always avoided discussions of sectarian religion. His remarks pertaining to the Divinity would not impress a theologian. He frequently spoke of "the Man upstairs." He seldom said anything which would indicate that he was a Catholic. Nevertheless, on occasion, he would be criticized for alleged religious posturing. In 1975, he was interviewed by a writer for an Irish newspaper. The writer, an anti-cleric, prodded Daley about the role of Catholicism in his life. The Mayor replied: "Anyone who doesn't have faith and confidence in the Lord misses something." He went on to say that his religion had "helped tremendously to make decisions. . . to pray and hope that your decisions will be right. I think it [religion] has a lot to do with a man making the right decision."

Asked if he was disturbed by the secularization of American life, he replied, "I think it's a temporary thing. I am told by religious leaders that more and more young people are coming back to religion." For these less than profound observations in response to questions, Daley was roundly criticized by the Irish writer for "frequently invoking the name of God."

Daley was a religious man but he kept his religious practice intensely private. A daily visit to church before going to City Hall was part of his routine but he never sought to spotlight it.

His unspoken rules for keeping tight control over City employees made him a superb administrator working with all top subordinates on a one-by-one basis—never through intermediaries. He dealt directly with these department heads, thereby not only learning firsthand what they were doing and giving them direction, but also causing them to be completely loyal to him. He spent much of his working day allowing supplicants for favors to see him alone on a personal basis.

He was legally astute. He mastered parliamentary procedures.

His other "rules" for power included:

— Prepare for all future events so that nothing relating to your political or governmental goals takes place without thorough preparation;

— Set aside time each day to take part in the public and private events which will advance your political and governmental goals; and

— Make certain that appreciation is expressed publicly for everyone sponsoring such events;

— Get up early every day, rarely go to bed late, and enjoy hobbies and recreational activities to break up your work week. Whenever possible, spend your evenings doing homework for the next day, and proceed through each day on a thoroughly organized basis, making use of every minute.

He worked strenuously to block potential political rivals and make certain that his governmental subordinates continuously sought his approbation. He often created work situations which would result in rival subordinates clashing with each other in order to gain their leader's ear. An example of this was the relationship between him and Earl Bush, my predecessor as press secretary, and Colonel Jack Reilly, Daley's Director of Special Events. Their jobs were such that they often worked on the same projects and were often in conflict. Both men were frequently forced to seek out the Mayor to resolve their differences. On more than one occasion, Bush expressed to me his annoyance at Daley for failing to appreciate him and favoring Reilly. It was the sort of situation dear to Daley's heart.

One practice by the Mayor especially pointed up his knowledge of human nature and how to develop political power. Many executives, when possessing a surfeit of tickets for a public dinner, for example, might ask their secretaries to inquire if some subordinate would like to have a couple. Not Daley. Every favor, no matter how small, flowed directly from his hand so that the recipient would forever remember to whom he or she should be grateful.

Over and over again he followed this practice. As Mayor, he received tickets for games being played by the Bears, Cubs, White Sox, Bulls, Sting, University of Illinois, University of Notre Dame and De Paul University. He treated each ticket as if it were a treasure. An example: I would be working at my desk at 5:30 p.m. The Mayor's secretary, Kay Spear, would call: "The Mayor would like to see you." I would enter his office and be seated. "Do you like hockey, Frank?" the Mayor would ask. I would lie and say I did. "How would you like to take Sally and the kids to the game tonight?" The game would begin in less than two hours. I would have to go home, pick up my family, and drive to the Chicago Stadium as quickly as I could to be on time. But, reluctantly, I would tell the Mayor that I'd like to have the tickets. He already knew that I did not like to go fishing. It was always a question of how many negatives I could compile regarding sports that he enjoyed. For Daley, the conveying of a ticket was a personal matter. His intent was that you always were to be aware from whence the favor came.

Another Daley trait was always to praise, never to criticize his colleagues or employees in public. This policy was to result in intense loyalty from those who worked with him or for him. It also resulted in great annoyance by the news media. Almost always Daley would respond to criticisms about public employees by observing that there were failings among those engaged in every type of endeavor, law, medicine, business and—especially—in the media. An exception to the Daley rule, of course, was the criticism of Superintendent Conlisk for not issuing a shoot to kill order to his police.

Those aspiring politicians who wish to emulate Daley should emphasize his rule of wake-going. At no time in an individual's life is an act of kindness so appreciated as at the moment of the death of a loved one. Richard J. Daley incurred the gratitude of thousands of Chicagoans by his lifetime of attending wakes and funerals. This practice did not come about as the result of any intentional desire by the Mayor to curry favor. It was part of his being. It was part of his neighborhood tradition and the tradition of the nationality of his ancestors that stretched back across the ocean. When somebody he knew died, Daley went to the wake and, in many instances, the funeral.

He once came to a wake at my house. He had known my father distantly decades before in Springfield. My father had gone there with his father, an attorney, to seek redress for the operators of cleaning shops from whom the state had wrongfully collected excessive amounts of taxes. Daley was the minority leader of the Senate at the time and helped provide legislative assistance. All of that was long ago.

My father was waked in his house and the word reached my mother and me that the Mayor was standing out front in the line of mourners waiting to pay their last respects. I quickly went out of the house and down the steps to the Mayor who was standing bare-headed holding his hat amidst the light falling snow. Ahead of him, waiting to enter the house were 20 or more people. "Mr. Mayor," I said, "please come in." "No," said he, "I'll wait my turn." And that he did. When he finally approached my father's casket, there was one more Daley touch. I thanked him for coming, and there was something in the way I said it that implied his visit was to please me. He quickly and gently let my mother, who was standing beside me, know that his visit was because of the respect he had for her husband and had nothing to do with me.

On thousands of nights during the decades of his political career, Daley found time to express his sympathy to the relatives of departed men and women he had known. In his lifetime, those visits forged bonds. In his death, they evoke continuing memories of fondness and loyalty toward him.

His appearance and manner were important factors in his political image. He always walked briskly, evidencing certitude and confidence. No ambling, slouching or strolling for Richard J. Daley and it added to the legend. Oh, what fun it was to walk with him through the airport terminal of another city! He would go through the terminal with his swift and deliberate strides and two bodyguards and me trying to keep pace. The fun came from the looks in the eyes of the people coming the other way when they recognized that Mayor Daley was walking through their terminal. What, in the name of God, they must have thought, is Mayor Daley doing here? New York, Washington, San Francisco and any place he went, they knew his face; they had seen him on television dozens of times. They may have disliked him. They may have admired him. Either way, they knew they were looking at a legend and he walked like he knew he was one.

He was always meticulous, never casual, in his appearance. Every hair on his head was in place. He had a well-scrubbed gleam no matter what hour it was and his clothes were always perfectly tailored. Richard J. Daley didn't work in his shirt sleeves. After all, he was the Mayor; he was the leader; he was not one of the boys.

Daley recognized the importance of some elementary trappings of authority. Let governors striving to be close to the people drive about in compact cars or converted taxi cabs. Mayors, Daley believed, should be driven by drivers in limousines. His ways of remaining close to the people were different.

And he had another trait. He always asked the other person how their children were doing and, surprisingly, he always asked for them by name. Too few of us really even go through the routine of inquiring about the members of another person's family. Almost none of us ever remembers the names of another person's children. Can you image what impact this trait had on others?

How many of Daley's intellectual critics could emulate his practice of befriending the relatives of deceased friends and showing personal interest in their families? The critics were always somewhat baffled by his political successes. They never understood the attractiveness of these traits that the ordinary people of Chicago understood.

He gained and maintained influence over other people in many more ways. Unlike Mayor John Lindsay of New York, who saw a political advantage in attacking Daley over his shoot to kill order, Daley rarely criticized his political opponents. He, unlike Lindsay, knew that the momentary victory of scoring points at another man's expense was outweighed by the defeat of incurring what might be a life-long enemy. He knew that his actions and policies would sometimes create enemies. He did not have to add to this list with critical words about anyone.

And he was blessed with the inability to speak with precision. *Time* magazine's editors once referred to him as the "blunt speaking" Mayor Daley. How wrong they were. Daley more often than not obscured his meanings. I, like the other reporters who covered City Hall on a full-time basis in the mid-1960s, was not often sure what he had really said at a press conference. My newspaper colleagues had $19 tape recorders, previously given to them at Christmas by a Republican alderman. These tape recorders were essential for analyzing what Daley had said at a news conference. His usual style was Hegelian—the first sentence was positive, the second sentence was negative and the third was a combination of the first two. Editors were rarely sympathetic to their reporters' plight in trying to figure out what Daley had said. What a skill! It was hard to pinpoint a man with that ability. Circumlocution was one of his strong points.

And Richard J. Daley rarely fell into the Jesuit practice of defining his terms and making distinctions. He knew that people are usually either for or against something. Unlike theologians, lawyers and accountants, the public does not get involved in qualifying its likes and dislikes. The best example of this Daley "rule" for influencing others was the public position he took regarding police conduct during the 1968 Democratic National Convention. Privately he acknowledged the terrible flaws in the police operations. But that was a qualification. The public was either with or against Daley and his police. He knew nobody wanted to talk about distinctions.

Daley was a master of the financial technicalities and budgetary ingredients of government. The politicians who succeeded him in Chicago lacked the financial and budgetary knowledge which was his greatest professional asset. His job titles through the decades underscore this point—Deputy Comptroller of Cook County, Minority Leader of the Illinois Senate, Director of Revenue for the State of Illinois, Cook County Clerk and Mayor of Chicago. In this last capacity, he brought about mayoral control of the City budget that emasculated the former budgetary power held by Chicago's aldermen. His encyclopedic knowledge of the city budget and how to control it was his greatest governmental strength.

On the personal side, a Daley strength was his incredible ability to relax. As a youth, he had been a good softball player and a participant in other sports. As Mayor, he continued his enthusiasm as a sports spectator. No matter what the governmental crisis, he was able to momentarily block it out of his mind and focus his attention on a sporting event. His concentration could be directed at a problem, for example, with the Board of Education, and instantly be diverted to a brief discussion about how the White Sox had responded to a tight situation during the previous night's game when the Yankees had men on second and third with no outs in the first of the ninth. This ability to not view each day's problems as life or death matters blended with another "rule"—never look back.

Like all good politicians and leaders, he could make a decision and move on, never anguishing over what he had done. Mayor Daley did not second guess himself.

He had one more trait that should be noted. Although he has been universally portrayed as the Boss who handed out thousands of favors to others—which was true—he did not engage in the practice usually considered to be the Boss' other side. By and large, he did not punish. Wards which failed to deliver votes did not have their services reduced. Politicians who had not always been faithful followers did not necessarily receive rebukes. He did not dispatch building inspectors to harass those owners who might have incurred his disfavor. When harassment tactics occurred, they usually were brought about by his disciples and employees who thought that might be what he wanted. Many times Mayor Daley was blamed for misconduct by his employees of which he was never aware. An example was the so-called undercover reports of the police anti-subversive unit. Such reports were frequently prepared by misguided policemen with a weak understanding of democratic procedures. Daley was not a man who sought derogatory intelligence information about others. He knew only too well that those kinds of chickens could come home to roost. When it came to punishing those political subordinates who did not serve him well, Jane Byrne found fault with the Mayor for being too soft.

Considering the fact that Daley was in the political limelight for two decades and that political sycophants around him watched his every move during those years, it is surprising that almost no one has sought to emulate the practices that contributed to his power.

When Daley was alive, one of his major critics was a man who knew all of his traits and observed him firsthand for more than two decades. He knew the Mayor's attractive qualities but, in private, chose to continually allege negative ones. He was one of Daley's closest employees, his press secretary, Earl Bush.

# The Critic from Within    *11*

*"The only principal guiding [Democratic] party
leaders [in Chicago] is 'don't get caught.' "*

From the days when Daley was Clerk of Cook County,
until the time of the insurance scandal involving his
son, John, the Mayor's press aide was Earl Bush. He
was generally viewed as a liberal influence on the Mayor. Bush took
pride in being what he thought was a bridge between the intellectual
community and the party organization. In his early fifties, married
and with grown children, he lived in suburban Skokie. His lack of interest in being fashionably attired had long since become a subject of
ridicule in the local press. He was abrupt, knowledgeable, and, in my
relations with him, first as a reporter and later with the Police Department, always helpful.

One thing Bush loved to do was talk. And that is what he did during a luncheon we had at the beginning of March in 1969. He specialized in gossip. The Mayor, Bush related, was angered by the criticism
of Chicago after the 1968 convention by Senator Hubert Humphrey
and other Democratic leaders. Humphrey had been on the telephone
several times the previous day, Bush said, trying unsuccessfully to
speak with the Mayor after Daley had made some public remarks critical of the former vice president.

Daley, Bush went on, had been asked to go on a lecture tour in the
aftermath of the convention for which he would receive $3,000 for

each appearance. Bush said he wanted the Mayor to take $2,500 and give him $500 for the speech-writing he would contribute. (Daley never conducted any lecture tour.)

"A half-dozen firms want to sponsor the Mayor on a proposed national television program to be called 'Mayor Daley Views the News,' " Bush continued. And there were offers after the convention for the press aide to write a mayoral biography. "Do it after I'm dead," Bush quoted Daley as saying.

As the summer of 1969 began, Bush continued in private conversations to criticize the Mayor. He was especially annoyed by the increasing amount of time Daley spent with his four sons. They ate lunch with their father frequently. Bush no longer did.

I was not certain whether Bush's criticisms were true but they reflected his growing personal disloyalty to the man who provided his livelihood. Three of the Mayor's sons were on the payroll at City Hall that summer, Bush whispered. Moreover, he continued, the Mayor had proposed that Bush leave the city payroll, start a private public relations firm, and, through a consultant's contract paid with city funds, serve as Daley's public relations advisor. "The Mayor actually considered going to Europe while the Illinois Legislature was in session," Bush said, sounding dismayed, "and there are several serious things which need correcting but he is not paying any attention to them." All this indicated to Bush that Daley did not plan to seek another term in 1971.

Bush confided that he wanted to write a biography of the Mayor but that Daley would not cooperate. The press secretary said an example of the cooperation he needed was to get the details of "how the Mayor made $20 million for the lawyers in the creation of the CTA [Chicago Transit Authority]." The Mayor, Bush said, was annoyed by the question. Daley was the Democratic leader in the Illinois Senate at the time when Chicago's Mayor Edward J. Kelly and Republican Governor Dwight H. Green worked together to bring into existence the Transit Authority. Daley's law partner, William J. Lynch, later to become a federal judge, handled much of the legal work for the CTA at its inception.

If Bush had at one time admired Daley, there was little indication of affection in any of the press secretary's conversations from 1969 on. In addition to grumbling about his employer, he continued to complain about his own economic status and how difficult it was to make ends meet with a son away in college. His finances were to become a matter of public interest within a few years.

As 1970 drew to an end, Bush continued to engage in his favorite pasttime—talking about the Mayor. In a conversation on December 2, he rambled at length about Daley and the 16 years the two of them had been together. He told of how the Mayor's parents wanted Daley as a youth to enter the priesthood. Consequently, Bush said, the Mayor could understand the feelings of his daughter, Patricia, a few years earlier when she was in a religious order, "thinking about her family getting ready for the visit of the Queen and all she was missing." Patricia had decided not to continue in the religious order. Bush said Daley, as a youth, considered the possibility of a priestly vocation but "thought of all he would miss."

The press secretary said he had decided years before that he would maintain only a working relationship with the Mayor and would never want to be a social friend. In this way, he contended, he would be able to best help Daley by maintaining a degree of objectivity and not fall completely under his influence.

Bush moved on to a new subject and told the hard-to-believe story that, in 1966, Dr. Martin Luther King, Jr., had demanded and received a Cadillac from Democratic fundraiser Charles Swibel as one of the civil rights leader's conditions for ending his Chicago open-housing campaign. Then, speaking of the Chicago rioting which followed King's murder, Bush blamed Director of Special Events Jack Reilly and Fire Commissioner Robert Quinn for inflaming the Mayor's anger leading to the shoot to kill order. This anger resulted, Bush said, not only in his being temporarily dismissed, but in the Mayor firing, at least for a few minutes, his entire cabinet. Bush credited former Corporation Counsel Raymond Simon as being the "calm head" throughout those 1968 days who helped to restore the jobs of all cabinet members who had been momentarily fired.

Bush was filled with chagrin toward Daley. The Mayor, he said, was "surrounded by second-rate minds." Daley had been "betrayed by so many" that he had withdrawn psychologically to the 11th Ward where he also "was betrayed by them."

Bush described Circuit Court Clerk Matthew Danaher (who was to be indicted for corruption) as being like the Mayor's "adopted son."

The long-time press secretary was especially critical of the Mayor's family, which he described as "almost incestuous because they are so close." The Mayor reacts in two different ways, Bush added. One is "his gut reaction" and the other is a result of "what his mind thinks."

Continuing, Bush described Daley as being opposed to "birth control for blacks" because of the moral teaching of the Catholic Church "but he knows intellectually this is what should happen."

The press aide credited his and Simon's influence on the Mayor as being crucial in preventing confrontations with Dr. King in 1966. Moreover, he said, he and Simon were the only ones in the Mayor's cabinet who would disagree with Daley if necessary. He added that Daley at that moment in December of 1970 was vacationing in Florida to decide whether to seek a fifth term. One thing was clear from these remarks—whatever bond there might once have been between Bush and Daley was long since severed.

From the days of Daley's first campaign for Mayor in 1955, Bush had provided him with speeches containing liberal rhetoric. Throughout most of this time he was the only Jew working on the Mayor's staff (with the exception of one secretary inherited from the preceding administration). More than a few of the members of that staff could be described as racists. Bush's presence, therefore, was essential to mitigate their influence. The press secretary's role, however, had diminished considerably since those days in April of 1968 when he unwisely remained on a Caribbean vacation while rioting tore apart the West Side. He had been fired and rehired upon his return, but never regained his previous position of influence.

At the end of August 1971, while I was still with the Police Department, I met with Bush again and we went for a long walk through the Loop. The Mayor, Bush said, was "thinking with his stomach. It was as if nothing had been learned from all the years as Mayor. It was like it was in 1955 when he first ran for Mayor all over again. He's thinking with his stomach, emotionally, not rationally."

Bush complained that the Mayor's sons were his main advisors. For years, Bush said, Daley and he had lunched frequently. The press secretary would talk about books he had recently read, hoping to have some of his liberal views and ideas, as he put it, "seep through." "Now," Bush declared, "I never get to eat with the Mayor. The four sons are the main lunch companions and I have absolutely no respect for their political views." He added: "They think I am a communist."

As we walked the Loop streets, Bush continued. "The only principal guiding [Democratic] party leaders [in Chicago] is 'don't get caught.' " I injected my concern that the city administration should show greater interest in the black community. Bush agreed but added: "The Mayor doesn't even think in terms of police protection for blacks; only for the whites."

This man who had worked with Daley for 18 years was describing his employer in the same terms used by Daley critics. They said the Mayor was primarily emotional, not intellectual; defensive; anti-black; a man who worked for his cronies; a man who was insulated. All the while Bush kept emphasizing that he personally was working in government only for the money.

As time progressed, Bush's bitterness toward Daley grew. At the same time, I was struggling with my own views about the Chicago Police Department where Daley had asked me to assist.

# Why I Went to Work for Him

**12**

*"Daley was doing more to help ordinary
people...than any of his media critics."*

I left the *Chicago Sun-Times* to go to work for Mayor Daley because he offered me more money. My pay went up from $10,000 a year as the paper's City Hall reporter to $16,000 a year as Director of Public Information for the Police Department.

And there were other reasons, of course. There comes a time in a reporter's life when he tires of running about asking questions, especially when those giving the answers grow less and less enlightening. That is what happened to me. I just didn't care any more what the Superintendent of the Bureau of Parking thought about anything. When that happens, a reporter should move up to an editor's job and when no one wants that reporter to be an editor, it's time to look elsewhere—away from the newspaper.

But there was one more reason. It became clear to me that to advance one's career as a reporter at City Hall or anywhere in Chicago journalism, you had to "get" Daley. He was the kingfish and, if a reporter was going to gain fame and money, he had to spear the Mayor. Mike Royko had shown all of us how to do it. His columns in the *Chicago Daily News* were the best read and best written journalism in Chicago. And Royko was relentless with his humorous barbs at Daley and his fellow politicians. Follow the Royko path and your editors would be pleased. And that is what more and more reporters were doing. In fact, that is what a whole generation of Chicago reporters did. In a way, it was natural. Daley had made himself the biggest target. And many newsmen and women also were enamored of his power. They wanted some of the same.

Objective journalism? That was impossible, they said, and, what is more, it was undesirable, if not boring. They knew what Daley should be doing. They had their special causes and those causes were not usually Daley's.

These reporters began to be, in my eyes, untrustworthy. Information given by me as the City Hall reporter—to my colleagues, covering other aspects of the city—became information they relayed directly to Daley's political opponents. The *Sun-Times* city room was becoming less a newspaper office and more the clearinghouse for the beginnings of a social revolution. My attempts at objective journalism were not the route to follow.

Amidst this media desire to "get" Daley, I felt more and more uncomfortable. Amidst the increasingly disruptive "civil rights" marches and Dr. King's attempts at confrontation, my respect for Daley grew. And then it became clear. Daley was doing more to help ordinary people—black and white—successful and unsuccessful—than any of his media critics. Granted, as Mayor he was in a position to do more good. But the fact was he was doing it better than all of the newspaper editors and television journalists who sat in judgment. I began to see Chicago as a barroom. At one end of the bar was a group of the big name newspeople of the city—critics to a man. At the other end sat Daley. I felt more comfortable sitting with him.

# The Police: Years of Valor—and Disgrace

*13*

Mayor Daley's police department dominated the local news for almost three years following the 1968 Democratic Convention. The Walker Report, calling the police conduct a "police riot," had been issued in the final month of 1968, and the controversy it engendered swirled through the opening months of the following year. By March, there were indictments of those who had come to Chicago to lead the convention disorders. These indictments were to lead to the Conspiracy Seven trial which added to the concentration of Chicago Police news coverage, with Daley always in the center. Then came the "Days of Rage" in October, with the Weathermen faction of the Students for a Democratic Society rampaging through the streets of the Near North Side and the Loop. Their destructive tactics aimed at "bringing the Vietnam War home" generated widespread support for the police even from the local media. Instead of stopping the Weathermen before they smashed store and automobile windows as they ran through the streets, the police stood by and allowed the vandalism to occur. It was poor police work but good public relations. Chicagoans were outraged by the conduct of Bernadine Dohrn, Mark Rudd and the other revolutionaries who had gained notoriety earlier by disrupting Columbia University.

Then, just at the moment when the media was letting up on its anti-police vendetta, an event occurred which plunged the city into a savage controversy which was to go on for years. On Dec. 4, 1969, 14 Chicago police officers assigned to the State's Attorney's office for investigative work, raided a three story slum building near the Chicago Stadium on the West Side, killing in the process two Black Panthers. The State's Attorney, Edward V. Hanrahan, had been advised by informants that the Panthers were storing a cache of weapons in an apartment. The Chicago Police command had refused to make a raid to recover the weapons because it decided the risk of injury to any raiding officers outweighed the good that might be achieved by confiscating the guns. But Hanrahan went for the idea. His decision was to be a poor one resulting in the deaths of the two Panthers, years of judicial turmoil for himself and the raiding officers, and the destruction of his political career. There was more. The raid played a part in the eventual division of the city into two Democratic parties, one black, the other white.

A chain linked all of this to the Mayor and the chain was forged by well-intentioned men. When they started, they had no idea of where their decisions would lead them. The chain began with Press Secretary Earl Bush and Charles Livermore, a former director of the Illinois Youth Commission, trying to bring an end to the youth gang warfare which was causing so many shooting deaths and injuries on Chicago's streets. Their determination to beef up police operations against the gangs and to make the city's anti-gang activity the primary item on the Mayor's public agenda  became obsessive. Day after day, memorandum after memorandum, the problem of youth gangs was sounded over and over by Bush and Livermore to Daley. Daley's reaction was, in the summer of 1969, to summon the city's top police, judicial and prosecutorial officers to his office to map strategy. At the news conference which followed, he readily accepted a newsman's suggestion that this was to be a "war on gangs." It was Daley who set into motion the forces which eventually would bring about the two Panther deaths, the destruction of Hanrahan's political future and the intense racial animosity which was to sever his political organization.

Prodded by his desire to please Daley and an ambition to succeed him in office, Hanrahan ordered the raid. Then the Chicago Police, saddled with the responsibility of determining whether there was any wrongful conduct on the part of the raiding officers, entered into a giant cover-up. The department's crime laboratory did ballistics tests on the Panther weapons recovered from the apartment. No tests, however, were performed on the police officers' guns. There were federal and county grand jury probes. There were lawsuits which stretched on for years. One conclusion was that, because one bullet had been fired through the closed apartment door by the Panthers against the police seeking to enter, the return police fire of more than 100 bullets was justified, as were the resulting deaths of Panthers Fred Hampton and Mark Clark.

Three years later, Hanrahan, because of the controversy over whether his raiding party killed in self-defense or murdered the Panthers, was dumped as his party's candidate for re-election. The animosity of so many voters had caused his running mates to fear his presence on the ballot would defeat the entire ticket. But Hanrahan ran in the primary anyway and beat the organization's candidate. Then he ran again in the fall of 1972 but lost to his Republican opponent. Black and white voters in substantial numbers had left the Democratic column to support a Republican. Daley was to be elected again as Mayor in 1975, defeating three opponents, one of whom was an embittered Hanrahan, but the racial rupture caused by the Panther raid was never to be healed.

It was the summer of 1970 when the public, including me, learned that the police had not sought the truth in the investigation of the officers who conducted the Panther raid. This was one more reason for my growing conclusion that the police command under Conlisk did not provide the leadership which his department and the city deserved. In the months ahead, the number of these reasons for my disillusionment with the police was to be increased. I made frequent visits to the Mayor recommending that Conlisk be replaced. Daley took no action. I believe he felt that, because of the controversies in which the police had been involved, including the convention and the Panther raid, he could not make a change in the department's leadership without seeming to acknowledge that some of his most important decisions had been wrong. I believe he felt trapped. The bottom line, however, was that he failed to do what was needed. The police and the city were to suffer much more from errant police conduct before the Fall of 1973 when the department would finally get new police leadership.

# In the Middle of the Lake     *14*

*"Why was I so disillusioned?"*

A s the days of 1968, 1969 and 1970 fade into history, it
is difficult to convey to a younger generation how
terrible they were. This was not due only to the divisions in the country over participation in the Vietnam War, but also
because of the domestic assaults on the American governmental struc-
ture, culture and society in general. The onslaught came, to a substantial degree, from university professors, priests, nuns, ministers, rabbis,
the news media and others who had been viewed, erroneously, as the
keepers of our traditions. The protectors really were, what some might
have thought, the most unlikely groups to have assumed this role
—the hardhats, low level politicians, policemen and ordinary people
who had never claimed to be the defenders of our system. They were
the ones who held it all together and there was no group that played a
bigger role in this than did the police. From coast to coast, in city after
city, they were the ones who did their dangerous work to keep society
going amidst an unprecedented wave of crime and violence.

The role of the writers, public speakers, clergy, academia and the
media in inciting violence on the streets of our country was never acknowledged. After all, they were the only ones who had access to the
means of conveying their negative role to the public and this was something they were never going to do. And never have done.

The list of those who sought to stimulate violent actions, against law enforcement men and women in particular, was long. Ministers and "civil rights" participants like the Reverend C.T. Vivian warned whites not to walk or ride in the predominately black neighborhoods of Chicago for, if they did, they risked being the victims of violence. Reverend James Bevel showed films of the arsons and violence in the Watts section of Los Angeles to Chicago youths, who then, shortly thereafter, engaged in similar activity in their neighborhoods. Television commentators like Hugh Downs maintained that there was only one word that could describe Chicago policemen—pigs.

The toll, affected to some degree by violent rhetoric, was high. During the approximately 18 months from January 1969 until mid-June 1970, ten Chicago police officers were murdered. Six of them were white, four black.

Nevertheless, the police role was not unmixed. Along with the bravery of the majority of officers patrolling the streets of Chicago, there also was a hidden sickness in the Police Department. The media, despite its generally antagonistic view toward the police, did not address themselves to the problems of police corruption during those days. Yet, behind the scenes it festered.

There is a dangerous strain within the police that forever presses its officers to view their prime responsibility as being toward each other rather than the public. At the same time, in the midst of the violence from street gangs and the inflammatory rhetoric of those pleading various causes, there existed a pattern of police dishonesty which increasingly disturbed me.

As a former newspaper reporter and Mayor Daley's personal representative with the Police Department, I had hoped that my efforts in some way would help to cause the high command to take firm action to assure an attitude of hostility toward police corruption.

But as time progressed, I grew more disillusioned with the likelihood that police operations would be conducted basically in the public interest. Once, during a particularly dramatic moment following the accidental fatal shooting of a police officer by his inebriated colleagues in a saloon, I asked James J. Riordan, my long-time personal friend who had been promoted to Chief of Patrol, why I was so disillusioned. "Because," he said, "most people wade in from the shoreline; you started [with the police] in the middle of the lake."

I had been placed by Mayor Daley in the midst of the Chicago Police high command. I did not spend years working up from patrolman to detective to sergeant and higher. Instead, because of Daley, I was put in a position where I could see and be involved with much of the department after just a few months.

And so, once the turbulence of the 1968 Democratic Convention began to subside—and it did not do so for almost a year—I began to be more and more involved with day-to-day police activities. Eventually it became clear to me that the police operated, to a substantial degree, to support each other regardless of their conduct. The climax was to come when the department's command did everything it could—except risk imprisonment—to thwart federal investigations of police corruption. Daley had asked me to go with the police to help in their public relations. To have quit because of earlier instances of frustration at bringing about a better attitude by the command staff toward allegations of corruption would have been a disservice to Daley and the city government that employed me. The Mayor, more than most people, knew that the proper functioning of government is difficult. He knew the history of the Chicago police and their possibilities for abuses. So I remained with the department and tried to bring about improved police operations during the time of the convention, after the Black Panther killings by policemen under the control of the State's Attorney, during the street demonstrations pertaining to the Vietnam War and the Conspiracy Seven trial, and in hundreds of other controversies.

I think the end of my desire to stay with the police—of whom I admired so many—was due to the killing of Tommy O'Malley. His story was never known to Mayor Daley. One day, long after it was over, when I mentioned it to him, he looked puzzled. Nevertheless, the corruption of the police in the Austin District on the West Side where Tommy O'Malley was shot to death was one of the factors which brought down the power of the federal government on Daley's administration and caused him much grief.

# The Gun in Tommy O'Malley's Belt

*15*

*"We take care of our own."*

During 1968 and 1969, a period of almost daily controversy involving the Chicago Police, there had been, strangely, little attention given to the subject of police corruption. Although frequently condemned by newsmen, the police were, by and large, heroes to much of the city because of the role they played in restraining the criminal conduct of street gangs and violent radical movements. The subject of police corruption, however, was rarely mentioned in the press. In fact, the police were so highly regarded by the general public that, during the 1971 mayoral election campaign, for the first time in many decades, police operations were not a major issue. Daley's opponent, Republican candidate Richard Friedman, made only a few subdued references to alleged excesses by the police task force. Even Friedman, a so-called reform candidate, knew there were few votes to be gained and many to be lost by attacks on the Chicago Police.

The subject of police corruption, which has recurred throughout most of the history of Chicago, did not come into the open again until November 1971. But behind the scenes during these months of 1969 and 1970, the tragedy, which police corruption causes, was taking place.

Some people—even newsmen—minimize the seriousness of bribing police officers with small amounts of money. Those who express this kind of indifference do not understand what the bribes lead to. Twenty dollar and $50 bribes only appear to be unimportant. They are significant, however, when the time comes for the briber to collect the police "service" that has been bought.

This is the story of Tommy O'Malley, a story involving police corruption which was to have an impact on Richard Daley's career, although he really never knew much about it. O'Malley was a heavy-set, 26 year old member of the International Brotherhood of Electrical Workers, the oldest of eight children, with a father who was a long-time member of that union. One night after work in May of 1969, Tommy O'Malley stopped in a saloon on West Chicago Avenue to have a beer. During the course of the evening, there was an argument at the bar and O'Malley was shot to death by an off-duty Chicago Police officer named Tommy McConville, age 25. At that moment all of the $20 and $50 bribes in the Austin Police District were called in for an accounting.

Detectives who arrived at the shooting scene drove McConville around the block to get black coffee in an attempt to sober him up. They rehearsed his defense over and over. Meanwhile, uniformed police officers, who arrived at the saloon, took the fatally wounded O'Malley to St. Anne's Hospital. As he was being wheeled into the emergency room on a stretcher, his coat was moved back and a nurse called out that there was a pistol tucked into his belt.

O'Malley was pronounced dead in the emergency room. The shooting was later deemed a justifiable homicide by the police. McConville told how there had been an argument and how O'Malley had reached beneath his coat as if to draw a weapon and how McConville shot first in self-defense.

So the crucial evidence became the weapon in O'Malley's belt. Did he have it in the saloon? Where did it come from?

O'Malley's bereaved father sought a further police investigation. His son did not own any firearms, the father said, and, in fact, had a strong dislike for guns. The pistol was traced back to the Kale Police Uniform Shop on West Roosevelt Road. It had been purchased by an unidentified person who asked that it be mailed to a "Tom Johnson" on North Avenue in Oak Park. The Police Internal Investigation probers went to the address and found a beauty parlor. The two female operators said they had never received a gun in the mail and never heard of "Tom Johnson." Perhaps, they suggested, he was a handyman who once worked there briefly.

So the efforts of Deputy Superintendent John Mulchrone and his IID investigators came to a halt. Somehow or other, the pistol had gone from being mailed to a beauty parlor to being tucked inside the belt of Tommy O'Malley. The official police investigation ended.

Then, months later, McConville, the killer-policeman, was arrested by the Chicago Police for two armed robberies. Once again, Tommy O'Malley's father asked the Internal Investigations Division (IID) to reinvestigate what happened the night his son was shot to death by McConville. Art Petacque, the veteran *Sun-Times* reporter, brought a police relative of the father to me at the Police Department for help. I looked in the IID file to see if there was any clue about the mysterious death weapon. Almost leaping off the pages were the names of the two operators of the beauty parlor on North Avenue— Nan Partipillo and Mrs. Ruth Skally. Mrs. Skally's husband was a mobster who had been shot to death several years before and his body found in a wooded area in suburban River Forest. Nan Partipillo was widely known as the widow of hoodlum Sam Cesario. He recently had been fatally shot in her presence while they walked near Polk and Loomis Streets on the West Side. She was even more famous as the long-time girl friend of crime syndicate boss Felix (Milwaukee Phil) Alderisio who was serving time in the federal penitentiary. The murder of Cesario was a warning to anyone who planned to fool around with a mobster's girl friend while he was in the penitentiary.

There was no indication in the IID file of any background check of these two women. As far as the IID was concerned, they were only two beauty shop operators. The mysterious weapon which was in Tommy O'Malley's belt, however, had not been delivered to just an ordinary beauty parlor. It was mailed to a place owned by two women deeply involved with crime syndicate figures. There the trail of the pistol stopped. Somehow or other, it had been transferred from Nan Partipillo and Mrs. Skally's beauty shop to Tommy O'Malley's belt. Could the trail have led through officers assigned to the Austin Police District? Could the trail have led to the Austin Police Station itself? Could the weapon have once been in a desk drawer in the Austin Police District? Could it have been a "throw-away" gun that an Austin police officer kept for that moment when all the $20 and $50 bribes had to provide a service for a briber—when the entire mechanism of police corruption had to go into operation, when a liquor licensee had to have his license protected, when there had to be a cover-up, when there was a need for not telling the truth about firing the fatal bullet into Tommy O'Malley's face?

A witness who was with Officer McConville quoted one of the initial detectives on the scene as saying "We take care of our own." Other policemen at the station "coached" the witness to make a statement friendly to McConville. Tommy O'Malley's father and his friends fared no better with the second IID probe than they had with the first. Reporter Petacque ran a story about Nan Partipillo and Mrs. Skally, but there was no way for anyone outside the Police Department to produce evidence of how the gun got to the St. Anne's Hospital emergency room that night.

The investigation of police corruption in the Austin District was not over, however, as far as the U.S. Department of Justice was concerned. The failure of the IID under Deputy John Mulchrone was to lead to a federal probe which would rock the entire Chicago Police Department and Mayor Daley's administration. Before the FBI was through, the tavern pay-offs to policemen in the Austin Police District would become public knowledge. Commander Mark Thanasouras and Matsanobu Noro, one of the detectives who took McConville out that night to sober him up, and many other officers assigned to the Austin District, would be indicted, convicted and sent to the penitentiary. Thanasouras, after his conviction, would become a witness against still more policemen. Then, one early morning he would pay the price for testifying against crooked cops. He would be shot to death on a city street.

But all that lay ahead. In February of 1970, Conlisk removed Thanasouras as the commander. He had been assigned to the Austin District by O.W. Wilson in 1966. Reporters for the Austinite newspaper said they could trace Thanasouras' corruption back to shortly after that appointment. They told Conlisk of the commander's lavish lifestyle, including a secret Lake Shore Drive apartment and of the working relationship he had with prostitutes and illegal liquor operations in the district.

Three months before Thanasouras' removal, the alderman from

the Austin area, Edward McMahon, told me how he, State Senator Thomas McGloon and Alderman Thomas Casey had been pleading unsuccessfully with the Mayor to oust Thanasouras.

A month after Conlisk's action against Thanasouras, I met with the Mayor and told him nothing had substantially improved within the Police Department. As yet, no public scandal had erupted and the police were still popular.

On June 5, civilian investigator Jack Clarke, a man about whom we will hear more later, visited the Mayor and gave him a proposed plan for revising police intelligence and IID operations. Clarke later told me he had come to the conclusion there were limitations on what the Mayor could accomplish.

I was beginning to come to the same conclusion.

# Farewell to the Police                    *16*

*"The blue curtain goes down and you're damn
right it goes down everytime an accusation is
made against a policeman."*

In a private meeting in October 1971, Daley had told me
he feared Chicago could have a police scandal similar to
the one then being exposed in New York City if Superintendent Conlisk were not on the alert. Daley said he had heard rumors
of 18 officers being involved in narcotics traffic on the West Side and
that policemen on the North Side were involved in what he described
as a sex ring. I told him there was a serious problem because federal
agents did not trust our department. Meanwhile, at police headquarters, Conlisk was telling his top personnel how important it was to fun-
nel any information of police wrongdoing to the top of the department
in order to avoid any New York-type scandal.

Wise observers have commented on the inappropriateness of selecting a veteran police officer to command a police department. A
man is a policeman for 25 years during which, on countless occasions,
he is aware of misconduct by fellow officers. He sees people being
beaten and abused by the police and money being wrongfully taken by
the police. Through it all, he turns his head and says nothing. Then, at
the end of the 25 years, this man, who has lived in a continuing atmosphere of tolerance for police wrongdoing and constant compromise
with corruption, is chosen to command the police personnel with
whom he has worked. It is unreasonable to expect that a person with

92

this kind of background could provide the discipline needed to bring about police concern for individual rights and an abhorrence of police corruption.

In Chicago in the Fall of 1971, the police were still benefiting from the popular good will which had been created by their struggles to protect the city and its citizens from the criminal activities of street gangs and the violence-prone radicals. From the days of the rioting following the murder of Dr. King through the 1968 Democratic Convention and the 1969 Students for a Democratic Society rampage, public opinion, despite the contrary efforts by many in the media, sided with the police. Police corruption, always a danger and always present in varying degrees, was not in the forefront of the public's and the media's consciousness. Such a time, however, was coming.

A Nov. 3, 1971, *Chicago Tribune* headline said it all: "U.S. Probes Chicago Police." The accompanying article, written by Bob Wiedrich, told of an FBI and grand jury investigation of alleged ties between gamblers and the police. Conlisk described the article as "dirty." He was "very upset" because he thought "someone upstairs had leaked the information to Wiedrich."

When I showed the headline to a high ranking officer, he exclaimed "goddamn FBI." Later he, too, expressed concern about which police official might have leaked the story. Absolutely no one in the police command voiced concern about police personnel possibly being involved in criminal activities. No one expressed determination to get to the bottom of the whole thing.

The following week, President Nixon came to Chicago for a Republican fundraising dinner. On the same night, I had a discussion with one of the top men in the department. In the course of our conversation, we talked about the book *Honor Thy Father* by Gay Talese and its accounts of the meeting habits of New York mobsters. The high ranking officer, who for many years maintained a close working relationship with the crime syndicate, said that he took part in meetings in Queen of Heaven Cemetery west of Chicago. He did not say why or with whom. He added that, like the organized crime figures in Talese's book, he used pay phones for transacting his non-official business. Outdoor public phones on Lake Shore Drive and pay phones in elevated station were the ones most utilized.

The official then told of how policemen under his command once arrested a minor gambling figure who operated a peep show on South State Street. The man's name was Louis Arger and, shortly after his arrest, he came to this high ranking officer to talk about the "gambling situation" in the 1st Ward. Prior to that, the officer told me, Arger had been viewed by the mob as just a "runner." He became "a big man," however, because of his new relationship with the police official. Arger asked if the official would be willing to talk about "the situation" with someone else. He replied that he was always willing to talk with anyone.

Subsequently, a meeting was arranged with Pat Marcy, the Democratic boss of the 1st Ward and its alleged link with the mob. Arger drove north from Chicago on the Illinois Toll Road and, at the service plaza near Lake Forest, parked his car and raised its hood. The high ranking officer then arrived at the plaza, picked up Arger from alongside his car, and the two drove together for a short distance. Then they exited the officer's car, were picked up by a third vehicle and driven to meet Marcy at a restaurant on the far Northwest Side.

Marcy, according to the officer, said he was interested in protection for what was described as "nine strip joints" in the Loop. The officer said he was asked if he would meet with someone else to discuss the matter further. Once again, he replied that he was always available to talk with anyone.

The next meeting was arranged to take place in an empty room in the Gaslight Club on the Near North Side with Turk Torello, a major crime syndicate hoodlum. Torello told the officer there were 30 places which needed police protection, that is, "non-interference;" 18 in the East Chicago Avenue Police District, nine in the Loop, and three in the "Old Warren Avenue District." Torello said the protection money he was about to offer would pertain only to those syndicate establishments outside the Loop. The high ranking officer would be free to work out a deal with someone else regarding the Loop.

Another meeting with Torello was arranged. This time it was in a parking lot at Ohio Street and North Lake Shore Drive next to the Ohio Street beach. Torello brought with him a briefcase containing $60,000 "which was to take care of everyone." The agreement would be for a continuing protection payoff of $60,000 a month.

At this point, I asked the high ranking officer, "Why are you telling me this?"

"Because," he said, "I turned him down. I told him I couldn't deliver. But I was making $6,800 a year as a lieutenant at the time and $60,000 a month was hard to turn down!"

The officer went on to say, however, that he told Marcy and a key man at City Hall that he "would do anything they wanted regarding liquor licenses."

The following day I asked Lieutenant Michael O'Donnell, the commanding officer of the police unit which investigated organized crime, what he knew about Turk Torello. "We think he's going to be number one," O'Donnell replied. "All of them [the crime syndicate hoodlums] go to meet with him out at a restaurant on Harlem Avenue." Turk Torello did become number one but died of cancer a short time later.

Two days after my conversation with the high ranking officer, I asked Conlisk whether the department had called in the ten officers subpoenaed by the federal grand jury so that the department might interrogate them about the alleged gambling payoffs. The superintendent said investigations were underway but the department could not question the subpoenaed men because it could be viewed as a conspiracy by the police command to obstruct justice.

The department's Internal Affairs Division (formerly the IID) still had no commanding officer although 18 months had passed since the previous commander was removed for criticizing the department's probe of the Black Panther case. The leaderless IAD continued its policy of waiting for citizens' complaints to be filed and never actively seeking to uncover police misconduct.

Two days before Thanksgiving in 1971, I received a telephone call from *Tribune* newsman Wiedrich who asked me to meet with him at Tribune Tower. Accompanying Wiedrich was his long-time friend, Lieutenant O'Donnell, the commander of the organized crime division, who said he had been asked by Jack Clarke of the Mayor's Department of Investigation, to meet with the Mayor's press secretary, Earl Bush. The purpose, Clarke had intimated to O'Donnell, was to enable the lieutenant to relay information about police misconduct directly to Bush, who in turn, it was hoped, would tell Daley. I recommended that O'Donnell agree to the meeting. I was invited by Bush to attend.

It took place in the LaSalle Hotel's room 1000, which Bush had rented for the occasion. Very few verbal punches were pulled. O'Donnell, Clarke and I all said that the Bureau of Inspectional Services, which was responsible for internal investigations and anti-organized crime activities, must be reorganized and the units which carried out these two functions should report directly to the Superintendent, and not to his subordinates as was the procedure. Vice officers had to be removed from district control and made responsible to the police command at 11th and State. O'Donnell said that vice activities were operating openly in ten of the 21 police districts and that some form of illegal public activities was taking place in all 21. He cited specific places where gambling was underway with full knowledge of the district commanders.

Bush asked what could be done immediately to correct the situation. O'Donnell, Clarke and I recommended that the ten subpoenaed officers be called in, questioned and asked for cooperation. If they refused, they should be suspended. Bush said he would see to it that this was done. He said he would prepare a memorandum on all of this for the Mayor. The meeting ended.

Meanwhile heat was developing in the Austin District on the far West Side. Two of the men who had served as former Commander Mark Thanasouras' vice officers were in trouble. Allegations had been made to the state's attorney that they were key men in the district's tavern shakedowns.

On the Friday following the meeting with Bush at the LaSalle Hotel, Chief of Patrol Riordan, who was, I believe, the bravest and probably the brightest of all the police, advised me that he had visited the Austin District and found police personnel to be in a state of "hysteria." They were, he said, "falling for the oldest of police tricks." The FBI agents were asking individual policemen to talk with them. Some of the officers were agreeing. "Don't they know their rights?" Riordan asked. He made it clear he believed no policeman should cooperate with the FBI.

The Austin District, where Captain Mark Thanasouras had so long ruled and Tommy O'Malley had met his death, was the target of the largest investigation by FBI agents ever undertaken in Chicago. Eight officers had already talked to the federal agents. The subject of the inquiry was police shakedowns of taverns. "It was a fishing expedition," Riordan said. On the following day Lieutenant O'Donnell telephoned me to report that more than 100 policemen from the Austin, Town Hall and Foster Avenue Police Districts had been subpoenaed to appear before the federal grand jury. Conlisk remained publicly silent regarding these developments. Within the department there was an all out attempt to hide the fact that a major federal investigation was underway.

I had been with the department for three years and nine months. During the first nine months the police had been under attack before, during and after the 1968 Democratic Convention. It was obvious, almost from the beginning, that there was a need for a change in the command of the department in order to eliminate police misconduct and to provide aggressive public leadership for police personnel. For three years I had worked for this change with no success.

The theme throughout the department was a defensive one which seemed to say, "We band of brothers must stand together against all criticism, right or wrong," or, as Deputy Superintendent John Mulchrone had put it: "The blue curtain goes down and you're damn right it goes down everytime an accusation is made against a policeman."

Conlisk was a man of personal integrity. He did not, however, take the steps necessary to ferret out the betrayers of public trust. He was not a public leader. As a result, both the department and the city suffered.

The bill of particulars against the department's high command was a long one. I was convinced that reform would not take place from within the system. I decided to resign as the department's director of news affairs. On Dec. 13, 1971, I met with the Mayor to tell him so. Conlisk had left the Mayor's office just as I entered. Daley was seated, looking flushed and old. After we shook hands, he asked me how things were going. I told him they were not good and that I was going to leave the department. He seemed surprised.

"The department," I said, "is engaged in a great cover-up similar to what it did at the time of the Black Panther case. At that time we could have conducted an honest investigation. The raid was legal but they (the police command) are so accustomed to lying that they can't tell the truth even when it is on their side."

"We should have examined the State's Attorney's policemen's guns before making ballistics reports. The policemen should have been questioned separately by the State's Attorney. Now once again," I continued, "we are having another cover-up."

I told Daley, "We seem to reward those who betray the people." I pointed out that one Deputy Chief had bungled the Panther investigation. As a result he had been at first demoted but was later, quietly, promoted to a higher rank. I also said the public had been betrayed in the investigation of the killing of Thomas O'Malley by an off-duty officer in an Austin District tavern. It was the alliance between crooked cops and tavern owners, I told the Mayor, and our failure to do anything about it, that was a factor in causing federal agents to engulf the district investigating the police. O'Malley's father had sought help from the department in uncovering the facts but was rebuffed. The Mayor seemed puzzled by my remarks and unaware of the O'Malley case I was talking about.

I again pointed out the superintendent's continuing failure to provide public leadership. "You and I have talked about this before," I told the Mayor. "The police believe that all politicians come and go, but the police go on forever. Few officers who have been with the Department for 20 or 25 years can put the public interest first. They are not," I continued, "primarily concerned about the welfare of the public but the welfare of the police."

I went through the whole bill of particulars. The department appeared to discourage cooperation with federal investigations. I added that I was aware that the federal probe was political to some extent. Nevertheless, it was very dangerous, I said, not to cooperate with a federal investigation. "Of course," the Mayor interjected, "it would be obstructing justice."

I said I believed that the police command was telling officers who were subpoenaed by the grand jury and those whom the FBI sought to question that they did not have to talk. "I heard that, too," the Mayor said. "That's why Conlisk called in a high ranking officer at my direction yesterday and questioned him, but he denied it."

I said that, instead of trying to root out wrongdoing, the department had gone on the defensive. After almost four years with the department, I told the Mayor, I had come to the conclusion that only a civilian could really run the police. "I once thought that it could be done by a career policeman, but now I am convinced that a veteran officer would have great difficulty putting the people and the city ahead of the police."

The Mayor injected, "But O.W. Wilson did a good job, didn't he?" I replied that I had nothing but respect for the former superintendent.

The Mayor's demeanor was one of sadness. Three times he stated that this was not what he had intended when he sent me to work for the superintendent almost four years before. "I had hoped," Daley said, "that Conlisk would listen and take your advice."

"Well then," he continued, "you view the whole thing as pretty hopeless?" I replied that "With the present leadership, yes. Basically," I added, "it's a good department. You've got a lot of good young men. There are young leaders who could be elevated." I named a few. "These are men you could trust who want to be good policemen. But now, the way the department is organized, young officers don't know where they can turn. There are men who have reported gambling operations to their superiors and have been transferred."

The Mayor asked me if I planned to stay in "communications." I said no. "We will help you get anything," he said. He wished me and my family a Merry Christmas. I said the same to him. We shook hands and I left.

The following day civilian investigator Jack Clarke said he had met with the Mayor and that Daley told him "the entire police command was part of the wrongdoing."

The day was about to come when the "wrongdoing" would be highly visible to all.

# Corruption Unlimited          *17*

*"What the blacks say is true. We are the oppressors!"*

In the Daley years before 1972, relatively few indictments for police corruption had been returned. Within the next two years, however, federal juries, following the greatest exposure of police corruption in Chicago's history, would convict 54 police officers, including men who held the ranks of chief and district commander.

I had told the Mayor on Dec. 13, 1971, that I was going to seek another job. Then, in the two months following Christmas, I decided against accepting two job offers. Events subsequently occurred which absorbed my daily concerns and postponed my departure from the department.

The hostility of the department toward federal investigators continued. Early in February the commander of the Police Intelligence Division stated privately: "There is a war going on between the FBI and the Chicago Police Department, and the Chicago Police Department is going to win." He instructed subordinates to retain some degree of relationship with FBI agents "but don't say nothing." At the same time, Superintendent Conlisk was ordering the department personnel who were responsible for the department's magazine to prepare an article telling how the police were cooperating with the FBI. The magazine cover was a photograph of Conlisk with J. Edgar Hoover. Meanwhile,

FBI agents were developing cases in the Austin District against vice detectives with the cooperation of tavern owners.

The Mayor began his own investigation of the Austin District outside police channels through the City's Department of Investigations. Its commissioner assigned a retired police officer to conduct the "independent" probe. The retired official's first step was to go to the FBI for information!

When Captain Thanasouras was removed as the Austin commander, he was succeeded by Captain Victor Vrdolyak, a brother of the 10th Ward alderman, Edward Vrdolyak. Commander Vrdolyak's administration collapsed early one Sunday morning when an officer under his command was shot to death in an Austin tavern. The dead man was one of a group of vice detectives who, while on duty, had been attending a party at a restaurant and cocktail lounge partly owned by former commander Thanasouras. Following the party, they went to a saloon and became involved with a black male patron who was accompanied by a white woman. During the course of the altercation, the black man was killed by a police officer after he had allegedly shot to death one of the carousing officers. The double fatal-shooting caused top brass from the department to rush to the Austin District station early on a Sunday to take personal command of the investigation.

The following day Chief of Patrol Riordan, conscience-troubled by what he knew of the event, privately exclaimed to me: "What the blacks say is true. We are the oppressors!" He intimated that the police had unjustifiably opened fire on the black civilian victim and that the white officer's death was subsequently caused by a stray police bullet. Certain policemen still hated the sight of a black man with a white woman. The police command, however, said the policeman's death was in the line of duty. The officer was buried with full honors.

Shortly thereafter, Vrdolyak was removed from his command and replaced by the officer who had been in charge of the unproductive, slow-moving, police internal probe of charges of police misconduct during the 1968 convention.

The relationship between the Chicago Police and the black community was rapidly deteriorating.

# The Black Revolt 18

*". . .you better watch it or you're going to go
the same way as the Post Office."*

In the early 1970s white politicians with the Democratic
organization knew that Chicago eventually would have
a black mayor. The population figures told them so. But
they thought it would take 20 years to happen. There just were not
enough voters to bring about a black victory before that time. The
white machine-politicians were proved wrong in 1983.

A decade of increasing black-white political divisions was to
speed up the timetable. One of the most far-reaching political–racial
clashes took place in 1972, tearing apart the once strong bond that had
existed between Mayor Daley and Congressman Ralph Metcalfe.

Prior to his election to succeed Daley's closest black ally, the late
Congressman William Dawson, Metcalfe had been a staunch supporter of the Mayor in the City Council. All of the six organization
black aldermen had sided with Daley during Dr. Martin Luther King,
Jr.'s forays into Chicago in 1966. None, however, had better expressed
the anti-King view than Alderman Ralph Metcalfe.

Because of his long-time service to Congressman Dawson, Metcalfe had been chairman of the Council's Zoning Committee, a position which could lead to lucrative under-the-table rewards. He also was
a true Daley man and for this he was rewarded with representation of
Dawson's South Side district after the congressman's death in 1970.

This close relationship to the Mayor was to fall apart in early 1972, leading eventually to an all out Daley effort to oust Metcalfe from Congress. It also was to lead, in about eight years, to a victory for the man who was Ralph Metcalfe's elected successor in Congress, Harold Washington.

Dr. Odom was a prominent black dentist who was stopped by the police for an alleged traffic violation on Feb. 17, 1972. He subsequently contended that he had been mistreated by the police and complained about this to an influential friend. The friend, in turn, sought to have the Police Department discipline the officers in the case. As frequently happened in those days, the police investigators dragged their feet and, after more than a month, no discipline was forthcoming. That was not unusual. What was different, however, was Dr. Odom's friend. He was Congressman Metcalfe and he was not about to accept the routine investigatory delays of the police. He complained directly to Superintendent Conlisk.

So a meeting was held in Conlisk's office with Metcalfe, Deputy Superintendent James M. Rochford, Deputy Chief Sam Nolan (the Department's highest ranking black officer), and Chief of Patrol James Riordan. I subsequently learned of the meeting from a reporter from the *Defender,* Chicago's black daily newspaper.

The following month, an elderly black doctor from Metcalfe's district was to become ill a short time after he was released from police custody following a traffic arrest. A controversy arose over the police treatment of the doctor and whether it contributed to his subsequent need for hospitalization.

On April 24, Congressman Metcalfe returned to Conlisk's office to complain that still no action had been taken regarding alleged police misconduct in the Odom case and none in the case of the black doctor. By accident I learned that Metcalfe was in the superintendent's office. The police command had not viewed this growing controversy as having a public relations aspect. The command also had not deemed this affair involving a congressman as significant enough to bring it to the Mayor's attention. Within a couple of hours, after two months of Metcalfe's involvement, Daley was to learn about it from the media.

The congressman, in his April 24 meeting with Conlisk, submitted a six point program for implementation by the police by May 31, with an answer due by April 28 whether implementation was intended.

Metcalfe implied that if his proposed program for improving police-community relations was not carried out, he would work to have the superintendent ousted. This threat to the number one mayoral appointee was not appreciated by Daley.

At the conclusion of this meeting, I immediately recommended to Conlisk that he leave his fourth floor office and go to the lobby of police headquarters where television reporters, tipped off by Metcalfe, had stationed themselves for an interview. I reminded the superintendent that Metcalfe was a congressman and had always been a loyal member of the Democratic organization. In no way, I said, should it appear to the public that the superintendent and the congressman were on opposing sides on the subject of proper police conduct in the treatment of blacks. Conlisk agreed and quickly went to the lobby where he joined Metcalfe in front of the cameras. The congressman voiced his complaints and Conlisk stated they would be promptly investigated and resolved.

Among the on-the-scene viewers of this television interview was Father George Clements, a Catholic priest and a supporter of Metcalfe's attempt to assure proper police conduct. Said Clements to a friend standing nearby upon seeing the Superintendent join Metcalfe before the cameras: "He [Conlisk] must have gotten the word from the fifth floor," (the location of Daley's office at City Hall). The priest added that "Daley goes to mass and communion every morning and then spends the rest of the day with his big fat Irish foot on the back of our black necks."

Weeks went by but there was no further contact between the superintendent and the congressman. Daley was outraged by Metcalfe making his complaints in public instead of seeking to resolve them behind the scenes. Metcalfe, the Mayor believed, was disloyal and was pursuing his own political agenda. What is more, rumors began to circulate that Metcalfe was under investigation by U.S. Attorney Thompson for allegedly taking bribes in zoning cases while an alderman. The congressman's sudden concern about police conduct was viewed by some as a means to protect himself from a federal indictment.

Daley ordered Conlisk to make no response to Metcalfe's demands. Another tactic was to be pursued. The Mayor planned a civic meeting in the City Council chamber on the subject of police-community relations.

During the preceding decade, black political opponents of the machine contended that white police officers routinely brutalized blacks. Along with the charge that public schools were in violation of the U.S. Supreme Court's anti-segregation decision, alleged police brutality was a major argument used against machine politicians by their black and white opponents. When one of the highest ranking machine blacks, Metcalfe, joined this attack against "police brutality," it was the first defection by a major member of Daley's organization.

By refusing to allow Conlisk to meet with Metcalfe in an attempt to smooth over the controversy, Daley was assuring a split with the black community that was to lead in a little more than a decade to a black candidate defeating Daley's son for mayor of Chicago.

Daley's planned civic meeting was scheduled for May 3. I wrote a statement for the Superintendent to read at this meeting and, on May 2, drove with him to City Hall. Daley wanted to review the statement.

Also attending the meeting in Daley's office were Rochford, Deputy Superintendent Patrick Needham, Corporation Counsel Richard Curry and the Mayor's administrative assistant, Kenneth Sain. After reading the statement I had prepared for the Superintendent, the Mayor directed that a number of changes be made to make it less liberal. Referring to a sentence which I wrote boasting how 39 percent of the Police Department's civilian employees were black, Daley leaned over his desk and said: "Jim, you better watch it or you're going to go the same way as the Post Office." He told Conlisk not to make the high percentage public.

Mayoral Press Secretary Earl Bush, who had come into the meeting late, announced that Metcalfe and his supporters were waiting at that moment to meet with the Mayor in a South Side church. "Forget the damn church," Daley said. He did not leave to join Metcalfe. Conlisk's proposed statement was revised later that day and sent to the Mayor's home for final approval.

Bush constructively suggested there be an addition to Conlisk's remarks calling for the city's commissioner of human relations henceforth to review Police Department investigations of citizens' complaints pertaining to the use of excessive police force. He telephoned the Mayor at home to relay his suggestion. Daley agreed and Conlisk was instructed to make the addition.

Conlisk had insisted that his statement contain a sentence which maintained that it was the Police Department which had originally uncovered most instances of police corruption being reported in the media. He honestly thought this was true. Bush and I knew it was not. When I arrived at work the next day, Daley was on the phone: "You can't let Conlisk make the statement," the Mayor said, "that it was the Police Department which uncovered most of the police misconduct. He will be ridiculed. It is so patently false." I advised Daley that the statement already had been deleted.

The Mayor's police-community relations meeting in the City Council Chamber was held with dozens of business and civic leaders in attendance, among them Clayton Kirkpatrick, the editor of the *Chicago Tribune*. The meeting, however, only caused a widening of the rift between Daley and Metcalfe.

# From Police Headquarters    *19*
# to City Hall

I never wanted to be Mayor Daley's press secretary. By the time I began covering City Hall for the *Sun-Times* in 1965, he had already been mayor for a decade. During that time he always had a good working relationship with Earl Bush as his press secretary. It is true I was pleased, late in 1967, to be asked by the Mayor to work for him as his spokesman with the police department. But I had no desire whatsoever to some day replace Bush.

Early in May of 1972, while I was still with the police, having been too busy with police crises since my December resignation to seek another job, the Mayor asked me to meet with him at City Hall. He had made a decision, he said. He was going to beef up his staff in order to operate more efficiently. Ken Sain would move up from administrative assistant to a title with responsibilities but no legal status—Deputy Mayor. Tom Donovan would be in charge of all patronage and a mayoral administrative assistant. I would join his staff as another administrative assistant. Daley's plan, he said, was to hire still another assistant—one who was Hispanic (he already had a black assistant—Erwin France).

By this time Daley had been Mayor for 17 years and clearly was set in his ways. He told me then, a year before I was named as his press secretary, that his plan was for me to replace Bush with whom he had grown increasingly displeased. I did not want the job and told the Mayor so. In subsequent days and weeks, when he would again raise the subject of my replacing Bush, I would suggest that it would be better for him to retain his long-time employee in that spot. To assume the responsibilities of dealing with reporters on almost an hour by hour basis on behalf of a politician with 17 years of accumulated grievances by the media, did not hold any appeal for me. Ideally, to represent a politician with electronic and print journalists, you should be with him from the beginning of his first race for major office so that you and he can work together as closely as possible. A politician and his press secretary should understand each other and agree on political objectives and media relations. If one of those components is missing, there cannot be an effective business relationship. In the case of Daley, I agreed sufficiently with his political objectives and could tolerate his media relations. Both of these elements, however, fell short of what were my ideals—especially his media relations.

In the best of all work situations, a press secretary and the politician should be so in tune with each other that the press secretary can speak freely to the media about the politician's future plans and how the politician reacts to new public developments. I could speak freely about what had happened yesterday to Daley but I could not become his verbal alter-ego. By the spring of 1973, when I became his press secretary, he had completed his 18th year in office and had long since become a legendary American politician. No one spoke for Daley.

My eventual job as press secretary was divided into many parts. First of all, there was the handling of dozens of telephone calls from the media each day. Without a press secretary these calls would have to be handled by the Mayor himself, totally disrupting his ability to lead the city. In most of these phone transactions, I believe I did a good job, quickly relating information to the callers. Some news personnel disagreed. I must add, however, that I did not have the freedom to speak the way I believe a press secretary should. New questions about new operations and hypothetical inquiries, for example, could be answered only by Daley. That was not an ideal arrangement.

A press secretary also should be a troubleshooter in the sense of continually being on the lookout for defects in the city government so they can be rapidly corrected. Moreover, the press secretary should be innovative in recommending new policies and services to better assist the public. In these areas, Daley was good to work with. He wanted this kind of assistance from his media aide.

Writing news releases and handling press conferences were also among the press secretary's day-to-day routines. So was the writing of speeches. Daley was easy to work with regarding speeches. He had been a politician so long that 80 percent of his public talks were ad-lib. For the remaining 20 percent, he read exactly what was written for him. The Mayor, unlike many politicians—for example, his successor, Michael Bilandic—did not quibble over words. Bilandic frequently had speeches composed by committee—three or four aides sitting in his office going over each proposed sentence so many times that an air of madness seemed to be loose in the room. Should the word be "that" or "the"? Should it be "these" or "those"? None of that for Daley; he knew that time was precious and he never wasted it on trivial matters.

As press secretary, I promoted certain journalists who sought interviews and screened out others. The criteria always was "which would help the Mayor politically?" I think my judgment was good but there were exceptions. One occurred when an Irish television crew wanted to do a documentary about the Mayor. I recommended his co-operation. The result was a visually engrossing hour program with the most anti-Daley television script ever written. He was portrayed as a man who got up each morning and tried to make life unpleasant for blacks. I later told a friend I had been startled by the vicious tone of these Dublin-based documentary producers. "They even made fun of the Mayor's religion," I said. The friend replied that he was surprised I did not know how anti-clerical certain Irish intellectuals were. I had made a misjudgment in my recommendation for the Mayor's coopera-tion. And yet, strangely, the resulting documentary was so visually at-tractive, I did not regret my decision. More than ever, it was clear to me that the television picture is far more important than the sound track.

Critics of Daley's relationship with the media usually overlooked the frequency of his news conferences during his almost 22 years in of-fice. They also downplayed the number of impromptu meetings with the media as he arrived and left City Hall and countless events. Daley as a front-page, prime-time star will never be matched by any mayoral successor.

For his press secretary, it was often difficult because of the num-ber of times media requests had to be turned down. For reporters, cameramen and photographers, there were no rides with Daley in his limousine and no visits inside his home. There were no trips by the Mayor to television studios for participation in any on-the-air news programs. If TV wanted prolonged interviews, they were conducted in the Mayor's office. He was never on call for the news industry.

The irony is that all of this ultimately made my job better because Daley's non-dependence on the media helped to transform him day by day, step by step, into a legend. He was a politician every newsman sought to question. He was the center of all local and much national attention. If it is true that familiarity breeds not necessarily contempt but, at least, increased familiarity, then Daley avoided this completely. He was not to be had. As a consequence, when he did appear on a filmed or taped television special, when he did grant an exclusive interview, it was a triumph for the particular media which had achieved it.

Daley's selectiveness and his distancing from hourly press demands expanded his legend. I was happy to be working closely with this remarkable politician. But the job of press secretary lay ahead. In May of 1972, I arrived at City Hall to become one of Daley's four administrative assistants, acting principally in the areas of police and fire department services. I did not know then how tumultuous the days ahead would be.

# The Critic Continues 20

*"Daley's philosophy is that the mistake is getting caught."*

ı

In the days that followed, Earl Bush continued to speak critically of his employer. He maintained that Federal Judge William Lynch, a bachelor, and the Mayor's longtime friend and former law partner, had drawn up a will which would leave $10 million to Daley's sons. Daley, Bush maintained, was "greedy for his sons," and anxious that they make large amounts of money in the insurance and law businesses. He said the Mayor had intervened in a lawsuit handled by one of the sons to make certain there was an unprecedented court ruling providing an interest payment for his son's client.

Bush maintained that former Corporation Counsel Raymond Simon had "thrown the sons out of his office" and gone off to practice law by himself. Bush described the construction of a new hotel at O'Hare Airport as a "scandal" and intimated sinister doings in the conduct of one of the most powerful aldermen and one of his law partners. There was a city construction job, Bush said, that was to cost $8 million, and the alderman had offered to reduce the cost by a million dollars if the contractor would split half the savings with him.

Many of the city department heads were under pressure from this alderman to engage in improper conduct regarding city matters, Bush said. Daley had attempted to block the alderman's demand for permits

to construct driveways in the Loop, the press aide added. The alderman retaliated by threatening to block Daley's requests for legislation
in the City Council. The Mayor, according to Bush, capitulated.

Bush added that, because of his "honesty," he had Daley's respect. The press secretary went on to say that "500 firms retained the
Daley sons (as attorneys) but will never use them." This was viewed by
many companies as a cost of doing business in Chicago, Bush said. He
continued: a Daley friend on the federal judiciary was an officer of
one of the major firms doing business with the city and Daley secretly
was a beneficiary. Moreover, all of the legal business from the race-
tracks in Cook County went to Daley's former law partners as a result
of the Mayor's intervention, Bush charged.

The press secretary went on, spilling out alleged grievances accumulated over almost two decades. Daley was "panicky" over federal
probes into Judge Lynch's finances and, Bush said, "possibly into the
Daley sons." Michael Daley was at that time a holder of racetrack
stock. Bush said, "Daley was willing to do anything for Nixon in order
to block the possibility of carrying these probes to their ultimate conclusion." This was the real reason, the press secretary maintained, the
Mayor "races to the airport to greet Nixon." Bush said he feared federal government investigations, then underway, would lead to indictments of County Clerk Edward J. Barrett, Clerk of the Circuit Court
Matthew Danaher and other high ranking Democrats. He added that,
on one recent occasion after having been "chewed out by the Mayor,"
Lynch stated that "everything he had was left to the sons but that now
he might tear up his will." Bush added, strangely, that he himself "had
been innocent for 14 years." He did not explain his implication how his
"innocence" would have ended about 1969. (A federal grand jury in
1973 would provide the explanation.) "Daley's philosophy is," his
long-time employee said, "that the mistake is getting caught." Bush attributed this philosophy to the atmosphere in which the Mayor grew
up in the Bridgeport neighborhood. "There was a passion for money,"
Bush said. He knew because he had seen the same passion, he added,
among West Side Jews.

"When Daley talks about Danaher's troubles," Bush continued,
"he speaks only as to how it will affect Daley. The sons are just like the
father. It is impossible to reform the organization. Daley's philosophy

is that there's no moral wrong if he arranges it but does not do it and is not the personal beneficiary."

This was the kind of conversation Bush repeated with many people during the summer of 1972. Most of what he said got back to his employer.

Bush eventually would be indicted and convicted in federal court for mail fraud connected with a city contract he secretly held.

# The Road to Miami and 21
# the Summer of 1972

*...the 21 year old had received a lesson in
"the power politics of the idealists."*

Meanwhile, the Mayor and the Chicago Democratic
Party were preparing for another national political
convention. In 1968, Daley had been depicted by
the supporters of Senator McGovern and other liberals as a villain. By
July of 1972, the South Dakotan and his allies would practice their alleged policy of inclusion by excluding one of the nation's most loyal
and powerful Democrats from his party's quadrennial meeting. It was
an opportunistic tactic performed under the guise of some form of
egalitarian principle. Daley was accused of ignoring the McGovern-
Frazier guidelines in assembling candidates to run for the position of
delegate that year. In reality, the Mayor and the great majority of the
elected Chicago delegation most likely would have backed Senator
Henry Jackson of Washington for the presidential nomination. The
way to assure that these pro-Jackson votes were never cast, in the eyes
of McGovern and his campaign manager, Gary Hart, was to bar Daley
from the convention. The liberals could not risk being liberal.

On June 30, 1972, the Credentials Committee of the Democratic
National Committee, meeting in Washington, voted 71 to 61 to block
the Mayor and the other 58 Chicago Democratic delegates from being
seated at the Miami convention on the grounds the McGovern–Frazier

rules for designating delegates had been violated. This happened although all of Chicago's delegates had been elected.

On July 5, the Mayor met in his office with Alderman Thomas E. Keane, chairman of the City Council Finance Committee and the second most powerful Democrat in city government. Also present were Corporation Counsel Richard Curry and Earl Bush. During the meeting Keane received a call from one of the attorneys representing the elected Chicago delegates. The caller said a three judge federal panel in Washington had rejected the contention of the delegation that it be seated at the convention. Moreover, the judges prohibited the delegation from seeking any state court order which might block the challenging delegates, headed by Alderman William Singer and Reverend Jesse Jackson, from obtaining convention credentials.

The Mayor was rested and in good spirits following a long 4th of July weekend at Grand Beach. Before the phone call, he had been telling of a conversation with a Democratic leader from the Bronx who reported how a 21 year old New York delegate had been ousted from the Credentials Committee following his pro-Daley vote. The Mayor said the 21 year old had received a lesson in "the power politics of the idealists."

After repeating his caller's message, Keane told Daley he recommended no further legal action in the delegate case. The Mayor amiably disagreed. He got up from behind his desk and kicked one foot in the air as if he were doing an Irish jig and said an appeal should be taken to the U.S. Supreme Court. "We might as well get knocked out at the top," he said, and gave one of his infectious laughs. There was no sign of being depressed by this major political setback.

The news media, however, was near-unanimous in its elation. *Chicago Today* stated that never again would the Mayor be regarded as a political genius. Political writers Jerome Watson of the *Sun-Times* and Joel Weisman of *Chicago Today* expressed the general news media view that the defeat before the Credentials Committee was due to Daley's unwillingness to compromise with a proposal to seat equal portions of each rival delegation. The media contention was not that he was the loser in a power struggle, but that he had destroyed himself.

Later that day, one of the young loyalist aldermen, Edward Burke, privately complained to me that Daley was the one at fault in the delegate debacle. Earl Bush added that the Mayor personally was responsible for the tactics employed by party regulars when they attended the meetings of the opposing "delegates" a few weeks previously. The regulars, as they had every right to, had sought to take over the challengers' meetings but had been universally criticized by the press for so doing. The next day the Mayor sat in his office reading aloud, with much amusement, a column by Mike Royko. Royko had written an open letter to Alderman Singer maintaining that the Daley delegates were truly representative of Chicago's Democrats while the Singer delegates were not.

One by one Royko listed the delegates whom the voters had elected from Daley's congressional district, contrasting their well-known political ethnic names—most of them held elective office—with the relatively unknown names of the Jackson–Singer challengers.

Earl Bush, always an aggressive liberal, convinced the Mayor that Royko's *Chicago Daily News* column be used as an ad in the *Miami Herald* on the following Monday when the convention was to open. Bush then arranged for reprints to be distributed to each delegate at the convention. Royko, journalism's number one Daley detractor, would be used to persuade the convention to reverse the decision by the Credentials Committee.

Bush privately blamed Daley for the committee defeat. The Mayor, Bush contended, had secretly ordered local party leaders to "disregard the McGovern rules" during the period leading up to the delegates' elections. Moreover, said Bush, "it was Daley who ordered the raids" on the Singer meetings.

On the Friday before the convention, Bush, 11th Ward Alderman Michael Bilandic, and many of the elected delegates left for Miami. Monday the convention opened and Bush called me to say he was hopeful that, if McGovern won his fight in the Credentials Committee to gain all of the California delegates, the Senator would not try to block the Daley delegation from being seated.

I spoke by phone with the Mayor in Grand Beach. He told me he had refused to take a call from Bush, because he "talks so much." Daley said he wanted me and Chicago historian Paul Angle to write a history of the delegate battle. The Mayor believed the attempt to reject elected delegates was outrageous and that the public should have the true story which was not being reported in the news media.

Daley said he had no plans at the moment to travel to Miami.

Nevertheless, he was hopeful that the full convention would soon side with him and the other elected Chicago delegates and that he could take his place in the convention hall. However, at 4:00 a.m. on July 11, 1972, the convention voted to block the Mayor and the 58 other elected delegates from Chicago and seat the Reverend Jackson-Alderman Singer group that had not been elected.

Later that week, when McGovern and Senator Thomas Eagleton were nominated, Bush and I agreed the proper course for the Mayor was to issue a statement that he, as a Democrat, would back the entire Democratic ticket. Several days after the nominations, Bush called me at home. He was greatly disturbed because the Mayor, who remained at Grand Beach, had phoned with different plans. Daley wanted to announce there would be a rally of precinct captains, ethnic groups and labor representatives to discuss what had happened to the elected Chicago delegates. He obviously had been receiving suggestions from persons who were embittered and did not want him to back McGovern.

On July 17 Daley returned to City Hall for the first time since July 6. His long-time friend, the former business manager for *Chicago's American,* Don Walsh, came to Bush's office to argue in favor of the proposed precinct captain rally, a device which was certain to lead Daley and the local party away from support for the national ticket. Bush, his assistant, Mike Neigoff, Daley friend and advisor Clair Roddewig, and I maintained that support for the ticket was the best approach so that he could continue as a Democrat and come back to fight another day. The two positions were again presented to Daley. The Mayor decided to issue a support-McGovern statement and, a few minutes later, did so at a news conference.

The rejection by the Miami convention of the 59 elected delegates evoked no outcry from the Chicago press. On the contrary, there was a tone of elation that Daley and his associates had gotten what they deserved.

# The November
# of McGovern

The date was Nov. 3, 1972. The place was the Auditorium Theater. The occasion was the major Chicago rally for Senator George McGovern's campaign for the presidency. Congressman Roman Pucinski, the Democratic candidate for U.S. Senator, was speaking. He named his running mates. At the mention of Edward Hanrahan, the candidate for State's Attorney, most of the audience began to boo. The head of the Democratic Cook County ticket was being booed at a Democratic rally!

On the stage were approximately 100 candidates, committeemen and other political leaders. The Democrats on the stage attempted to counteract the booing by applauding. Then those on the stage stood, with Jane Byrne, standing on a folding chair, leading the cheering on behalf of Hanrahan who remained seated. The audience hooted, yelled, and booed, while the party leaders cheered. And the deep sickness of Cook County Democracy was out in the open for everyone to see.

It was a McGovern crowd, and he and Dan Walker, the maverick candidate for governor, received the most enthusiastic cheers. McGovern arrived during the program and delivered a dull speech. Frank Mankiewicz, his aide, stood in the wings. He looked at the size of the hall. It had less than 3,000 seats. In previous years, Democratic presidential campaign rallies had been held at the Chicago Stadium, with almost 20,000 seats filled and people overflowing onto adjacent Madison Street and Warren Avenue.

This year, however, George McGovern was the candidate. The Cook County party was unable to muster the marchers or spectators for the traditional parade out Madison Street to the Stadium. It was unable, with McGovern at the top of the ticket, to even fill the Auditorium Theater. And now those who had come to watch and listen were booing a man who was on the ticket with McGovern, and the old politicians on the stage cheered back in support of their own. Mankiewicz, as he watched this scene, must have wondered if this was the powerful Cook County organization about which he had heard so much for so many years.

In the remaining days before the election, Hanrahan publicly expressed his deep friendship for Committeeman John D'Arco of the mob-controlled First Ward, and spoke sharply in a radio interview to the wife of the Republican candidate for State's Attorney. When the returns came in, Hanrahan lost by a narrow margin.

Walker was elected Governor, with Daley loyalist Neil Hartigan as Lieutenant Governor. Matt Danaher was re-elected as Clerk of the Circuit Court and Michael Howlett won the race for Secretary of State. Nixon carried Illinois by a large margin. Daley had been politically injured by being barred from the Miami Convention. But the harm to the Democratic National Party was to be much greater.

# His Politics                              *23*

*"You never get anything in this world, unless
you keep pressing for it."*

D aley won his first elective office in 1936 in the midst
of the New Deal. As a state legislator, his political
agenda was New Deal-type legislation for Illinois. He
proposed, unsuccessfully, a 2 percent income tax to prevent an increased sales tax. He helped initiate lunch programs for schools. He
fought to prevent home evictions and to lower sales taxes. The privately owned public tranportation system in Chicago was consolidated
under public ownership. A new public university was created for
downstate Illinois. He had legislative achievements despite the fact
that during most of the years he was in the state senate the legislature
was under downstate Republican control. For six of the eight years, a
Republican was in the governor's office.

Milburn P. Akers, later to be editor of the *Chicago Sun-Times,* described Daley in 1945 as "probably the best exhibit of the hard-
working, decent, honest organization politician that the Kelly machine
can provide."

Later, as Mayor of Chicago, Daley came to be intensely disliked
by many liberals. But a summary of his own liberal credentials is im-
pressive. Following his service in the legislature, he was named director
of the State's Department of Revenue by incoming Governor Adlai E.
Stevenson. This appointment came a few months after Daley's first ap-

pearance as a delegate at a Democratic National Convention. At that Philadelphia gathering in 1948, he bucked the Cook County Democratic Chairman Jack Arvey who favored drafting General Dwight D. Eisenhower for the presidential nomination. Daley, all along, supported President Truman. Then, at his party's convention in Chicago four years later, Daley supported Stevenson for the nomination. By 1956, Daley had become mayor. He again backed Stevenson for the nomination and, that same year, worked hard but unsuccessfully to help Jack Kennedy win the vice presidential spot.

In 1960, at Los Angeles, Daley was a major factor in Kennedy's presidential nomination. A small number of delegates from downstate Illinois, led by former Governor John Stelle, backed Missouri Senator W. Stuart Symington. Daley, however, worked on behalf of Kennedy in alliance with such big city Democrats as Gov. David Lawrence of Pennsylvania, Carmine DeSapio of New York, and Governor Michael DiSalle of Ohio, and delivered the great bulk of the Illinois delegates for the Massachusetts senator.

Later, the Mayor's role in JFK's squeaker victory over Richard Nixon was wrongfully attacked by Nixon supporters from coast to coast. Chicago, with a reputation for vote fraud, was an easy target for accusations that Daley had engineered massive thefts at the polls. During that particular campaign, however, I led a team of pollsters through downstate Illinois on behalf of the *Chicago Sun-Times*. Our polling predicted with pinpoint accuracy the victories of Otto Kerner, the Democratic candidate for governor, and Senator Paul Douglas who was seeking re-election. Kennedy would win Illinois, according to our poll, by 100,000 votes. His actual election victory margin was approximately 8000 votes. To this day, my polling experience in three presidential elections, convinces me that there were vote thefts in Illinois in 1960 but that most of them occurred in Republican-controlled counties. Over and over again, while conducting the 1960 poll, I encountered downstate precincts where Democratic voting judges had never been seen on election days.

Typical was one roadside tavern in Bureau County 100 miles west of Chicago. It was mid-day, but the large room inside the tavern was darkened, with only a naked light bulb glaring above a large circular table. Around it sat eight men playing cards. When I explained the reason for my sudden appearance and asked if they would mark a secret

ballot for the *Sun-Times* poll, the man who obviously was the dominant one of the group turned away from his cards and said to me:
"Just mark eight straight Republicans, buddy, and let it go at that."
The other seven laughed. I knew that on election day there would be
little, if any, poll-watching by the Democratic Party in Bureau County.

Added to the absence of an effective minority party in many
downstate counties was the vote-fraud-prone Illinois practice of not requiring voter identification in 101 of the state's 102 counties. Only in
Chicago and outlying Cook County were voters required by law to
have their signatures matched on election day with those on the voting
registration records. In the 101 other Illinois counties, the registration
records with voter signatures were kept locked up in county court-
houses on election days. The result was that all over the state, outside
Chicago, voters could claim they were someone else. To berate Daley
for alleged vote thefts on behalf of Kennedy was merely following a
long-standing Illinois Republican hate-Chicago tradition.

As a newspaper reporter, I subsequently covered the only vote
fraud case that went to a jury trial in Cook County. The evidence
showed that, during the 1960 presidential vote count in one of Chicago's West Side precincts, the Democratic election judges worked fever-
ishly erasing pencilled x's preceding Richard Nixon's name, while at the
other end of the counting table, Republican officials changed Kennedy
ballots to favor the G.O.P. presidential candidate. Observing this was a
Chicago police officer assigned to the polling place to assure fairness.

There were thefts on both sides in Illinois in 1960 but my opinion
is that the Nixon supporters stole more. Daley offered to put up a million dollars in Democratic funds to pay for a state-wide recount but
Nixon refused to go along.

In the presidential campaign four years later, Daley urged Lyndon
Johnson to pick Robert Kennedy as his vice presidential running mate.
Then, in 1968, at Chicago, Daley's first choice for the presidential
nomination was Teddy Kennedy. After Teddy declined to run, the
Mayor supported Humphrey but only after it became clear he would
be the sure winner at the convention. In 1972, the Mayor, certain that
Senator George McGovern was a sure presidential loser, favored Senator Henry Jackson for the nomination. Subsequently, despite being
barred from that year's convention by McGovern strategists, Daley
campaigned whole-heartedly for the McGovern-Shriver ticket.

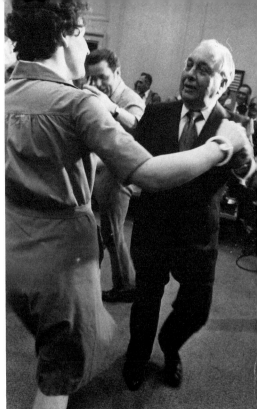

Above Left: On the reviewing stand for one of the Mayor's most enjoyable annual events, the St. Patrick's Day parade. *(© Laszlo Kondor)*

Above Right: With a visiting Irish dancer outside his office. *(© Laszlo Kondor)*

Below: Campaigning in a Mexican neighborhood. *(© Laszlo Kondor)*

Above Left: With the author and his family in 1967. *(© Chicago Fire Department)*

Above Right: The "topping off" ceremony for the world's tallest building. *(© Laszlo Kondor)*

Below: Leading the St. Patrick's Day parade flanked by movie actor George Hamilton (left), labor leaders, Illinois Governor Dan Walker (second from right) and Lt. Governor Neil F. Hartigan (far right). *(© Laszlo Kondor)*

Above: Mayor Daley talks with the media while members of the Chicago Board of Education look on. *(© Laszlo Kondor)*

Below Left: The 1975 primary night victory celebration with Mrs. Daley, some of their sons, daughters and spouses, Jane Byrne (third from right), her daughter, Kathy, and family friend Father Gilbert Graham. *(© Laszlo Kondor)*

Below Right: On a fishing boat in Lake Michigan wearing City Hall clothes. *(© Laszlo Kondor)*

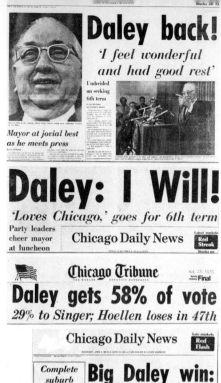

Above Left: The author, when he was press secretary, in his City Hall office in 1973. *(© Laszlo Kondor)*

Above Right: Chicago newspaper headlines announcing Daley's return to City Hall following surgery, his decision to seek a sixth mayoral term, the result of the primary voting and that of the mayoral election. *(© Laszlo Kondor)*

Below: With his cabinet, including Jane Byrne, at the city's water purification plant. *(© Laszlo Kondor)*

With Jane Byrne at a 1975 campaign fashion show in the Ambassador West Hotel. (© *Laszlo Kondor*)

Daley, 74, in an aldermanic softball game less than a year after suffering a stroke and undergoing surgery. (© *Chicago Today*)

Muhammad Ali is made an honorary Chicago citizen, backed by then Alderman, later Acting Mayor, Eugene Sawyer (left) and other politicians.

*(© Laszlo Kondor)*

Conferring honorary Chicago citizenship upon Frank Sinatra, who Daley always called "Frankie." *(© Laszlo Kondor)*

With the "Polish Prince," singer Bobby Vinton. *(© Laszlo Kondor)*

With President Truman.

With President Kennedy.

At a Democratic dinner in Chicago with former President Lyndon B. Johnson.

At a 1972 Democratic dinner in Chicago with Senator Edward M. Kennedy.

With Senator George McGovern during Chicago hearings on the proposed delegate rules for the 1972 Democratic convention. *(© Laszlo Kondor)*

Introducing President Ford to some of the Mayor's grandchildren at Meigs Field in Chicago. *(© Laszlo Kondor)*

With Senator Walter Mondale during a news conference at City Hall while the senator was testing the waters for a try at the 1976 presidential nomination. He dropped out of the race later to be selected as vice-presidential nominee. *(© Laszlo Kondor)*

1976 campaigning with Jimmy Carter and, to his right, Senator Adlai E. Stevenson III. *(© Laszlo Kondor)*

With his son, Richard. *(© Laszlo Kondor)*

Mayor Daley's home at 3536 S. Lowe Ave. in Chicago's Bridgeport neighborhood photographed during the 1975 mayoral campaign.
*(© Laszlo Kondor)*

Celebrating a birthday with his sons, left to right, Michael, Richard M.,
William and John. *(© Laszlo Kondor)*

Flanked by the Shannon Rovers bagpipers and drummers, the Mayor and
Mrs. Daley leave St. Patrick's Church prior to the annual St. Patrick's Day
parade. *(© Laszlo Kondor)*

The Daleys, especially happy on the day he was discharged from
Rush-Presbyterian-St. Luke's Medical Center following his 1974 surgery to
clear a carotid artery. *(© Laszlo Kondor)*

Headed for the firehouse polling place across from his home to vote in the 1975 Democratic primary. *(© Laszlo Kondor)*

One of his last photos. Walking past ice sculptures across from City Hall en route to a gymnasium dedication on Dec. 20, 1976. Four hours later, he died from a heart attack. Shown here with the Mayor are Alderman William Barnett (left) and an administrative aide, Thomas Donovan (right).

*(© Laszlo Kondor)*

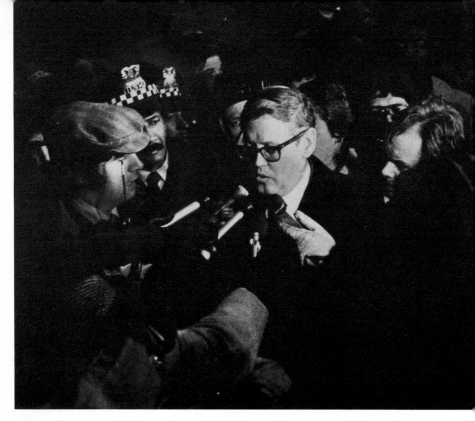

The author announces the Mayor's death, asking Chicagoans "to pray for the soul of this good man." (© *Chicago Sun-Times*)

A mourner signs a registry expressing sorrow upon Daley's death. The quotation on the poster, attributed to Abraham Lincoln, was a favorite of the Mayor. (© *Laszlo Kondor*)

McGovern later stated that no one in the Democratic Party had worked harder on his behalf than Daley. Forty-nine states went for Nixon. Chicago voted for McGovern.

In 1976, Daley believed that the candidacy of Jimmy Carter, as a former Southern governor, would be difficult to sell to voters in Chicago and Illinois. Nevertheless, he jumped on the bandwagon after the Ohio primary made it obvious Carter would be the convention choice at Madison Square Garden. In the election, Carter lost Illinois.

While Daley was supporting the political aspirations of Truman, Stevenson, LBJ and the three Kennedy brothers, the Daley-influenced congressional delegation from Chicago was a key and united factor in carrying out the Democratic Party's legislative agenda in Washington. Upon his retirement as Speaker of the House, Congressman John McCormack asserted that no elected official outside Congress had played a greater role in bringing about the legislative programs of the Kennedy and Johnson years than Mayor Daley.

At the annual meetings of the U.S. Conference of Mayors, and at hearings before the Democratic National Committee, Daley was the strongest champion of the Democratic proposals for inner city housing, urban renewal, the war on poverty, federal aid for education, Medicare, Medicaid and all the other Kennedy-Johnson-backed legislative programs. Despite this, he is generally remembered with disdain by many of the same people who supported this legislation. Why?

The reasons are many, and include Daley's refusal to assist Martin Luther King by providing him with a Selma-like psychological victory in Chicago, his immersion in machine politics, his wrong-headed shoot to kill order, his opposition to affirmative action on behalf of women and blacks in the selection of delegates for party conventions, and the simple desire by politicians on the outside to replace a man who had held office for almost a generation. The media and a major portion of the nation's liberals refused to credit Daley for the political strength he consistently provided for liberal presidential candidates and their programs. He could have easily reduced some of this liberal disdain if he had been willing to engage in liberal rhetoric on race relations. Words always seemed more important to his critics than actions. But Daley refused.

Words, obviously, were not among his skills. During my 12 years of association with him, he delivered only two truly fine speeches, and both were ad-lib. Both expressed his desire to assist blacks. The first came at the time of Dr. Martin Luther King, Jr.'s 1966 Chicago campaign for open housing. Daley, skillfully, with the advice of his press secretary at the time, Earl Bush, and Corporation Counsel Ray Simon, had avoided any confrontation with the civil rights leader. King had decided to leave Chicago after the Mayor offered a program which included such trivialities as the installation of a handful of portable swimming pools at inner city locations and the opening of fire hydrants on hot summer days for the enjoyment of inner city children. The non-trivial focus of the Daley program was an open housing agreement to spur resistant real estate brokers to practice racial fairness. It was at this time that he delivered his best off-the-cuff talk at City Hall.

Speaking before a news conference after the King agreements, the Mayor noted that for 100 years ten southern states had deprived their black populations of voting rights, equal education and job opportunities. During the preceding decade, a dozen northern and western cities had been called upon to make up for this century of southern injustices. Chicago, he maintained, had striven to rectify these wrongs and would continue to do so. The city had undertaken a massive program of new school construction beginning in 1950. There had been a vast program to provide adequate housing. The city, he said, was working for justice and opportunity for all of its residents and would continue to do so.

"These problems," he said, "were created thousands of miles away from here, in Georgia, Mississippi and Alabama. This deprivation of education can't be laid to the people of Chicago. They had nothing to do with it."

His other memorable talk came before a joint session of the Illinois General Assembly in 1975. Governor Walker was opposing an increase in the state funding for public schools, money desperately needed by the Chicago school system. Daley traveled to Springfield to plead for this legislation which, in Chicago, would have mainly benefited schools that were predominately black. In the course of his talk, he confessed having made a mistake when he supported Walker in the 1972 gubernatorial race over the incumbent Republican, Richard B. Ogilvie. Daley's remarks delighted the G.O.P. members of his audience.

Only two memorable speeches in a dozen years—he was not a man of rhetoric. He was, essentially, a back-room politician, masterful in building and maintaining political coalitions, effective in carrying out public programs, but woefully remiss with inspiring words in an era increasingly dependent on television and radio.

His coalition was made up of black and white voters. He would not engage in the rhetoric of the civil rights movement for three reasons. First, it might ruffle the people of his own heavily white neighborhood and adjoining areas on the Southwest Side. Secondly, it was not his style or his talent to utilize rhetoric for any cause. Thirdly, and sadly, he was a product of his time and place as far as race relations were concerned. He did not believe one race was superior to another. At the same time, he did not have sustained empathy for blacks nor a kindred spirit for their struggle. Most of his experience before becoming Mayor worked against the building of such a spirit.

It was to the neighborhoods just to the east of his that the black migration came during and after the First World War. It was in his neighborhood Stock Yards that these same blacks sought jobs. It was his Bridgeport neighborhood, which, for decades, has resisted black residents. His education at nearby Graham public school, Nativity parochial school, De LaSalle Institute and DePaul University Law School, provided no inspiration for racial justice.

On the other hand, because of his Irish background, he was well aware of the struggles of a minority people for social, political and economic fairness. His mother worked for suffrage for women. His father was an organizer for the sheet metal workers. He served with blacks in the Illinois legislature. He received life-long loyalty from blacks like State Senator Corneal Davis. He was first elected Mayor only because of black votes with the support of Congressman William Dawson. He retained the loyalty of the black members of the City Council, including, for many years, a man of no little talent, Ralph Metcalfe.

Nevertheless, no black secretaries were in his office. Black promotions to high levels in the police command were almost nonexistent. His fire commissioner disliked blacks and did everything he could to discourage their participation in the Fire Department. Only toward the end of his career did Daley retain a black man as one of his dozen bodyguards.

Once I telephoned Mrs. Daley to alert her that a black demonstration was going to take place outside of her home in protest of a black being roughed up by whites for venturing onto a Bridgeport residential street. She responded by noting that "You don't hear about our boys being beaten up when they walk through their neighborhoods."

Daley's support of the three Kennedy brothers and other heroes of the liberal pantheon was unimpressive to his liberal foes for other reasons. He was the personification of the machine politician. But to him, the Democratic organization of Chicago and Cook County was the grass roots organization which his political opponents wished they had.

For some of these opponents, he was too much of a Democrat, believing in the priority of elections over back-room or front-room caucuses. He could never subscribe to a mathematical formula for endorsing candidates on the basis of sex or race. He had come from a period when not much attention was paid to either of those accidents of birth at slate-making time and he certainly did not view women as equals when it came to holding office.

He was frequently criticized for favoring an excessive number of Irish appointees and candidates. This was increasingly true as his tenure in office grew. But he and the political organization which he led could never have achieved their success in Chicago if they had not always been sensitive to having a diverse ethnic make-up.

Tenure in office may have been the biggest cause for the disdain he received from his liberal opponents. He was there too long to suit them. Political conflict is often viewed as a struggle over principles and causes when, in reality, the conflicts of the Daley years could very well be viewed as combat by the outs to get in, using racial arguments about alleged principles as their instruments to gain power. At least that is how Daley viewed it.

During his time in office, Chicago politics was not a struggle between blacks and whites. During his last decade it was a battle between a small number of white and black politicians on the one hand and the huge majority of white and black residents on the other. The voting statistics of the Daley years show this. It was in the aftermath of Daley, when lesser politicians succeeded him, that his successful coalition ended. Even when State Senator Harold Washington ran against incumbent Mayor Michael Bilandic in 1977, Washington was able to get only 11 percent of the vote. Six years later, this figure grew to 36 percent, enough to get him elected mayor in a three-way race with incumbent Mayor Byrne and Daley's son, Richard, who together received 64 percent.

The liberals' dislike for Daley showed increasing strength after 1968 but his political foes faced continuing failure at the polls as long as he was alive. The heavy majority of Chicago voters liked the man who backed FDR, Truman, Stevenson, Kennedy and LBJ. They liked the man who worked for the defeat of Richard Nixon three times as a presidential candidate and twice when he was running for vice president.

Once, when a group of Puerto Ricans came to the Mayor's office for a ceremonial occasion, Daley got into a political discussion with his visitors. He advised them to always press those in government with their demands. "You never get anything in this world," he said, "unless you keep pressing for it." Daley had been the target for hundreds and hundreds of demonstrations by all sorts of groups pressing him for things that they believed in. His advice to the Puerto Ricans was to do more of the same.

# The Critic
# Is Silenced

# *24*

*"Now they know the whole story. Nothing
more can be disclosed."*

As 1972 drew to a close, Earl Bush came to me greatly
troubled. Long-time Democratic Party leader Joseph
Gill had died several months before. For many years
he had much of the city's insurance business without bidding for it.
Bush said that after Gill's death the Mayor ordered the insurance business
shifted toward his own son, John. It was the first known instance
that a member of the Mayor's immediate family had benefited from
city business.

Bush and I agreed that it was a tremendous mistake which Daley
should reconsider. Bush said he was going to try to get the Mayor to do
so. Gill's heirs thought they should inherit this city business. It would
not be long before they conveyed their bitterness to the news media.

Before January of 1973 ended, Bush reported to me that the news
media was investigating the Mayor's transfer of the city insurance.
Bush and I both believed it was imperative for Daley to have his son
disassociate himself from the city business. Although legal, the insurance
situation was clearly at odds with Daley's 18 year record of not using
the Mayor's Office to financially benefit himself or his immediate
family.

Early in February the story broke in *Chicago Today*. It was every
bit as harmful to the Mayor as had been feared. Shortly thereafter,

Bush telephoned me at home and said he was going to recommend that the Mayor apologize and for John to return the commissions. I agreed that this was the right thing to do. When I hung up, I told my wife and she remarked: "You have just recommended that Bush lose his job. If he does that [recommend a Daley apology], he will be fired." I did not want this to happen. I called Bush back to recommend that he hold off on his advice but he had gone out for the evening.

The next morning, after much thought, I reversed my opinion and decided that Daley could not apologize and still retain an effective position of leadership. He had built an aura of omnipotence. His style of leadership would not allow for an apology. What is more, one apology would not satisfy his critics; there would be demands for more. I thought John should return any commissions he might have already received and get out of the city's insurance business but with no public apology by the Mayor. I went to Bush's office at City Hall for a long discussion. Bush and his assistant, Mike Neigoff, favored an apology. Bush's other aide, Jack Bowen, and I were opposed. Finally, I told Bush I thought it would be all right for him to make the suggestion to Daley but that, if I were asked, I would recommend no apology. Bush, of course, had already decided that an apology recommendation should be made. A memorandum to this effect was forwarded by him to the Mayor.

Several days later, on St. Valentine's Day, the Mayor gave his answer. He told a cheering audience of Democratic committeemen meeting at the LaSalle Hotel: "If a man can't put his arms around his sons, . . . then they can kiss my ass." Bush's days as press secretary were numbered.

In May of the previous year, when the Mayor had asked me to become his administrative assistant, he said it was only a matter of time before he wanted me to replace Bush as press secretary. Bush's endless private criticisms of the Mayor and his family had gotten back to Daley. The animosity generated by Bush's gossiping caused the Mayor to be critical of almost everything Bush did and almost everyone associated with him. It got to the point, throughout 1972, during the months before the insurance controversy, that the Mayor would frequently keep the door to his inner office closed. The reason, he told me, was so that Bush would not enter unannounced.

The press secretary's comment to friends and associates that the

Mayor was "anti-Semitic" was especially galling to Daley. He and Bush disliked each other intensely long before the insurance matter arose. When that happened, Bush's recommendation that the Mayor apologize for his actions meant the time for a firing was at hand. The only questions were how and when.

On Feb. 20, 1973, the Mayor called me to his office and told me to prepare a news release announcing the appointment of City Public Works Commissioner Milton Pikarsky to the Chicago Transit Authority Board. Three days previously, Pikarsky and I and our wives had been among the guests of Bush and his wife at a dinner in their suburban Skokie home. The day prior to the dinner, the Mayor told me, in the presence of Deputy Mayor Sain, Tom Donovan and management consultant Paul Rice, that I was to take over Bush's operations. I replied by noting that the Mayor and Bush had worked together for 18 years and intimated that Daley should go slow in bringing this relationship to an end. Daley was annoyed that I appeared to be suggesting it was unkind for him to dump an aide after so many years. Later he told Rice privately, and on another occasion he told me directly, that he hoped I would not be soft in my new job. No date was set for the transition.

As soon as Daley told me to prepare the news release on Pikarsky's appointment, he called Bush into his office and told both of us that, henceforth, I would handle all press relations and Bush's job would be only to write the Mayor's speeches.

The next day, at the Mayor's direction, I prepared a suggested news release announcing that I was replacing Bush as press secretary. After reading it, Daley reversed himself. This was not the way to handle it, he said. The best tactic was to wait until Pikarsky actually moved to the CTA and then Bush could go with him to handle press relations for that agency. At that point, the Mayor said, he could announce that Bush was taking on a new job and that I was going to succeed him as press secretary.

The internal politics of City Hall moved on. For the next month, I was the administrative assistant who secretly wrote news releases and Bush was the press secretary who was not supposed to have much dealing with the press. The arrangement was secret until it was disclosed in a *Chicago Daily News* article by Jay McMullen.

Then on March 24, McMullen wrote a second article predicting that Bush would be replaced because he had recommended that the Mayor apologize in the insurance matter. This second article hurt Bush's public image of being close to the Mayor and probably accelerated his removal from his job. The source of the article was the Mayor's political confidante and McMullen's good and close friend, Jane Byrne.

On March 22, it became public knowledge that City Comptroller David Stahl was leaving city government because of the insurance controversy. Stahl, in response to newsmen's questions, had stated that Daley ordered him to transfer the city insurance to Heil and Heil, the insurance firm for which the Mayor's son, John, was serving as a broker. Stahl had quoted Daley as saying that John "should be given a crack at it." Daley, upon hearing this, immediately decided that Stahl must go. The Mayor was growing more and more defensive. Stahl was being fired for telling the truth.

Bush, fighting to hold on, then wrote a memo to the Mayor suggesting that he be named an administrative assistant as a face-saving device. Daley showed the memo to me before leaving for a Florida vacation and asked my opinion. I said to transfer Bush to administrative assistant would "institutionalize" him in the Mayor's office and would be a cause of future conflicts. The Mayor agreed. He was standing by his desk, loading his briefcase. He said he was leaving for Florida and by the time he came back  he wanted Bush out as press secretary and his press office completely reorganized. I told the Mayor I would try to find a place for Mike Neigoff in city government. Daley said: "Nobody wants him." Neigoff, who had an extensive background in TV news, had once been asked by a reporter what was the mayoral salary. "Thirty-five thousand dollars and all he can steal," Neigoff answered, and Daley never forgot. The Mayor and I shook hands and he departed on his Florida vacation.

Later the same day I told Bush I was going to have to reorganize his staff. I told Neigoff his position was terminated as of May 1. Always perceptive, he told a friend I was not responsible for his firing. Said Neigoff, alluding to Bugs Moran's alleged statement about Al Capone, "Only Daley kills like that."

*Sun-Times* reporter Harry Golden stopped by my office and asked if there was any truth to reports on the previous Friday that Bush was going to be replaced by me. I told him I had already replaced

Bush and was responsible for press relations for the Mayor. Furthermore, I told him, Bush was continuing to work for the Mayor but under me. It was the first and only time one of Daley's appointees announced his own appointment.

After the Mayor returned from his Florida vacation, I accompanied him on two political trips. In May, he traveled to Washington, D.C., to participate in a meeting of the advisory council of elected officials of the Democratic National Committee. Among those attending were Senators George McGovern, Hubert Humphrey, and Henry Jackson, along with House Speaker Carl Albert. Of the group, Daley spoke in the most liberal terms about the need for the Democratic Party to stand for specific economic programs. En route to the meeting, the Mayor's cab passed the White House and he ruefully commented, "If it was a few years ago, we could have stopped by for lunch."

The following week he flew to Springfield, Illinois, to attend a dinner honoring the Democratic majority leader, Senator Cecil Partee. Before the dinner, about 20 top Democrats met socially in a suite in the Leland Hotel. Everyone consumed an alcoholic beverage. No one went back for a second. Then Daley went to the bathroom. Cook County Board President George Dunne immediately stepped behind the portable bar, announced that the Mayor was momentarily absent and that this would probably be their only chance to get a second drink without the boss seeing them. Everyone raced for the bar.

May 16, 1973, was the day after Daley's 71st birthday. Before the flight to Springfield, Alderman Tom Keane called to wish him a belated happy birthday. "I wish I was 59," Daley said with a smile.

During this period, Dave Stahl finally packed up all his belongings and left City Hall for a new job. Daley's last comment to me before the departure was "get him out of here as quick as possible." Stahl was an outstanding public servant, but he was the victim of Daley's guilty conscience about the insurance matter. The Mayor, however, said privately to me that his son "never made a penny" on city insurance and told me to prepare a statement to this effect. I concluded that he meant John's profits had come from insurance written for other government bodies such as the Park District and that commissions on city government insurance had not been received as of that date. He also discussed with me the possibility of John writing a letter to the newspaper publishers explaining all this. I prepared a statement but Daley never issued it. He decided to let John keep the profits.

On May 23, the Mayor made his third out-of-town trip of the month. This one again was to Washington for a $500 a plate Democratic dinner kicking off the 1974 Congressional races. Accompanying the Mayor on the commercial flight were George Dunne, State Representative John Touhy, Alderman Michael Bilandic, Alderman Edward Vrdolyak, Deputy Mayor Ken Sain, Park District Superintendent Ed Kelly, Tom Donovan, County Commissioner Matt Bieszczat, Democratic Committeeman John D'Arco, Lieutenant Governor Neil Hartigan, Sheriff Dick Elrod, Alderman Claude Homan, Democratic Committeeman Bernie Neistein, Milton Pikarsky, County Clerk Stanley Kusper, City Treasurer Joe Bertrand and Congressman Morgan Murphy.

At the dinner, I sat with Neistein, D'Arco, Pikarsky, Alderman Homan, Elrod and Bieszczat. The evening at the Capital Hilton began with Neistein slipping the bandleader money so he would play "Chicago." When the band struck up the song, the group assembled at our table stood and waved their napkins, adding class to the $500 a plate affair. A CBS camera crew filmed this Chicago Democratic contingent. The following night CBS newsman Walter Jacobson reported that the public could tell a lot about the Mayor by the people he picked to accompany him. One of the film clips showed Neistein, me, Elrod and D'Arco. "There," Jacobson said, narrating the film footage, "you see Bernie Neistein, the white boss of the black 29th Ward sitting next to Frank Sullivan, the Mayor's press secretary. And he is next to Sheriff Elrod, who is sitting along side John D'Arco, committeeman of the 1st Ward and, reportedly, the organization's link with the mob. The sheriff is obviously sitting there so he can keep an eye on D'Arco."

"This group," Jacobson concluded, "tells you a lot about the Mayor's interest in reform." Then the newsman looked soulfully into the camera and exclaimed: "He has no interest."

After the dinner, the visitors from Chicago climbed aboard a chartered bus for the ride to the airport. En route Daley led the group in singing Irish songs. At one point, the lights went out in the bus as it circled the brilliantly illuminated Lincoln Memorial. It would have been a good scene in a movie, the darkened bus cruising past the imposing statute of Lincoln, with the strains of "When Irish Eyes Are Smiling" coming through the night.

The following month was the time for San Francisco and the U.S. Conference of Mayors. We arrived on Saturday, June 16. That evening the Mayor and Mrs. Daley served cocktails in their suite at the St. Francis Hotel for his aides and their wives who had joined him on the trip. Daley, in a tuxedo and making sure that everybody had a drink, ice, and hors d' oeuvres, was a different Daley than I had been accustomed to.

On Sunday morning, after Mass, he insisted that his employees spend the day sightseeing in the scenic areas north of San Francisco. That night there was another small cocktail party with the Daleys, followed by a sumptuous dinner in a large private room at Ernie's, with many toasts and much camaraderie.

The following day, longshoreman-philosopher Eric Hoffer and S.I. Hayakawa addressed the Mayors' Conference. Daley left the sessions early, at the request of San Francisco Mayor Joseph Alioto, to participate in the taping of a one-hour ABC-TV discussion program. Daley invited New York Mayor John Lindsay to ride with us to the television studio to meet Alioto and Los Angeles Mayor-elect Tom Bradley. Daley and Lindsay chatted amiably en route, but Daley privately remained annoyed by what he thought was Lindsay's gratuitous criticism at the time of the shoot to kill order five years before.

The next day Daley was the guest of honor at a luncheon given by Mayor Alioto. The location was a Catholic home for merchant sailors not far from the Bay Bridge. The weather was perfect. Waiting to greet Daley outside the hall were Alioto, Hayakawa, wearing a brightly colored tam, and a contingent of Irish bagpipers.

At the luncheon, Alioto presented the Mayor with the "St. Francis of Assisi Humanitarian Award" for his "service to the poor of America's cities." The guests, who were politicians, policemen, firemen, labor officials and priests, sang "My Kind of Town" and "I Left My Heart in San Francisco." Those in attendance were mainly of Irish or Italian descent. They included Mrs. Daley and long-time longshoremen's official, Harry Bridges. It was the 11th Ward along side San Francisco Bay and a colorful conclusion to five beautiful days.

But back home, the insurance question kept coming up. On July 12, the Mayor was to hold a press conference. I recommended that, if asked again, he should not offer any explanation of the insurance. No matter how thoroughly he explained it, his critics would not be satisfied and he would be on the defensive. He agreed.

He noted that the news media was now writing stories about the new insurance office which his sons, John and Bill, had just opened across from the Nativity of Our Lord Church. "What do they want them to do?" the Mayor asked. "Move to another city?" He added to me that he recognized the difference between "helping your sons when you're in private life and helping them when you're in politics." It was the only indication that he had a feeling of guilt regarding what he had done in the insurance matter.

During these months Earl Bush had been working for me, assisting with background information for some of the Mayor's talks. On July 25, Daley told me he learned that Bush had an interest in the firm which had the contract for providing display advertising in all the terminals at O'Hare Airport and was being investigated by the U.S. Attorney's office. Daley said this was "the worst thing" that had happened in his administration, considering his close relationship with Bush. He said the former press secretary would have to resign immediately or he would be fired. (It has always been my opinion that Daley gave Bush this business.)

Subsequently, Bush went to Daley's office and the Mayor asked me to be ready outside. After a short time, he called me in and said Bush was going to resign and that the two of them had discussed the wording of the letter of resignation. Bush insisted that the letter should be written in terms of a leave of absence. Daley disagreed. There should be an immediate resignation or, as he said to Bush, he would have to be fired.

Daley then gave me a letter of resignation which he had written for Bush to sign and told me to have secretary Kay Quinlan type it. I walked out of the Mayor's office and handed it to Quinlan who began typing. Bush then left Daley's office and went into an ante-room where he paced up and down. When the typing was completed, I showed him the letter and he said he did not want the "flowing language" about how he had enjoyed working with the Mayor. There should be "just a simple sentence" announcing the resignation.

Then the Mayor called the two of us into his office. Bush was visibly angry. He intimated that, once again, this was what he had referred to earlier in the Matt Danaher case as a one-way street for Daley. Bush asked me if I would leave the room for a moment. When the Mayor called me in again, he stated that Bush's suggested shortened version of the letter of resignation would be used. Earl signed it. Bush and I then left the office and the press was notified.

It was clear to me from Bush's remarks that, although he knew he had to step aside, he wished it did not have to be a permanent resignation. He was letting Daley know loud and clear that the U.S. Attorney would be questioning him about his 19 year political relationship with the Mayor and that Daley should always want Bush to remain friendly.

During these days both Bush and his wife, Sylvia, by the things they said, left the impression that Daley had better go along with them, or else. Earl had indicated previously that both he and Corporation Counsel Richard Curry were aware of the problems that the Mayor was having with IRS investigators. On July 28 Bush cleared out some of his belongings from City Hall.

The next day the *Daily News* broke the news about Bush's interest in the display advertising at O'Hare. Daley fundraiser Charlie Swibel had called me to warn that it was coming, but the newspapers were already out. The Mayor said later that it was a good thing Bush's resignation had been announced the previous day.

Then, Friday, August 3, *Chicago Today* printed a detailed story stating that Bush was the sole owner of Dell advertising company which had the exclusive O'Hare contract for all display ads in the airport terminals. Bush phoned me, seemingly undisturbed. "Now they know the whole story," he said. "Nothing more can be disclosed." He sounded as if he was unconcerned about the trouble he had caused Daley and himself and the destruction of his image as an idealist.

Bush was a wise man and a great help to Daley through much of his career. But the press aide suffered from an ailment too common with employees of highly successful men. Bush began to think he was the political genius shaping Daley, that the Mayor was basically a front man depending on his aide for political astuteness.

The truth is that some working relationships simply should have cut-off points. If those in the relationship begin to sour on each other, the relationship should be ended. Increasingly, Bush complained he was unappreciated by Daley. Among the Mayor's employees, the press secretary became the most frequent critic. Bush forgot the simple fact that if an employee wishes to remain an employee, he must act like an employee. That is what Daley wanted from him.

The Mayor had another close employee who, like Bush, was convicted in federal court. But unlike Bush, he never became a mayoral critic. His name was Jack Clarke and his story has never been fully told—until now.

# His Eyes and Ears                    25

*"You don't know the bagman after 12 years?*
*Get your ass out of here. We don't want*
*anyone in this unit who's as dumb as you are."*

One of the most mysterious figures in the Daley administration was a private investigator by the name of John Clarke. He was referred to from time to time by the media as Daley's "spy" or Daley's "eyes and ears." In the sense that he was an undercover agent and had the ear of the Mayor, he was a little bit of both those things. There were also some in the media who, after the Watergate scandal surfaced in Washington, claimed that they saw striking similarities between the actions of Daley's man Jack Clarke and the actions of all the President's men.

Jack Clarke was a multi-faceted individual who was roundly misunderstood and often unjustly maligned by the media. In the roles he played in government he earned the hate of some and the respect of others. For much that he did, I admired him. He was a tough, wily man who fought much of the wrongdoing at City Hall and police headquarters.

Jack Clarke's relationship with Mayor Daley spanned more than a decade. It ended in a sad irony, with Clarke, the combatant of crime and government corruption, convicted in a bizarre case and going off to spend a year at the federal penitentiary on McNeal Island in Puget Sound, Washington.

During the year he spent in the penitentiary, agents of the Federal

Bureau of Investigation would periodically arrive to question him. In fact, they came practically every week; their objective, to get him to give derogatory information which could lead to a criminal prosecution of the Mayor. Clarke not only refused to talk to the FBI agents, but finally wouldn't even go into the same room with them. His loyalty was well entrenched. Jack Clarke gladly served one year in the federal pen with the knowledge, at least the belief, that he was doing all of it to show his loyalty to Richard J. Daley.

During the year Clarke was in the penitentiary, however, the Mayor not only made no attempt to contact him, he never tried to assist Clarke's wife and children, actually never even wanted to raise the name of Jack Clarke, much less discuss his problem. Shortly after Clarke went to prison, Tom Donovan, Daley's administrative assistant, refused to pay Clarke $8,000 which the city owed to him. I interceded and he eventually got the money.

Jack Clarke was born in 1927 in a tough section of Chicago's South Side. He grew up in St. Sabina's parish and went to Leo High School in the same part of town. As a young man, he obtained a job with the Adult Probation Office of Cook County. For an inquisitive person who is willing to work hard—certainly chief among Jack Clarke's qualities—being a probation officer was an interesting job. He got to know many people who had been or still were criminals. He did favors for them and they did favors for him, and the biggest favor you could ever do for Jack Clarke was to give him information. As a result, Clarke had data on a lot of people in Chicago.

I met Jack in 1963 when I was a reporter covering the Criminal Court Building and he was a probation officer working there. He is a short, chunky, Jimmy Cagney of a man, with a shock of bushy, brown hair and a unique blend of charm and toughness. We got on well from the beginning.

In 1965, I was transferred by my newspaper from the Criminal Courts at 26th Street and California Avenue to City Hall where my job was to report on the activities of the Mayor and the city government. At about that time Clarke came downtown, too, and maneuvered a job as an investigator on a per diem basis with the City's Department of Investigations. This was a special department which consisted of only five people. It had been set up by Daley so there could be investigations of wrongdoing by city employees which would be under his control.

In 1966, Clarke was assigned full-time to the Department of Investigations. One of his major efforts was to clean up the Port of Chicago, where more than a million dollars' worth of thefts were reported each year. It was here where some of Clarke's problems later would be focused. He would make a lot of enemies on Chicago's waterfront.

Clarke had head on approaches to everything. When he was investigating the Port of Chicago, he made that clear. Among the first things he did was to demand that federal customs agents open their automobile trunks for searches on the way out of the Port at the end of each work shift. He had come to the conclusion that federal employees were among the major thieves at the Port. The indignity of having to open up their trunks was too much for many of the agents and a number of them felt enmity toward Clarke. Nevertheless, the thefts were reduced.

Members of the Longshoremen's Union also were annoyed by Clarke. He made each wear a badge displaying the worker's photo in order to gain entry and exit from the Port. Until then, badges of identification had not been required. Even less pleased with Clarke were those who previously had relatively free access to the Port and its spoils by posing as longshoremen. He cultivated a whole web of informants, and he paid them in the same way the FBI or the local police would. This practice would come back to haunt him.

In 1968, Clarke, still with the Department of Investigations, engaged in activities at the time of the Democratic National Convention. He had various operatives—people who reported to him—placed in the National Mobilization Committee's office, but his people, contrary to the aims of the Committee, spent much time on the phones trying to *discourage* potential demonstrators from traveling to Chicago for the convention.

He later contended that one reason a relatively small number came (not more than 5,000 took part in the street and park demonstrations) is that his people had discouraged so many others from coming to the city.

On May 16, 1972, at Daley's request, I left police headquarters to become his administrative assistant at City Hall and Clarke moved the base of his activities to the Police Department. At police headquarters he was able to obtain the confidence, even the friendship, of Superintendent Conlisk.

The initial contact took place in May. Clarke went to the superintendent to report an ugly incident which could have had far-reaching consequences in the black community. A police sergeant, Timmy Danaher, related by marriage to Alderman Edward Vrdolyak, had stirred black anger by entering a South Side restaurant and referring in a loud voice to the black women who were with their husbands as "whores" and "prostitutes." Clarke learned that blacks, led by veteran and highly respected radio personality Daddio Daylie, planned to ask the Mayor to discipline Danaher. Clarke thought the matter could be resolved by swift action by the superintendent.

Conlisk, after meeting with Clarke, agreed. Danaher was transferred and reprimanded. Clarke and Conlisk, however, incurred an enemy, Alderman Vrdolyak. In the months that followed, Conlisk and Clarke became good friends, each respecting the other. It was as if Clarke, with his blunt talk about the ways to improve police operations, was one of the few people Conlisk felt he could trust. Clarke, on the other hand, began to view Conlisk as a good policeman hampered greatly by the Mayor's intrusions and insistence on City Hall involvement in police promotions.

Conlisk was a "desk" superintendent. He went out onto the street only on the rarest of occasions, and was distantly removed from his men. Clarke encouraged Conlisk to leave police headquarters and get out on the streets. On one occasion he took the superintendent to meet with a black prostitute to learn firsthand about police shakedowns. Clarke felt that by bringing Conlisk out of his fourth floor office at 11th and State, he would ultimately become a better superintendent.

About this time, a black lawyer and former newsman, Mitchell Ware, was appointed deputy superintendent in charge of the Police Department's Bureau of Inspectional Services. A civilian, Ware would run all the internal investigations of police conduct, the Vice Control Division, and would be in charge of intelligence gathering. Clarke and Ware became friends. Through their efforts, a new police unit was formed called *C-5*. Its purpose was to investigate links between organized crime and Chicago police officers.

*C-5* had a short, stormy existence. Clarke played the chief role in recruiting personnel from police ranks to serve in *C-5*. A description of part of the screening process follows:

Clarke would sit in a room with Ware and a high ranking representative of the department's old guard. Other top commanders were fully aware that a civilian had been made deputy superintendent and that Clarke, also a civilian, had the ear of Superintendent James Conlisk. The old guard knew Clarke and Ware needed watching.

One by one, the police officers who had shown interest in serving in the secret unit to investigate the ties between the mob and the department would be brought in for questioning. Clarke would begin by asking to what district the prospective *C-5* member was assigned. After the policeman would answer, for example, Monroe Street, the conversation went like this:

> Clarke: Okay, how long have you been there?
> Cop:    Twelve years.
> Clarke: Who is the District Commander's bagman?
> Cop:    I don't know what you're talking about.
> Clarke: You know 'what.' Who's the bagman for the Monroe Street District?
> Cop:    I don't know any bagman.
> Clarke: How long did you say you were in the District?
> Cop:    Twelve years.
> Clarke: You don't know the bagman after 12 years? Get your ass out of here. We don't want anyone in this unit who's as dumb as you are.

The *C-5* candidates would look momentarily at the old guard representative who was in the room. Then, to their credit, every applicant answered Clark's questions. They wanted to help clean up the department. The screening process for *C-5,* however, was not something that made a lot of friends for Clarke.

By the end of 1972, *C-5* was fully formed and operating. It was probably the most sincere effort by the Chicago Police in 50 years to break the ties between the crime syndicate and the policemen the mob controlled. It was doomed.

The unit encountered opposition within the department almost immediately. It eventually was parodied by members of the news media who were anxious to seize upon any dissension within the city government to score points against the Mayor. Representatives of police associations also were angry. They expressed shock that the *C-5* officers had required two policemen, who were suspected of having accepted marked money as a bribe, to drop their pants in a search for the cash. This tactic, often used by police in searching civilian suspects, caused alleged outrage when used against the police themselves.

Conlisk, however, stood firm in support of his new anti-corruption unit. An early example of its work came when Clarke reported privately that *C-5* had infiltrated the Hawk Social Club near 32nd Street and Princeton Avenue in the 11th Ward. Among those present at the Club on certain occasions were crime syndicate figures Jimmy Cardovano and Jimmy "the Bomber" Catura, two high ranking police officers, and a U.S. Customs agent at the Port who would later play a major part in Clarke's eventual downfall. Clarke also reported that two of Catura's associates were trusted officers in the police organized crime unit.

Grievances by police officers against Conlisk for doing the right thing were to become grievances against Clarke who was working with the Superintendent to try to bring about the reforms which had so long been needed. One of the aggrieved was a North Side police captain who had been removed by Conlisk for covering up police corruption as a district commander. The captain's brother was an auditor at City Hall who had access to vouchers of funds legitimately paid to Clarke for informants in his efforts to clean up the Port and the Police Department. The two brothers were to be among those who would seek to settle the score with Conlisk by doing in Clarke. Working along with them against Clarke were an alderman and his policeman brother and their police brother-in-law who was eventually to serve time for corruption. As Clarke was taking on corrupt police officers and politicians, the number of his enemies was increasing.

He eventually found himself in deep trouble. He came under investigation by U.S. Attorney James Thompson and a federal grand jury. During the course of their investigations, the fact was brought out that Clarke had paid off a number of informants over the years. They were informants, he explained, who were helping him with his investigations—principally the investigation of the Port of Chicago. All sorts of vouchers from the City of Chicago regarding these payments to Clarke had been turned over to federal investigators without the government even having to ask for them. They had been turned over by the city employee whose allegedly aggrieved police captain brother was anxious to lash out at Clarke and Conlisk.

The government began to build a case that Clarke had made a misstatement in his income tax returns. The charge was that he should have shown the payments for informants on his personal returns. He took the position that narcotics officers did not cite the informants they paid in their personal income tax returns; therefore, he did not have to cite the informants who were paid by him. He said that before he followed that course, he had checked with Jack Walsh, who had been the head of the IRS Intelligence in Chicago, and his successor in that position, John Foy. Both, according to Clarke, had told him that he did *not* have to record in his income tax returns the payments he made with City money to informants.

Eventually, however, Clarke was indicted and brought to trial. An obstruction of justice charge, according to the government, grew out of a telephone call which Clarke had made to a Chicago police officer who was testifying before the Cook County Grand Jury about shipments of pornographic materials into Chicago through the Port of Chicago. Clarke said that in these conversations he had told the policeman that he had better tell the truth to Bernard Carey, the State's Attorney. (Clarke had been a major factor in breaking up the shipments of pornography through the Port of Chicago.) Clarke also told the officer to tell everything he knew to the grand jury. The policeman, however, charged that Clarke had threatened him and had told him to keep his mouth shut.

On Dec. 3, 1973, Clarke pleaded guilty to misstatement of income tax and to obstructing justice and was sentenced by Judge Hubert Will to one to three years in the federal penitentiary.

The reasons for the guilty plea go beyond face value. In the 1971 mayoral campaign, one year before Watergate, Clarke had a spy in the campaign office of Richard Friedman, who was the Republican opponent running against Daley. This campaign office worker leaked continuous information about Friedman to Clarke, and through Clarke to Daley. The operative was paid with City of Chicago funds. There is not the slightest evidence that Daley wanted such information or had any idea Clarke was using city funds to pay for it. In the subsequent federal investigation of Clarke, abetted by some of the enemies he made over the years, the federal investigators kept getting closer to the person who was paid illegally, the revelation of which could cause the Mayor much trouble. There were something like 70 people who served as paid Clarke informants over the years and the federal investigators were going through their names one at a time. He felt that eventually they were going to get down to *the* man who had worked in the Friedman office and learn that City money from the Daley administration had gone to pay him for his political information. Rather than have this story come out, rather than exposing for everyone the parallels between Watergate and this phase of his political activities, Clarke decided to plead guilty.

As a public investigator, he had seen law enforcement from just about every angle except one. The missing link was actually serving time in the joint. So it was not without some degree of pleasure that he went off to spend a year behind bars. He did it in true Clarke style. He went to Tacoma, the place where incoming prisoners for the McNeal Island penitentiary usually reported to the Federal Bureau of Investigation office. But Clarke bypassed the FBI and headed directly to the dock. He traveled by ferry to the penitentiary out on an island in Puget Sound. He rode along with a rock band that was scheduled to perform at the penitentiary. When they landed, he went to the prison gate and knocked on the door, announcing that he was John J. Clarke, prisoner, who was there to serve his term. It is doubtful that anyone had ever entered McNeal that way before.

Meanwhile, back in Chicago, Jack Clarke had become a nonperson to Daley—relegated to a limbo reserved for those who were potential or real sources of embarrassment to the Mayor.

When Clarke returned to Chicago after completing his penitentiary term, there was a long delay before there was any contact between the Mayor and him. His calls to Daley, even to the Mayor's assistant, Tom Donovan, went unreturned. Then one day, Clarke finally got through to Donovan and was told to come down to Democratic headquarters in the LaSalle Hotel to see the Mayor.

That session was a teary-eyed one, with Daley putting his arms around Clarke's shoulders. The Mayor professed his friendship to Clarke and how he was going to help him get back to a normal life. Months went by but nothing happened. Nothing would ever happen.

# A Policeman
# Says Good-bye

# 26

*"Don't be [sorry]. Now I'll never have to deal
with that Police Board again."*

The Summer of 1973 had turned into Fall and the
Mayor was unable to resolve the problem of what to
do about the police superintendent. One day, toward
the end of September, while we were riding together in his car, he said,
"Maybe Conlisk should go." For the first time in more than a year, I
told the Mayor that I thought this was the way it had to be. Since the
summer of 1972, I told Daley, I had tried to do everything I could to
help Conlisk but it was just not in the interest of the City or the Department for him to remain as superintendent. Chief Clarence Braasch
and 22 other officers from the Chicago Avenue District were on trial
for shakedowns and a verdict was expected soon.

Then, on October 5, Braasch and 18 of the 22 other officers were
convicted. The following Tuesday was the annual ceremony honoring
the City's outstanding police and fire heroes. Daley and Conlisk were
present. The Mayor told me that he was going "to talk to that fellow"
and that I should wait outside the Mayor's office.

Conlisk went in to meet with Daley and, after about five minutes,
I was called in. "Frank," Daley said, "the superintendent has decided
to resign. I would like you to prepare a letter for him." The Mayor said
it should be effective November 1. Conlisk and I then went to my office. I said I was sorry. He said, "Don't be. Now I'll never have to deal

with that Police Board again." I drafted a letter and he agreed with the wording. I told him it would have to be typed and forwarded to him for his signature. We shook hands and he departed.

The suggested letter was approved by the Mayor. Daley set 3:30 p.m., Wednesday, October 10, as the time for a news conference announcing the resignation. The time was selected because it was the first opening in his appointment schedule. Daley said an acting superintendent would have to be appointed. I said Rochford was next in the chain of command. The Mayor said, "No. It can't be him." He suggested Needham.

On Wednesday morning I accompanied the Mayor as he rode from a speaking engagement at McCormick Place to City Hall. I handed him Conlisk's signed resignation. The Mayor's attitude had changed somewhat. The previous day he had been determined that Conlisk had to go and I agreed with him. Now he talked about how the newspapers did not seem to be pressing for the superintendent's resignation and that maybe it did not have to take place.

When we arrived at City Hall, the Mayor said we would talk in the afternoon about whether to go through with plans to hold the press conference to announce Conlisk's resignation. He then held a series of meetings until about 1:00 p.m.

When I saw him at that time, he was still reluctant about having Conlisk resign. I told him I thought it had to be done and that this would give him enough time to pick a successor by the first of the year, giving the department a clean slate to begin 1974. He said to call the press conference for 3:30 p.m. Then he left for a luncheon and the opening of a new public building.

Moments later, when I returned to my office, I learned that Vice President Spiro Agnew had resigned. At about 2 p.m., Daley returned to City Hall. When informed about Agnew, the Mayor expressed sadness.

At 2:30, I notified the media that the Mayor was going to hold a 3:30 p.m. press conference. Before it began, Daley told me he was still sad about the plans to announce Conlisk's resignation. "You know," he said, "[former commissioner] O'Connor came in himself and told me he had had enough." The Mayor made it clear he wished Conlisk had done the same thing. A few minutes later, Daley met with the press and announced that Conlisk's six years as superintendent were over.

By coincidence, the vice president and the superintendent had quit within two and one half hours of each other. At least one newspaper was to later view the timing of Conlisk's departure as being deliberately planned to closely follow the Agnew announcement and, therefore, receive less media attention. Another sharp reporter contended that Conlisk's letter of resignation and the accompanying news release from the Mayor's office were typed on the same typewriter.

On the following Friday, Daley said that he was going to confer with Conlisk about the designation of an acting superintendent and that no decision should be made until close to November 1.

In November, James M. Rochford was named acting superintendent.

# Flashbacks 27

On June 28, 1972, the Mayor traveled to Washington to testify before a House subcommittee on the need for firearms control legislation. En route on the plane his bodyguard pointed out to me that the man napping across the aisle from the Mayor was Senator Abraham Ribicoff. It was the first time he and Daley had been together since the 1968 convention when the Senator denounced the Mayor for allegedly being responsible for "Gestapo" tactics by the police. The Mayor had spotted Ribicoff as he boarded the plane but had avoided him. About an hour out of Washington, the Senator awakened and noticed the Mayor sitting nearby. "Dick," he exclaimed. "I didn't see you." Ribicoff got up and moved next to Daley. The Mayor and he shook hands and the two engaged in almost an hour of pleasant small talk.

---

After testifying on behalf of proposed gun control legislation at the 1972 U.S. House hearing, the Mayor went to Congressman Dan Rostenkowski's office for a private meeting with Frank Mankiewicz of Senator George McGovern's staff. Upon his return to the airport, Daley spoke with Congressman Morgan Murphy and Roman Pucinski about Paul Simon's unsuccessful primary campaign for the Democratic gubernatorial nomination that year. Simon's defeat had been attributed, in part, to a statement he made expressing the need for an increase in the state income tax. Daley told the congressman: "I called him on the phone, and asked him 'Paul, Paul, what are you doing? Why did you say that?' And he started to give me all that Adlai Stevenson let's talk sense to the people shit."

On the return flight, the Mayor spoke at length about a number of subjects. He said he could have been governor of Illinois in 1960 but that he wanted John Kennedy to be elected president. He did not believe there could be a successful ticket with Irish Catholics for president and governor. "I was thinking of my four sons," Daley said, "and I wanted John Kennedy to be their president."

A flight attendant asked the Mayor if he cared for a drink. Daley ordered a Bloody Mary. I normally would not have had a drink at lunch but, to be sociable, I ordered, inexplicably, a beer. When the beverages were served, I began drinking the beer when suddenly the Mayor exclaimed: "Do you drink a lot of beer, Frank?" I replied that I did not, but he seemed to be oblivious to my answer. For the next 20 minutes he spoke of the Irish and the curse of alcohol and how many families in his neighborhood had been "destroyed because of fathers and husbands who took to drink." During the rest of the flight I never took another sip of beer. The Mayor ordered a second Bloody Mary.

He described a saloon in his neighborhood. It was called Sheehan's and, he said, it was at 38th Street and Halsted. Sheehan was a man with white hair and "a real sweet turkey face. Everyone had to check his gun when he came in," Daley continued, "the policemen and the hoods." I thought to myself that must have been one tough neighborhood that he grew up in.

When Hirohito came to Chicago for a visit in 1975, I prepared a suggested introduction for the Mayor to deliver at a formal dinner for the Japanese Emperor. After reading my suggested words which lauded Japanese-Americans for their contributions to our city and country, the Mayor exclaimed: "Didn't you lay it on kind of thick about the Japs, Frank? You know, Sis and I saw the Arizona out at Pearl Harbor. Along with us was a group of visiting Japs, and a guy from the State Department pointed out that one of them had burns on his face from the Hiroshima bomb, and I said 'He's a hell of a lot better off than the 900 guys buried here in the Arizona.' And the State Department guy didn't like what I said. I didn't give a damn. Remember, Frank, we always forgive, but we never forget."

That night at the dinner, Daley delivered a decidedly neutral introduction. I cannot help but think that his street instincts were at work again and that they told him for every Chicagoan who felt friendly to Hirohito there were at least two who were made unhappy by his visit.

When Anwar Sadat came to Chicago also in 1975, he had not as yet made his momentous visit to Jerusalem. In view of the fact that many of the dignitaries at the dinner Daley hosted in honor of the Egyptian president were Jewish, my suggested remarks were cautious. Again, Daley took me by surprise when he put aside the prepared remarks and ad-libbed one of the most laudatory introductions I ever heard him give. Sadat, he said, was a man who worked tirelessly to better the living conditions of his people. He was a man who wanted peace and a man who had suffered much during years of imprisonment by the British government because of his determination to end its colonial rule. As I sat there listening to the Mayor, I concluded that, because of his Irish tradition, there was a bond between him and any national leader who struggled to end British colonialism.

# Daley vs. the Media —Round 2

## 28

*To gain fame, money, and power as a reporter take on Daley!*

E. B. Long, in his biography of Huey Long, points out how the Louisiana politician, at the start of his career, was able to single himself out for voter attention amidst a multiplicity of candidates. When he initially came to a Louisiana parish, he would determine who was the most powerful person in the community. Then he would proceed to verbally attack that person. Quickly the unknown politician became known. By zeroing in on the most powerful, Huey Long was able to place himself on the same level of power in the eyes of many voters.

Of all the Chicago journalists, one separated himself from the pack by his continuing attacks on Daley and his administration. This journalist was the most gifted writer in Chicago and he was to become the finest national satiric columnist. His journalistic weapon against Daley was the most effective one against any politician—humor. Mike Royko could make his readers laugh at the Mayor and those around him. Royko also could be deadly serious. The combination of ridicule and unrelenting exposure of frailties and wrongdoing was devastating. But Royko's greatest harm to Daley came not from his column or even from his national best-selling book, *Boss*. It was due to the fact that he became the idol of most of Chicago's media. The lesson to other journalists became clear. To gain fame, money, and power as a reporter, take on Daley! At the same time, it could make your conscience feel good.

All of this came about quite logically. First of all, there was this politician who was the most powerful by far in Chicago's history. Secondly, he had a personal disdain for newsmen and newswomen, and never sought to curry their favor. On the contrary, quite frequently he was in open combat with the media. Thirdly, Daley's political opponents challenged him with a racial argument—that blacks were treated unfairly by the local government. And finally, the tenure of Daley as mayor made him an increasingly vulnerable target. Just as the number of public achievements increased, so did the number of mistakes. There is a fundamental rule of elective office. Never overstay your welcome. Daley obviously never did that as far as the electorate was concerned but he overstayed his welcome in the eyes of the city's media and a large portion of the local intellectuals. His decline began after his election for a third term in 1963. That year he had been opposed by Benjamin S. Adamowski, the former State's Attorney of Cook County who had challenged Daley as early as the 1955 Democratic mayoral primary. Adamowski, whose credentials included being an anti-machine candidate and a Polish-American, was able to win 19 of the city's 50 wards and come within six percentage points of securing a majority of the city's votes. But he could not penetrate Daley's greatest bloc of voters, the blacks.

That same year, 1963, was the beginning of civil rights demonstrations which gave local newspeople a cause. Moreover, a new breed of journalists was on the scene, the disciples of advocacy journalism. A reporter was not someone who objectively wrote or told what happened. He was someone who knew who the good and bad guys were and on which side lay justice and morality. The reporter's job, or so the young ones thought, was to shape history. They did not see local politics as a struggle between groups that wanted self-serving power. They saw it as a fight between good and evil, and Daley was evil.

Oddly, the advocacy journalists were enamoured of both political power and Daley as a power broker. They did not want to be great reporters. They wanted to be shapers of political power. The advocacy journalists played an important part in Daley's career. They magnified his power. They helped build his legend.

*Boss* became the Bible of those who saw Daley as a racist tyrant.

It quickly became required reading in high school civics classes and college political science courses from coast to coast. Royko was later to be quoted saying that he did not seek to write a balanced book about the Mayor. How would such a book sell? The book presented Daley as a national scandal, a politician who would compromise with political corruption and practice racial bigotry. Royko's reputation as a fearless journalist and a perceptive writer soared even higher. The adulation he received from his peers grew.

*Boss* was a grossly unfair depiction of Daley. If he had been the man portrayed in that book, I would not have worked for him. *Boss* is not the real Daley.

I believe it is unlikely that the Mayor ever read *Boss*. Like most successful politicians, Daley was a strong optimist and rarely devoted time to viewing or reading negatives about himself. Mrs. Daley, however, perused Royko's columns with some regularity and also read *Boss*. She intensely disliked him.

As a result of *Boss,* more and more local news people vied to become little Roykos. The journalistic onslaught on Daley expanded.

The only counter-weapon left to the Mayor was television. The news about him and his administration which was filtered through reporters and editors in print usually portrayed him as a knave and a scoundrel. It was only through television that he could continue to speak to his voters. And that he did.

# The Personal Man                    *29*

*"People like it when every now and then you
make a mistake in grammar and in your way
of speaking. They feel you're more like them."*

When, as a reporter, I first met with Mayor Daley, I
was surprised at what I thought was his awkward-
ness with people. That was in March 1965. Daley
was 62 years old. He was the opposite of a gregarious Irish-American
politician—the kind played by Spencer Tracy as Frank Skeffington in
*The Last Hurrah*. Daley was close-mouthed. He had an engaging
laugh and a broad smile. But his face was basically emotionless. This
factor was in contrast to his reputation through television for becoming highly emotional and shouting, with words tumbling forth, often
ungrammatically. That was all true. But the basic Daley, the one who
met privately in his office with thousands of people, one by one, over a
period of almost 22 years—this was an impassive Daley. Visitors by
and large never knew exactly what he was thinking. That was part of
his great skill as a leader. He did not reveal himself. The late Speaker
of the Illinois House, Jack Touhy, used to say that Daley always gave
the impression that he found the visitor's thoughts and ideas interesting  even though the visitor might know intellectually that this was not
true.

Countless politicians, telling Daley of their intent to run for elective office, for example, left the Mayor's presence thinking they had his

support when in reality all he had said was that everyone had the right to run for office.

Daley was a politician who always played his hand close to his vest. He had one confidante—his wife, Eleanor. No one else did he trust. In later years, when I served as his press secretary, he asked me to fire an aging speech writer who long had been employed at City Hall. I asked the Mayor to reconsider because, I said, the man had served the City and the Party for many years with talent. Daley acquiesced. Two years later, however, I reversed my position. The press was questioning exactly what the elderly ex-newsman did. I thought he should be transferred out of the Mayor's office to another City department. The most powerful Mayor in America replied negatively. The old man could not be transferred to another City payroll, Daley said, because "there is no one we can trust."

Richard J. Daley was well known for his misuse of words. Some people thought he did it intentionally. This was not the case. I do not know what his I.Q. was, but I think it probably was very high. His mind leapt ahead of others, but his words did not keep pace.

Even he was prone to explain his malapropisms as intentional. He once told me that a candidate for State's Attorney made serious mistakes by his use of an extensive vocabulary. "You know," Daley said, "people like it when every now and then you make a mistake in grammar and in your way of speaking. They feel you're more like them."

On the subject of so-called reformers, Daley had strong views. In his vocabulary, reform was a dirty word. Reformers, to him, were fakers. This was a word he used repeatedly, most notably during the 1968 Democratic Convention when, angered by Senator Abraham Ribicoff's accusing the Chicago Police of "Gestapo" tactics, Daley stood up, cupped one hand by his mouth and shouted it over and over. Television pundits to this day think he was using another word. He would never have used the other F-word, even under extreme provocation. In all the time we were together, I never heard him say it. He would have considered it a mortal sin.

As Daley saw it, reformers were simply other political factions seeking to gain power with no intent to bring about better government. Historically, in his opinion, these factions were opposed to immigrants and the sons and daughters of immigrants. Daley viewed himself as the champion of the immigrants. Frequently, in his mind, so-called reform was a tactic used by white Anglo-Saxon Protestants to regain some of the political power they once had in certain American cities. A tableau involving Daley, the grandson of immigrants, and a WASP publisher took place one day in the Mayor's office. Marshall Field V had come to ask a favor, namely, to allow the Art Institute of Chicago to take over additional land in Grant Park to construct a new building. One of Chicago's most revered traditions was the so-called Montgomery Ward ordinance which forever required that this land be kept for park use. Now, the heir of Chicago's greatest fortune, the publisher of the *Chicago Sun-Times,* was asking Daley to violate the spirit of Montgomery Ward and amend the ordinance.

The Mayor sat behind his desk, his face immobile. His critics were forever pointing up his occasional public outbursts which took place most often during City Council meetings. In day-to-day encounters, however, Daley had magnificent control over his facial muscles. He had the great ability to hide his emotions. And that is what he did when he faced Marshall Field. As I sat across the room from both of them, I looked at Daley's eyes. I knew he was thinking that he represented all of the immigrant families of Chicago and now he was sitting there behind his desk with a man who represented the city's entrenched wealth and former political power. Here was Marshall Field asking Daley for a favor. A favor which, if it had been requested for anything other than the Art Institute of Chicago, would have been editorially denounced by Field's newspaper.

Daley granted the favor because he recognized the importance of the Art Institute to the city. But he did so with a sense of satisfaction that Field had to come to him and beg.

Daley was constantly aware of the gap existing between him as the elected representative of the people from the side streets on the one hand and WASPS who retained great economic power on the other. It showed at the dedication of Water Tower Place in 1975, the nation's first vertical shopping mall. After the ceremony, as we drove away in his limousine, the Mayor turned to me and said, chuckling, "Well, there you have it, the entire entrenched power of Chicago sitting on one platform." He was referring to the other participants in the ceremony—the presidents of various banks and the executives of Marshall Field & Company. As the grandson of Irish immigrants, Daley knew they were not his people.

His Irish ancestry, however, is often depicted as having an exaggerated influence on his life. Daley first and foremost was a Chicagoan. Even before that, he was a product of his particular neighborhood on the near Southwest Side of the city. He was closer to men and women of Lithuanian and Polish descent from the 11th Ward than he was to any Notre Dame professor who was of Irish descent. This was one of Daley's greatest strengths. He felt comfortable with all ethnic groups save, perhaps, blacks and Jews. Many in other ethnic groups felt a particular bond with him despite his Irish ancestry. To them he was a family man, good husband, father—a man with whom they shared many values.

Daley's bond with the ethnics of Chicago was exemplified toward the end of his life when he made one of the most atrocious statements of his career. He was speaking before the Sons of Italy in the Sheraton Hotel. Toward the end of his remarks he told his audience of Italian-Americans that "World War II was won by the sons of the Irish, Polish and Italian families of America." The audience erupted with cheers and applause. People stood on chairs and waved handkerchiefs. They loved it. He had just ruled out most of the American people as having had anything to do with winning the war but this particular audience was in agreement. The press was on hand but, strangely, never reported his outrageous remark!

All this took place shortly after his recovery from a mild stroke. There was a general attitude, even in the press, that it was good to have him back in action and, for a while at least, he was free from criticisms.

Daley was a man of immense self-control. His life was completely ordered. Every hour of every day was planned. In his daily work his emotions were completely under control. During the 12 years I worked with him, I never once heard him raise his voice to a member of his staff. Never once was there an indication in his work conduct of losing his temper, or of even expressing serious annoyance in dealing with secretaries, bodyguards and other city employees. He never threw a pencil down on his desk. He never complained in an emotional way about a mistake that an employee had made for the 14th time, never indicated exasperation with someone or something.

The same was true in his relationship with his wife and children. His conduct was always moderate. When I tried to encourage him to visit a particular restaurant because the owner was a great admirer of his, Daley replied: "Frank, Sis and I decided many, many years ago when I was in the legislature that you only get in trouble by going to taverns and we decided that we were going to stay out of them and always eat at home." This he did with few exceptions.

During those years as a state representative and senator in Springfield, while many of his colleagues, while away from home, frequently partied, Daley was one of the few members of the General Assembly well known for spending his evenings in preparation for the next day's work. Others could go out drinking with the boys but he went back to his room each night to study proposed legislation and plan tactics.

To be a great mayor, you have to act courageously. But to act courageously, you must first survive.

Daley survived for more than 21 years as Mayor because he was able to out-fox all of his political rivals. He was the master of deviousness. A case in point was his role in filling a North Side vacant committeeman position with his choice. An aspirant for the job was the ward's Alderman, Paul Wigoda. He was the law partner of the Mayor's City Council floor leader, Alderman Thomas E. Keane. Keane wanted Wigoda to fill the committeeman vacancy. Neil F. Hartigan, a mayoral administrative assistant was also competing for the position.

One Saturday morning, while Alderman Keane was taking a shower, the Mayor called and asked to speak with him. Mrs. Keane, who had answered the phone, relayed the message to the showering alderman. When he came to the phone, the Mayor told him not to worry, that his law partner, Alderman Wigoda, was going to be the next committeeman of the 49th Ward. All Wigoda had to do, the Mayor said, was "sit tight" and the job would be his. Keane thanked the Mayor profusely. Then he telephoned Wigoda with the good news.

Early the next week, however, Wigoda began to hear rumors that the top precinct captains from the Ward were being called in to see Hartigan whose office was just outside that of the Mayor's. The precinct captains also were being summoned to see Raymond F. Simon, the City's Corporation Counsel, a Hartigan ally in the Ward. Wigoda became jittery and called Keane who reassured him. "Don't worry," Keane said, "you have the Mayor's word that you're going to

be the committeeman." Later that week the precinct captains met officially and unanimously voted for Hartigan to be Ward committeeman.

Subsequently, a stunned Wigoda obtained an appointment with
the Mayor. He asked Daley why he had misled him. The Mayor, according to Wigoda, responded that he did not know what the alderman was talking about. Wigoda reminded him about the promise that
he was to become the ward committeeman. Daley allegedly denied that
he had ever made any such promise. Wigoda, trying to pin him down,
asked about the telephone call Daley had made to Alderman Keane at
his home while he was in the shower. Said Daley: "I never made any
telephone call to Keane." Said Wigoda: "Now I know what it feels like
to have a knife stuck in my back."

As press secretary, one of my jobs was to write suggested remarks
for the Mayor for all his public appearances. One such appearance was
for the dedication of improvements at the site of a downtown statue of
three Revolutionary War patriots: George Washington, Gouverneur
Morris and Haym Salomon, the last a Jew who helped finance the
struggle against England. My suggested remarks for the Mayor praised
Salomon and American Jews for their outstanding role in our national
life. Said Daley to me after he had looked over my suggested remarks:
"Don't you think you have gone a little overboard about the Jews,
Frank?"

Few people within the Democratic machine ever voiced criticisms
of Daley. There were rare exceptions, however, and, among them, criticisms by my predecessor as press secretary, Earl Bush, a Jew, that the
Mayor was anti-Semitic. Alderman Wigoda, also a Jew, denied this
was the case. Others pointed out the near-impossibility of anyone holding the top elected urban office for more than 21 years while being a
bigot. Wigoda described Daley more precisely when he said, "He just
isn't comfortable with Jews."

I believe emphatically that Daley was fair-minded to all people. I
also believe, however, as Wigoda said, that he was not comfortable
with blacks and Jews. This can be best evidenced by enumerating the
men and women he chose to be closest to him on his office staff and
his bodyguard detail. As I noted earlier, Bush and one woman secretary from a previous administration were the only Jews. Until shortly
before his death, there were no blacks.

Another example of the devious Daley exemplified in the Paul

Wigoda incident was visible when he dumped John Stamos as Democratic candidate for State's Attorney in 1968.

Stamos, a long-time prosecutor, had been named by the Cook County Board in 1966 to fill the unexpired term of State's Attorney Daniel P. Ward when the latter was elected to the Illinois Supreme Court. Stamos, however, was a man who put his legal professionalism ahead of ward politics. On one occasion he refused to order his aides to seek a search warrant for the Chicago police who maintained that a youth gang was hiding guns in a South Side church. Stamos believed there was insufficient evidence for such a raid. Moreover, he feared that if no guns were found by the police, they would plant narcotics in order to justify their intrusion. His decision brought about substantial enmity from within the Police Department.

On another occasion, then State Representative Henry J. Hyde (later to become a congressman) complained to Stamos that two of his State's Attorney's policemen had offered to delay service of a subpoena for one of Hyde's clients over a weekend if $200 were paid. When he learned of the shakedown attempt, Stamos directed that the two officers, both of whom were part of Daley's 11th Ward organization, be transferred out of the State's Attorney's office. This angered Daley's top aide in the ward, Matthew J. Danaher.

Stamos, in other words, did not play ball. Danaher and other committeemen convinced the Mayor that Stamos should not be slated to run for a four year term in his own right. But the Mayor knew that any dumping of Stamos from the ticket would incur the wrath of Greek-Americans who regularly contributed large sums to the local Democratic Party. The same contributors, if they had advance warning of the Mayor's dumping plans, would beseech him that Stamos be retained. Daley, therefore, kept his plans secret.

On the morning when Democrats were to choose their party ticket for 1968, a Chicago newspaper headlined that Stamos was to be replaced by the U.S. Attorney for Northern Illinois, Edward V. Hanrahan, as the candidate for the county's top prosecutorial office. Still, however, Stamos had heard nothing from the Mayor. Soon after arriving at Democratic headquarters in the Sherman House, Stamos was congratulated by some of the party leaders on being chosen to run for Illinois attorney general instead of state's attorney of Cook County. Said Stamos: "I don't want it." One of the leaders, thereupon, went back into Daley's private office to advise him that Stamos needed some talking to before an official announcement of the slate was made. The Mayor invited the unhappy Stamos into the inner office where they sat at opposite ends of an eight-foot long table. Daley told Stamos he was going to be the Democratic candidate for attorney general. Stamos repeated: "I don't want it." Then, according to Stamos' account, the Mayor said what a great opportunity it would be. Stamos replied that the state office would require two residences, one in Springfield and one in Chicago, a situation which, he maintained, was not desirable. "But you get your own private plane to fly back and forth," Stamos quoted the Mayor as saying. The prosecutor could not believe what he was hearing. Daley was trying to convince him, a grown man, that it would be so wonderful to get a private plane to fly back and forth across the state that it would outweigh any inconveniences. Moreover, Daley added, as Stamos recalled, that the Democrats would have "a great ticket," with Sam Shapiro for governor, Paul Simon for lieutenant governor, and John Stamos for attorney general. Stamos replied that it would be "a great ticket on Ellis Island" but he did not know how well it would do in downstate Illinois. He then thanked the Mayor for his offer but told him that he could not accept. With that, Stamos got up and left party headquarters. A substitute candidate was quickly selected for the attorney general candidacy.

If Stamos had even an hour's advance warning, he could have telephoned his Greek allies who would have put the pressure on Democratic committeemen to make certain that he was not dumped. Daley had seen to it, however, that there would be no advance warning.

Daley the personal man had differing views about the Kennedy brothers. For John Kennedy, he had an emotional attachment right up to the time of the Mayor's death. The relationship with President Kennedy had been one of the great experiences of Daley's life and he would not tolerate criticisms of the murdered president. He was most disturbed about the stories that were printed after Kennedy's death regarding his various sexual affairs. Daley believed attacks of this nature, against a man who did not have a chance to defend himself, were unmanly.

On the other hand, the Mayor grew to dislike Teddy Kennedy, especially because the senator did not attempt to support Daley at the 1972 Democratic Convention in Miami. Teddy allegedly was cruising on his yacht at the moment when the Massachusetts delegation voted to bar Daley and the other elected Democrats from Chicago. Jane Byrne subsequently met Teddy and told him that it was a good thing for his brother, Jack, that Daley had not been out on a yacht in 1960 when the Democratic Convention at Los Angeles was taking place. When, in 1976, Senator Kennedy said he did not want to be a candidate for the Democratic nomination, Daley told me he did not believe him.

Daley was a "non-intellectual" man. He had no interest in art. He rarely saw movies. (During the last few years of his life he only mentioned watching one, a loser called *Hindenberg*.) He had no interest in music. He had no interest in drama. He had no interest in the theatre. Even more disturbing, I don't believe he had a clear concept of what a city is or should be.

Irish statesman Daniel O'Connell has been described as having no great political convictions as far as a course of policy was concerned and yet the people of Ireland loved him. He was their champion. He spoke for them. In the same way, the majority of Chicagoans of all nationalities and, for at least the early years of his administration, blacks, believed that the Mayor was a man who would fight for their interests. Nevertheless, it is questionable whether Daley ever had a philosophical view of what a great city should be. Once, while being interviewed on the local public television station, the Mayor was questioned by reporter D.J.R. Bruckner about what a city should be. Daley responded he would like to see a city with each neighborhood like a suburb.

At another point in the program, Bruckner asked whether the Mayor thought Chicago were better today than it was when he was a boy. The camera then moved in close on Daley's face and, for a split second, he paused. He had been Mayor for 20 years. It seemed, in that split second, he was seeing a kaleidoscope of Woodlawn, Lawndale, Uptown—neighborhood after neighborhood that had changed in the 60 years since he had been a boy. One would have thought he'd give an instant reply of, "of course the city is better." Instead he answered, "I like to think that it is." Daley had seen the urban decay that had taken place in those six decades. He knew the Chicago of 1976 was not a better place than the city of 1916.

Daley was the top urban politician in America. Yet he never articulated what a city is or can be, what his concepts were. There never was a single discussion with any of his aides on this subject. Moreover, most of his time in office was devoted to politics rather than the city. I would describe the time split as 70/30. Before working for the Mayor, I would have thought these numbers to have been reversed. It must be emphasized that the Mayor believed very strongly that, in order to get things accomplished for the people of the city, he and the city had to have support from the Illinois General Assembly and the federal government. This meant that a considerable amount of time had to be spent on political matters assuring that legislators from individual districts in the city and downstate would be supportive of the city's interests on key votes. The same assistance was needed from members of the Chicago delegation in the U.S. House and the state's two senators. Nevertheless, one might have wished that some time had been devoted to brainstorming or engaging in serious reflection with his staff for more ideas and ways to improve urban living.

On the subject of organized crime, the Mayor publicly denied it existed. Despite this, he saw to it that politicians who represented organized crime never had real influence in his administration or access to his office. Daley set a definite barrier between himself and the outfit politicians. He sought to prevent any form of inroads by the mob into his administration. By and large, the Police Department was the only city agency into which organized crime could make real infiltration. The degree of this infiltration, however, was vastly reduced from what it had been in administrations prior to Daley.

During his years in office, there were four police superintendents, all of whom were honorable men. Timothy O'Connor had been appointed by Daley's predecessor, Martin H. Kennelly, and was retained for five years until the Summerdale police scandal involving eight police burglars. O'Connor was succeeded by Orlando W. Wilson, James B. Conlisk, Jr., and James M. Rochford. None of these men was susceptible to the crime syndicate.

The mob's influence in the Police Department also was reduced because of Daley's relationship with the 1st Ward Democratic organization which was run by the successors of Al Capone. It was a strange relationship in that Daley never confronted the 1st Ward's leaders head on, but he did not do their bidding. He maintained that the people of the ward had the right to elect their own representatives. He certainly was not consistent in this position in that, on certain occasions, he challenged the leadership of other wards. Nevertheless, 1st Warders Pat Marcy and Buddy Jacobson were not welcome in Daley's office shortly after he was elected Mayor. The mob's influence at City Hall and in the Police Department—though ever present—was substantially reduced from what it had been in the 1940s.

There was a saying in the Cook County Criminal Courts regarding jury compositions that all stereotypes were true. Certainly Daley as a street kid from the South Side would be prone to think that way. Throughout his life he had been exposed to racial and ethnic stereotypes.

As a newspaper reporter, I watched one day when Chicago's Polish-American aldermen rose one by one to speak on a subject dear to their hearts. A court battle had finally been won after many years directing that the name of Crawford Avenue be changed to Pulaski Road. The Polish aldermen gave their speeches stating what a momentous moment it was in Chicago history. While this was happening, I kept my eyes glued to the Mayor's immobile face. He was presiding over the City Council session, indicating in no way any emotion. There was no smile, no frown. Nothing. A few feet form him, sitting in his council chair, was Alderman Keane, Daley's floor leader. He, too, evinced no emotion while listening to the would-be Polish orators. Keane and Daley were thinking, "poor fools"—twenty-five years of political activity to change the name of a street while, during that time, Irish politicians were handling all the jobs, making all the appointments, slating candidates for office, and controlling all contracts. No Irish politician in the history of the world ever thought the name of a street was important.

Daley knew the weaknesses of other people. This knowledge seemed to be part of his being. He learned that Polish politicians were greatly reluctant to form political alliances with any group; that black politicians, who had a special responsibility to remain loyal to their constituents, often were among the first to be bought; blacks also wanted mayoral proclamations—proclamations honoring Muhammad Ali, Elijah Muhammad, proclaiming Nancy Wilson Day in Chicago, Lou Rawls Day, etc. No Irish politician ever asked that a day be proclaimed in anybody's name. But each day the Mayor's office was besieged by black politicians seeking to have days proclaimed.

Boston's legendary rogue mayor, James Michael Curley, in his autobiography, stated that whenever Italian-Americans would ask him for a favor and, especially, when they wanted to slate members of their group for political office, he would arrange, as a substitute, to put up a new statue of Garibaldi, Mother Cabrini or Columbus. As a result, Boston to this day is filled with such statues as a reminder of how an ethnic group can be dissuaded for a while from attaining its rightful objectives.

One of Daley's greatest PR triumphs took place the day singer Bobby Vinton came to his office. All of the city's elected Polish officials were on hand to cheer for a pleasant but mediocre entertainer who, by recording a few words in Polish in a song called "Melody of Love," had revived his career. He presented the Mayor with a "Polish Power" T-shirt and Daley seized the PR initiative by joining him in a chorus of his popular song—in English, that is.

Richard Daley was a total politician. Everyone else in his drama was a person to be used. He did not seek to be loved. He did not believe that love from those outside his family was important. He became a legend only as the years went by. For much of his time in office, he was not viewed as a charismatic politician. As late as 1965, ten years after he had first been elected mayor, he was awkward in greeting people. He could not make them feel comfortable. He was not a back-slapping politician. The events which shaped him were compressed into one year, 1968. That year contained the happenings for which he is best remembered. The legend grew from the way he shaped those events, the way he reacted, and the way he conducted himself for the eight remaining years of his life.

His critics often exaggerated his power. They exaggerated because they were enamored of it. The limits of his power could have been seen in a meeting that he held during the year before his death with some residents of Chicago's Marquette Park neighborhood. About 60 white men and women, ages 50 to 75, asked for an appointment to express their concern about their neighborhood. It was the usual Southwest Side complaint—blacks were moving in and crime was going up. The people in the room were primarily of Lithuanian extraction. With the Mayor were Ken Sain, his deputy, bodyguard Mike Graney, and me. The visitors expressed their grievances regarding abandoned housing in the neighborhood which resulted from unwise federal housing programs, poor quality schools and crime. Daley, responding, said he had tried for many years to work with the Chicago Board of Education but had been unable to have any positive impact. He said he had tried for many years to get the U.S. Department of Housing and Urban Development to stop its practice of making houses available with no down payments. HUD's federal programs had continued, resulting in increased numbers of abandoned houses. The people who had obtained them with no money down could not keep up payments. Despite the Mayor's negative tone, members of the audience continued to say: "But you're the Mayor of Chicago. Can't you help us?" And Daley kept returning, over and over, to asking his visitors about their police protection and police patrols. He would turn to his deputy and suggest that more squad cars be detailed to the neighborhood. Here was the most powerful urban politician in America who had really no substantial influence over the city's school system, no real influence in shaping the policies of the federal government regarding housing, who, altogether by 1976, had very limited power. The only instrument of government he still had under control was his Police Department. So over and over again he would suggest that neighborhood problems could be solved by greater use of the police. Before the end of his life, even his power over the police would be diminished by federal courts.

As far as blacks were concerned, Daley's inability to empathize to any substantial degree with the civil rights movement was the major weak point of his career. He came from a neighborhood which for more than two generations had resisted any form of integration with blacks.

At the same time, Daley was well aware that he had been elected Mayor in the first place because of black votes. His great ally in that first election in 1955 was the black boss of Chicago, Congressman William Dawson. To the end Daley was, unfortunately, when it came to race relations, a product of his very limited neighborhood and its people. He was able to hold together his coalition of white and black voters for 21 years. But after him, the great change was to take place.

Two nights before his stroke the Mayor and Mrs. Daley attended a Frank Sinatra concert at the Chicago Stadium. Daley rarely went to see any entertainer. Sinatra, however, was special. His views of the press and his reputation for standing by his friends, along with his musical promotion of Chicago, appealed to Daley.

During the Mayor's illness in 1974, Sinatra engaged in one of his recurring attacks on the press, describing reporters as parasites who lived off people of talent. In one of my telephone conversations with the Mayor at Grand Beach, Sinatra was mentioned. "He's right, Frank," Daley said. "He's telling the truth."

In September of 1975 Sinatra was invited by Daley to his office to receive a medallion symbolic of what was called honorary citizenship in Chicago. A mayoral proclamation was issued lauding the singer. Daley and Sinatra met privately and instantly hit it off. They obviously were two men who had done it their way. The 71 year old Daley then introduced the 60 year old Sinatra at a news conference as "Frankie."

In May of 1976 Sinatra returned to the Stadium. During his singing of "My Kind of Town," he turned toward where the Mayor and his family were sitting and injected the words "Mayor Daley, Chicago is." With that, the almost 20,000 people attending the concert stood, turned toward the Mayor, and gave him one of the most memorable ovations of his career.

# Scandals                                         *30*

L ooking back, it's hard to believe. The indictments
     from federal grand juries in 1973 cascaded forth. One
     after another, Daley's colleagues, both elected and ap-
pointed, would stand trial and—almost to a man—be convicted.
Rarely, if ever, has the federal government spent so much money and
so many staff hours in the prosecution of members of one political organization. At any given time during 1973, multiple grand juries were
probing into the dealings of the top Democrats of Chicago. At the
apex of the Justice Department's activities was John Mitchell, President Nixon's attorney general. Nixon had harbored grievances against
the Democratic Party of Cook County since November of 1960 when
he claimed his election had been stolen by Mayor Daley and his organization.

Now it was 1973. Nixon's appointee, James R. Thompson, was the
U.S. Attorney for Northern Illinois. Thompson, after he had personally prosecuted U.S. Court of Appeals Judge Otto Kerner and obtained
a jury conviction, received a telephone call from Air Force One and an
exuberant, grateful Richard Nixon.

Members of both political parties were unaware of the remarks
which John Stamos had made in early 1968 during his brief period as
Cook County State's Attorney. Stamos, then under pressure from

Mayor Daley to seek indictments against the Republican Sheriff and the warden of the Cook County jail for conditions in that institution, had refused to do so. In extemporaneous remarks which he made before the Cook County Board at the time, Stamos spoke of the reasons that he believed the Founding Fathers had subscribed to certain articles of the Bill of Rights. The Founders were concerned, he maintained, about protecting politicians. They had seen the civil warfare in England during the preceding century and were determined in this country that there would be legal obstacles to thwart the "in" group of politicians from spending their four years in office trying to imprison the "out" group. "As long as I am State's Attorney of Cook County," Stamos said, "there will be no political indictments."

Daley was unhappy by Stamos' refusal to seek indictments of the Republican Sheriff and warden. He did not know then how many Democratic politicians in Chicago were to be indicted by the Republican U.S. Attorney within the next few years.

Political motivation certainly was part of the prosecutorial attack on Chicago's Democratic organization in the first half of the 1970s. It was not, by any means, the sole explanation. In most instances, it was juries that found these politicians to be guilty. And the guilty list was substantial.

On May 2, 1974, Alderman Keane was indicted on 17 counts of mail fraud and one count of conspiracy in connection with having assembled and sold off 1900 parcels of tax delinquent land to various public agencies with enormous financial profits for himself.

In the previous year, Governor Otto Kerner had been convicted of bribery, conspiracy, mail fraud, income tax evasion and perjury in connection with a racetrack stock deal.

Convicted in March of 1973 was County Clerk Edward Barrett for accepting $180,000 in bribes from a voting machine conspiracy.

Matthew Danaher, the Circuit Court Clerk, shared in $300,000 in payoffs from two Chicago builders who needed zoning changes and private financing in order to build two subdivisions. This was disclosed on Dec. 20, 1973. Danaher was indicted for conspiracy and income tax charges on Apr. 10, 1974. He died before the case went to trial.

Alderman Paul Wigoda was indicted on income tax charges in connection with a $50,000 bribe.

In February of 1974, Earl Bush was indicted regarding advertising contracts at O'Hare Airport.

The list went on and on.

# Daley Reminisces

*"I loved LBJ. There was nothing he wouldn't
do for Chicago."*

The first three months of 1974 were downhill months
for Richard J. Daley. Every day seemed to bring a new
accusation of corruption in the local Democratic organization. But, as Spring began, more and more the headlines were
about Watergate. Nixon was being exposed. Few public officials
wanted to be seen with him.

In March, the President was invited to Chicago to speak before
the Executives Club. Initially, the Mayor did not plan to accept an invitation to participate in the luncheon. Colonel Reilly, however, argued
that not only should he attend, but he should also greet Nixon at the
airport upon his arrival. I disagreed. Reilly prevailed. The Mayor decided that courtesy for the Office of the President demanded he drive
to O'Hare to meet Nixon.

I rode with the Mayor and his son, Bill, from the Mayor's home to
the airport. "What should I talk about?" Daley asked as we drove out
the Kennedy Expressway. I suggested that Nixon be reminded of the
need for federal funds for more senior citizen housing. Chicago had a
backlog of 13,000 people waiting for apartments in senior citizen
buildings constructed by the Chicago Housing Authority. Much more
federally supported housing was needed.

At the airport the Mayor was met by its manager, Patrick Dunne, who suggested that Nixon be asked to have the federal military acreage at O'Hare turned over to the city. Lyndon B. Johnson had agreed to this but it had never cleared the bureaucracy of the Pentagon.

En route to O'Hare, the Mayor reminisced about the 1948 Democratic National Convention in Philadelphia, the first he had attended as a delegate. He recalled that Jack Arvey and Jimmy Roosevelt had publicly announced in advance of the convention that they favored General Eisenhower for the Democratic nomination and demanded that Truman be dumped. The Mayor said he was the only Chicago delegate who was openly for Truman. All the others, he said—Al Horan, Joe Gill, et cetera—declined to make any public endorsement of the President.

A caucus of the Chicago delegation was held on the train, Daley continued, with no one joining him in backing Truman. The Mayor said he then went to Edward J. Kelly who had been succeeded as Mayor the previous year by Martin Kennelly. "They're planning to get rid of you as chairman of the delegation," Daley told him. "You can assure yourself of staying on if, when this train gets to Philadelphia, you announce you're for Truman as we get off the train." That is what Kelly did and he was not removed as chairman, Daley said. He went on with his reminiscences.

At the Philadelphia convention there was much tenseness and animosity over the proposed civil rights plank. "I went to J. Howard McGrath who was presiding," the Mayor recalled, "and urged him to have the band play 'Dixie.'" Daley quoted McGrath as replying, "Aw, they're nothing but a bunch of Ku Kluxers." But Daley said he prevailed. James Petrillo had provided musicians who accompanied the Illinois delegation. They began to play "Dixie" and the emotions of the delegates in sympathy with Alabama and Mississippi were appeased, somewhat. At least for the moment.

The Mayor said a lot of "rather rough fellows" from Bridgeport also had accompanied the Chicago delegation to Philadelphia. When the Alabama and Mississippi delegates who had walked out of the convention returned to the hotel that evening, Daley said, "They were pushed around a little bit and hit with signs" by the Bridgeport contingent in the lobby. "I sometimes wonder," he added, "what would have happened at Miami [in 1972] if we had brought that same group with us."

Daley talked of his admiration for the speaking power of Senator Alben Barkley who gave the keynote address at Philadelphia. The Mayor said he noticed the Kentuckian did not consume water while orating and later asked about this. "Water makes the throat dry," Daley quoted Barkley as saying. "The throat has natural saliva which is sufficient. Speakers who drink glasses of water often end up coughing because it makes their throats dry." Then, according to Daley, Barkely said: "Young man, I'd be delighted to have you join me for a glass of Kentucky bourbon." Daley accepted the invitation.

At the conclusion of the convention, the Mayor said, he talked with President Truman who thanked him for his support.

Daley also reminisced about the late Congressman William Dawson who had been one of the Philadelphia delegates in 1948. The Mayor exclaimed he "loved" to attend Negro rallies arranged by Dawson in the 1955 mayoral campaign, and listen to the oratory. "We don't have that any more," Daley said. "The young black leaders are well educated but they don't know the biblical references and they have lost the art of great orations." He must have momentarily forgotten his foe, Jesse Jackson.

At the airport the President of the United States arrived and no Republican from the State of Illinois was there to greet him. The only persons on hand were the Mayor, his son, Bill, Alderman Roman Pucinski, and me. Daley and Pucinski went forward to shake hands with Nixon as he came down the steps from Air Force One. Bill and I reluctantly followed, at the Mayor's direction, to multiply the size of the Chicago contingent.

Daley introduced me to Nixon. Then Bill and I climbed into the police tail-car and followed the presidential limousine carrying Nixon, Daley and General Alexander Haig for the trip over the Kennedy Expressway to the Conrad Hilton Hotel.

In spring of 1974 the Mayor made another of his periodic trips to Washington. The purpose was to press for construction of the Crosstown Expressway. He attended a private dinner arranged by Congressman Dan Rostenkowski for members of the Chicago congressional delegation and the Mayor's traveling companions. Daley and Rostenkowski talked about the days of LBJ. The congressman recalled a meeting in the Oval Office at which, he said, Daley told the president that our military commitment in Vietnam was a mistake. Thereupon,

Rostenkowski continued, Johnson summoned his military aides who produced various maps and charts pertaining to Southeast Asia. "It was quite a sight," Rostenkowski declared, "seeing the president with the maps spread across his desk, waving his arms and excitedly trying to explain to Dick why the LBJ position on the war was right."

At one point during this Washington visit, the Mayor exclaimed to those who traveled with him: "I loved LBJ. There was nothing he wouldn't do for Chicago."

Before returning to National Airport, the Mayor journeyed to Arlington National Cemetery. He got out of his car by John Kennedy's grave and stood in silent prayer. Then he walked a short distance, for the first time, to the site where Robert F. Kennedy was buried, and stood in the quiet of Arlington, praying silently. From there he was driven the short distance to the Tomb of the Unknowns to view the changing of the guard. He then left to catch his plane.

April 1974 was the time the Mayor made one of his rare acceptances of an invitation to appear on national television. The program, on NBC, was called "The Loyal Opposition." Edwin Newman was to moderate from a studio in New York City and NBC newsman Bob Jamieson was to talk with the Mayor in Chicago. Joining in the discussion from a studio in Washington were Senators George McGovern, Edward M. Kennedy, and Henry Jackson, along with Democratic National Chairman Robert Strauss. Daley had agreed to the invitation because of the high level political company he would be in and Jamieson's reputation for fairness.

I rode with the Mayor and Mrs. Daley from their home to the NBC studio in the Merchandise Mart. He recalled a similar journey they had made almost 14 years before as the guests of Senator John Kennedy to attend the telecast of his first debate with Richard Nixon in Chicago's CBS studio.

In the NBC studio, before the program, the Mayor spoke with and saw the men in the Washington and New York studios through a closed circuit monitor. While studio personnel adjusted Daley's microphone and dusted powder on his forehead, Senator Kennedy took his place before the cameras in Washington, and Edwin Newman exclaimed: "You know that gentleman out there in Chicago, don't you, Senator?" Kennedy replied that he did and the Mayor immediately said: "Good evening Senator. How is young Teddy coming along?"—a reference to the Senator's son hospitalized for a cancerous leg condition. It was an example of Daley the man and Daley the politician.

The program was only a few minutes on the air when Newman announced that they were about to show some film which would be of interest to the Mayor. It showed him standing alongside Nixon at the Executives Club luncheon three weeks previously. "Well," said Newman, "what do you have to say about that, Mr. Mayor?" The Mayor responded by stating that he was not the mayor of the Democrats of Chicago but of all the people, and that he had gone to the airport to greet Nixon out of respect for the presidency the same way he had greeted Presidents Eisenhower, Lyndon Johnson and "our late beloved, martyred President, John Kennedy, God rest his soul."

Quickly Daley added that if Newman or anyone else had any questions about his loyalty to the Democratic Party or where he stood regarding the party, "There is a man sitting there in Washington who can give you the answer." Senator McGovern immediately responded to this reference by making a strong expression of appreciation to Daley for the way he had supported the South Dakotan in the 1972 presidential election campaign. No one did more to help to fight against Nixon than Daley, McGovern maintained. Newman did not address any more questions to Daley but the audience could clearly discern which of the "loyal opposition" had the most dominant personality.

# Stroke 32

*"I was, I regretfully concluded, a front man for thieves."*

April of 1974 was a particularly bad month for Daley. The full power of the Republican U.S. Attorney's office continued to be used against some of the Mayor's key political colleagues. Then, in April, something significantly different occurred. The federal government began to focus on Daley himself. The Nixon-Mitchell-created Thompson started a course aimed at sending the almost 72-year-old Mayor to the penitentiary.

On Saturday, April 26, private attorney John P. Coghlan, Jr., telephoned me at home. He asked if I would arrange for the delivery to the Mayor of certain records which belonged to Daley but were then in the possession of the Mayor's long-time accountant and friend, Peter Shannon. Rather than discuss this with Daley on the telephone, I drove to his home. After being greeted by Mrs. Daley, I was escorted by her to the basement family room. Moments later, the Mayor came down the steps dressed in a tuxedo. He and Mrs. Daley were preparing to attend a cocktail reception to be hosted by Chicago Stadium owner Arthur Wirtz before a Frank Sinatra concert. I told Daley that I had received the call from Coghlan and that he had told me the IRS was investigating Shannon and might at any moment seize all of the Mayor's financial records which were in Shannon's possession. To avoid this, I said, Coghlan believed the records should be turned over to the Mayor. He agreed and asked me to bring them to him.

The following day, Sunday, I met with Coghlan in my parked car outside Shannon's office at 55th Street and Damen Avenue on the Southwest Side. The only papers he gave me were a copy of a federal subpoena issued for Shannon, and an IRS agent's list of printed documents which he wanted to view. The Daley financial records, all originals, Coghlan said, were numerous and he had not finished getting them all together. I delivered to the Mayor what Coghlan gave me and relayed that the attorney wanted to meet with him. Daley agreed to a meeting.

The following day they met in the Democratic party headquarters in the LaSalle Hotel. Coghlan was retained as the Mayor's attorney, a relationship which was to last only a few days. During those days, however, Coghlan turned over to the Mayor:

— all financial records of income and expenditures of the Democratic Party of Cook County from the time Daley became its chairman in 1953 to 1974;
— all financial records of Daley's political campaigns from 1954 to 1974;
— all records of expenditures of City money from the Mayor's contingency funds from 1955 on; and,
— all previously non-subpoenaed records pertaining to Elard Corporation, which had been created for the ownership of the Mayor's Michigan and Chicago homes, "Elard" being a combination of the first two letters of Mrs. Daley's first name and the last three of the Mayor's.

This material, Coghlan said, "filled seven large boxes." He added that he had retained a Xerox copy of each document "in order to protect" his client, Shannon, but that none of the Xerox material was now in either his or Shannon's possession but was located in the South Side home of a Coghlan friend.

Coghlan said he believed the Mayor and his sons were "vulnerable" on possible tax charges.

The well-intentioned Coghlan, however, made a serious mistake during his LaSalle Hotel meeting with the Mayor. Present with Coghlan and Daley was the Mayor's son, Michael, an attorney. Coghlan knew that Michael could not later claim a privileged relationship if questioned about the hotel meeting by government attorneys. Coghlan insisted, therefore, that Michael leave the room, stating that he would speak only after the son's departure. Instead of appreciating Coghlan's legal alertness, Daley saw it as a slight to one of his children. Before the week was over, and after Coghlan had turned over all the Daley documents, the South Side attorney was dismissed by the Mayor and replaced by long-time criminal attorney, Harry Busch.

It had been a bad week. When I met with the Mayor in his home on April 27 to turn over the copy of the Shannon subpoena Coghlan had given me, Daley said: "I've been betrayed by people who were very close to me—by Matt [Danaher] and Earl Bush."

Alderman Thomas Keane, Press Secretary Earl Bush, Cook County Circuit Court Clerk Matthew Danaher, County Clerk Edward Barrett, Alderman Paul Wigoda—the list of Daley associates being investigated by U.S. Attorney Thompson continued to grow. On Sunday, May 5, independent alderman and Daley opponent William Singer went on television to contend that the Mayor was morally responsible for, what Singer described as, "the political corruption in Chicago." No elected official had previously held the Mayor personally responsible. I lay awake in bed that night until midnight. For part of the night, I watched a public television program re-enacting portions of the Watergate scandal. The events of the past two weeks were having a decidedly negative impact on me. The atmosphere at City Hall had been increasingly unsavory.

I went through my chronology with the Daley administration. I had left the *Sun-Times* in January of 1968 for idealistic as well as financial reasons. I admired John Stamos and wanted to help him stay on as State's Attorney. But then he was dumped as a candidate the following month. I accepted the Mayor's offer of the job as spokesman for the Chicago Police because I believed strongly that he was a good man and the Police Department needed public support, not endless criticism. But seeing firsthand how the Police Department continually put its misguided or outright crooked interests always first, I grew disillusioned. Almost every effort at openness and reform was thwarted. The hostility to the media was succeeded by insensitivity toward the black population and, ultimately, strong resistance to the FBI and all outside probers. By December of 1971, my conscience was disturbed that I was part of police headquarters. I told Daley so. He had refused to replace Conlisk with a dynamic Superintendent who could discipline the police, reach out to minorities, and provide the public police leadership Chicago deserved.

Then Daley asked if I would come to City Hall to work for him directly as his administrative assistant. And that is what I did in May of 1972. In March of the following year, I became his press secretary.

A city must have public employees who continually seek public improvements. In the imperfect art of government, only the naive are shocked by official corruption. The problem is in the degree of corruption. And, for me, in the first few days of 1974, the degree and my role became unacceptable. I began to conclude that my job as press secretary consisted mainly of being a front man for people who were using politics for the sole purpose of enriching themselves. I was, I regretfully concluded, a front man for thieves.

My job, regretfully, was to get up every morning, come to City Hall and relay explanations as to why this official or that official was not a crook. For Daley foes, my conclusion may appear to be too late. For Daley admirers, my conclusion may seem unwarranted. In the midst of thousands of decisions and actions, each of us has to make personal judgments. For me, the time was then—late at night on Sunday, May 5, 1974.

The time had come, I told my wife, to terminate the job and to pursue something more wholesome. Monday would be the last day. And then I said to my wife, if all these accusations of corruption are so adversely affecting me, "imagine what they are doing to the Mayor." The impact on Richard J. Daley was to be more dangerous than I had thought.

The next morning was Monday, May 6. I met with attorney Coghlan for an early breakfast in a restaurant across from City Hall at his request. He was annoyed that Daley had retained him only long enough to obtain all mayoral records in Shannon's possession and had then dismissed him. Coghlan said he had been prepared to go to jail for the Mayor. (This, I thought, was an all too frequent expression by South Side Irish to point up their devotion to the Mayor.) Now, Coghlan continued, although he would never hurt Daley, his responsibility was to help only Shannon. Coghlan had with him a large envelope containing some Shannon, that is, Daley, records which were going to be delivered by him to a federal grand jury that morning in response to a subpoena for all the books and records of Daley's Elard Corporation.

This would be the day I'd resign. I knew it was foolish to leave one job without having another one waiting. Nevertheless the job of press secretary was so fast-moving there was no time to be scouting for other work. Besides, I was confident about the future. I had the same attitude two and one half years earlier when I told Daley I was going to leave the Police Department because of what I believed to be a refusal by Department leaders to pursue reform. On the day of that resignation in December of 1971, I had no future job arranged. Now, as then, it seemed to me the most important thing was to act and to sever my relationship with an administration with which I was no longer comfortable. I would seek out the Mayor at a time when he and I could talk for a few minutes.

But, upon arriving at City Hall after the breakfast with Coghlan, it was apparent from the morning newspapers that reporters were zeroing in on the city's car rental arrangements at O'Hare Airport. So there was immediate work to be done. I was convinced that Corporation Counsel Richard Curry, a bright and good man, could provide honest and satisfactory explanations and handle all press questions. I went to Daley and recommended that Curry respond to the newsmen on the subject. The Mayor was opposed. "He will only keep things going," Daley said. But, after summoning Curry to his office, the Mayor reversed himself and said the Corporation Counsel could respond to newsmen if asked.

Daley told me he was then going to attend a memorial service for the late Cook County Commissioner Lillian Piotrowski in the Cook County Commissioners' Board Room. Afterwards, at about 10:00 a.m., I accompanied him to the City Council Chamber to attend a Junior Officials Day program. While the Mayor was presiding over this program, I telephoned Curry and asked him to come to the City Hall press room to explain the car rental negotiations at the airport. I asked City Collector Marshall Korshak to do the same. Both men subsequently did excellent jobs in explaining the City's transactions. Then

I went to Daley's office to tell him how well they had done. It was about 11:10 a.m.

Prior to my arrival, police officer Michael Graney, who was in command of the Mayor's bodyguards, had telephoned Daley's physician, Dr. Thomas Coogan, to report, at the Mayor's request, that Daley had "a cramp" in his right leg. An appointment had been made for the Mayor to see Coogan at 11:30 a.m. At 11:10 a.m., in his office, I told Daley that Curry and Korshak had taken care of the airport matter and that the question should not arise again from newsmen when he attended a Palmer House luncheon at noon. Daley said he was pleased and would see me at the luncheon.

Upon arriving at the Palmer House, I learned that Daley was not going to appear after all. At about 12:10 p.m., as the luncheon was beginning, I received a telephone call from Kay Spear, Daley's secretary. She said Graney had phoned to say that the Mayor had been admitted to Rush-Presbyterian-St. Luke's Medical Center and that I should go there immediately.

A police officer drove me to the hospital. I arrived at 12:20 p.m. One of the Mayor's bodyguards who was standing on the sidewalk escorted me to the 10th floor. A small group of newsmen stood around the ground floor emergency room entrance. I told them I would return as soon as I learned what had happened. On the 10th floor I found Mrs. Daley sitting in a chair in the corridor alongside the closed door of the Mayor's room. I walked up to her and took her hand for a moment. Then I tried to learn from others what had happened.

That afternoon I was to hold four news conferences. I was trying to gather and relay information as quickly as possible. The first time I met with the press was 12:55 p.m. I returned to the emergency room entrance and started to talk with newsmen when a member of the hospital's public relations staff told me I would have to get out of the corridor. She led me to the office of the hospital's finance director. There, for about ten minutes, I gave my first report. John Callaway of CBS asked me if I would repeat my remarks before his camera and I did.

The gist of my report was that the Mayor was in a private room on the 10th floor. He had gone to see his doctor for an 11:30 a.m. appointment. The doctor had recommended that the Mayor go immediately to the hospital and had accompanied Daley in his limousine. The Mayor had entered the emergency room and was there for about 15 minutes when he was taken to the 10th floor where he was to undergo a series of tests.

I then returned to the 10th floor to try to learn more.

Within a short time the *Chicago Daily News* was to be on the streets with a headline stating that the Mayor had been stricken. His children joined his wife in rushing to the hospital. Rumors were to sweep the city that the Mayor was in critical condition.

It was at this time when I first met Dr. Coogan. Michael Daley was with us. He told Coogan that he could say whatever he wanted to say but he should understand that the "family has no concern nor feels any obligation to provide information for the news media." Coogan should understand this at the very beginning, Michael said.

There were to be three more press conferences that afternoon. The first of these was a crowded session again in the finance director's office. More than 30 people were jammed into the small room. All local television stations were represented. I repeated the information I had given at the previous conference. I added that the Mayor had walked into the emergency room and, since going to the 10th floor, had talked with Mrs. Daley. Bob Crawford of CBS asked if the presence of the Mayor's family didn't indicate that it was something serious. I replied it showed the love and affection which the sons and daughters had for their father. I avoided the use of all descriptive words like "serious" or "not serious" because I had no medical report and such words could lead to inaccurate speculation. I declined to characterize but only to report facts. This greatly annoyed the media representatives. My efforts were to no avail because the media began to attribute to me descriptive words I had never used. The second conference was at about 2:00 p.m.

The third conference at 3:00 p.m. and the fourth, at 4:45 p.m. were held in a hospital auditorium. On these two occasions, I told newsmen I could not pinpoint the Mayor's ailment. I assured them he was not in an intensive care unit. He was conscious. He had visited with members of his family. Dick Kay of NBC and Ellen Warren of the *Daily News* were among those who wanted to run through a list of ailments—Had he suffered a heart attack? Had he suffered a stroke?

I said I had to decline to answer such questions because they could be answered only by doctors. The press wanted to know why the doctors were not there. I said they were with the Mayor and had asked me to represent them. This made the press very unhappy, but no one in the room wished more than I that a doctor had been present.

After the third news conference of the afternoon, Michael Daley told me that was enough. I thought, however, that the newsmen and women and, more importantly, the people of Chicago, should not be left in suspense as to what was happening or whether they would hear any additional reports about the Mayor throughout the night. Someone had to say that there would be no more news conferences that day but there would be information provided the following day, Tuesday. Michael Daley disagreed with me strongly.

If I had concurred with his wishes and simply vanished, the serious credibility problems I encountered on Tuesday would not have arisen. I believed, however, the news personnel were reasonable in expecting someone to talk with them in detail about the Mayor. I had thought State Senator Richard M. Daley, the Mayor's oldest son, should be that person because this was a very personal situation. At the fourth and final news conference on Monday, I said there would be another press statement on Tuesday about 10:00 a.m. This was distorted by some media people to give the impression that the Mayor's doctors had agreed to appear at that time.

A conclusion began to form. The conclusion was that the lack of a detailed report on the Mayor's medical condition meant that something mysterious was happening. Newsmen began to assume that there was a plot to conceal information. No media pointed out that assurances were given that the Mayor was not in critical condition and not in intensive care, that he was conscious and was being examined to determine precisely the nature of his illness. Instead, the media representatives began to talk and write about the hospitalization as if Daley were Woodrow Wilson and there was a conspiracy under way to prevent them from knowing about any disability. Nothing short of a total medical analysis by the physicians could hope to satisfy newsmen's appetites and only the patient or patient's family could authorize such medical disclosures.

Daley remained behind closed doors in his 10th floor room. A television monitor relayed his heartbeat to medical personnel outside his room. A room adjacent to the Mayor's was provided for Mrs. Daley. She was to spend that first night and the succeeding ones at the hospital until the Mayor was discharged. Other members of the family took turns joining with her in this vigil. Outside the Mayor's room and at other locations on the 10th floor corridor, members of his police body-guard detail were stationed. Mike Graney, whose quick thinking and actions had earlier played an important role in assisting the Mayor, had been replaced by Captain Jack Townsend in command of the body-guards. Townsend had raced to the hospital to take the key position outside the door of the Mayor's room.

I had planned to stay overnight at the hospital but Senator Daley recommended that I go home and return in the morning. I left at 10:30 p.m. and came back at 7:30 a.m. on Tuesday. Before I left the hospital, Sheldon Gardner, who headed the hospital's public relations staff, met with me and implied that the Mayor was to undergo a test on Tuesday to determine if he had suffered brain damage.

At about 9:00 a.m. Tuesday, I met with Mrs. Daley, Michael, and Dr. Eric Oldberg, the president of the Chicago Board of Health, in Mrs. Daley's room adjacent to the Mayor's. Oldberg emphatically stated that "only one person could be the spokesman on the Mayor's condition and Frank Sullivan is that one person." Oldberg then left the room and, shortly thereafter, became the most garrulous mischief-maker connected with Daley's illness. He was replaced at this Tuesday morning meeting by Dr. Coogan.

I told Mrs. Daley that hospital officials had indicated to me that the Mayor was to undergo testing to determine if he had suffered brain damage. I further stated that this would probably be in print before the day was over. Mrs. Daley made no response and in no way indicated agreement or disagreement with what I said. I asked her and Dr. Coogan what I should tell newsmen about the Mayor's condition. They said I could tell them he had suffered for some time from high blood pressure and had a mild diabetic condition for which he was tak-ing medication. They said that when he visited Coogan's office on the previous day, the Mayor had complained of dizziness and the doctor recommended admission to the hospital for a series of tests.

I had made it clear to Mrs. Daley and Coogan that there were go-ing to be rumors, probably in print, about possible brain damage. Nei-ther she nor the doctor made any mention of a mild stroke.

I left the room to prepare a brief press statement based on what Coogan had said. In a small office on the first floor, I had just started to write the statement when suddenly *Daily News* reporter Ellen Warren entered and said, "My newspaper has information from a most responsible source that the Mayor has suffered a stroke. Is that true?" That was the question I had feared. I had no knowledge which would justify a "yes" answer. At the same time, in view of Sheldon Gardner's early comment, how could I respond "no" with certainty. The *Daily News'* information came directly to its publisher, Marshall Field, from his suburban neighbor, Dr. James Campbell, who was the medical center's chief of staff. The Daley family viewed information about the Mayor as being a favor for the news media instead of an obligation toward the people of Chicago. Despite their non-cooperation, however, the information was getting out.

Lacking information regarding Warren's statement, I tried to bluff. I said to her, "How could you ask such a question?" And added, "There is only one word to be used to describe someone who would ask such a question—you're really a cute kid." Other reporters saw and heard me shouting at her. Then she went to a telephone to report all this to her city desk. I was concerned. What had my remarks indicated? A positive answer? A negative answer? I telephoned her city editor, Bob Schultz, to complain about her conduct. Schultz gave me a brief lecture on my lack of professionalism and asked what she had done that was so wrong. Nothing, I admitted. I knew her question was legitimate. I was reacting strongly against it because I did not know the answer.

My assistant, Dennis Church, and I knew that at the press conference, which was to take place in a few minutes, Warren would again ask the question. Mrs. Daley and Dr. Coogan had been unwilling to provide me with an answer. To respond to newsmen by saying "I don't know" would obviously accelerate their demands for me to find out and I had been unable to find out. I weighed the facts as I knew them. I had told Dr. Coogan and Mrs. Daley that the hospital personnel implied the Mayor was going to be tested for brain damage. Neither she nor the doctor indicated that this was true or that Daley had suffered a stroke. No one on the hospital staff had said he suffered a stroke. I had made every effort I could to get an answer. I had no evidence to support an affirmative answer. I could only conclude, from the silence that surrounded me, the answer was negative. The answer ultimately was a matter for the patient and his family and they were noncommunicative. And 24 hours earlier I had been planning to resign! I wish

I had been able to do so. But now everything was different. The Mayor was hospitalized and it was no time for me to walk away from the job.

I went into a crowded news conference to point out that the Mayor's specific health problem had not as yet been determined and that he was to undergo days of testing. The gist of my remarks was reported that evening on NBC's local television news: namely, that all of us would like to have known exactly what was the Mayor's condition but that many of us had relatives or friends in the hospital and knew that doctors could not always provide an immediate diagnosis—that it sometimes took from three to five days to complete all necessary tests, and that was what was going to have to happen in this case. In answer to the inevitable question as to whether Daley had suffered a stroke, I responded, "No."

The media later reported that I had said that the Mayor only suffered from high blood pressure and a mild diabetic condition. Overlooked completely was the emphasis I had made that no final medical report could be given until a series of tests was completed. I never used the expression often attributed to me, "not serious." No reasonable person could have concluded that the hospitalization of a 72 year old man was not serious.

For the first time in his adult life, Richard Daley was unable to speak in public. Part of his political strength had come from his practice of speaking for himself, not through spokesmen. It was my belief that, because he was not permanently incapacitated and not in critical condition, the detailed report of his illness had to come only with his authorization. Unfortunately, he did not authorize it for six days.

From Wednesday, May 8, through Friday, May 10, there were many inquiries from the news media regarding the Mayor's condition. My answer was that he was resting comfortably. By Saturday morning, however, I was deeply concerned. The patience of the media was being severely tested. They did not know exactly what was wrong with the Mayor. Neither did I. Their wrath had yet to be unleashed but I knew it was destined to come. Dr. Oldberg was issuing what seemed to be hourly statements and interviews. He was giving inane explanations for Daley's hospitalization to the effect that because he was admitted to a hospital and "his pants had been removed," the opportunity was present to subject him to a checkup.

I went to the hospital early Saturday hoping to talk with Mrs. Daley. Instead, I met with Senator Richard Daley and his brother, William. I put the question to them directly. Had the Mayor suffered a stroke? "No," replied the Senator. "That word has never been used," said William. I took their comments as assurance that there had been no stroke. I told the Senator that by Monday morning, a detailed statement must be issued regarding the Mayor's health. The media's patience could not be tested beyond Monday morning, I said. Daley replied that his father had instructed Dr. Coogan to prepare such a statement. I asked the Mayor's eldest son to please be at the hospital the following day, Sunday, to review Dr. Coogan's statement so it would be ready for issuance on Monday morning. The younger Daley had been talking in terms of a Tuesday announcement. I told him that would be too late.

On Sunday afternoon, I returned to the hospital but Senator Daley was not present. I spoke with Mrs. Daley who said she was pleased with the Mayor's condition. Because of the absence of Senator Daley, there was no statement from Dr. Coogan and no chance to review it for Monday morning issuance.

On Monday morning, the Lyric Opera strike was in the news. Mrs. Daley called my office at City Hall and asked me to work with William A. Lee, the president of the Chicago Federation of Labor. Lee had been asked by the Mayor to act on his behalf in resolving this dispute. It was typical of Daley's mode of operation that he asked the head of Chicago's labor organization to resolve a labor dispute.

Dr. Oldberg, who, unlike me, knew Daley's medical condition, telephoned and irritatedly told me that I had "to do something to make Mrs. Daley issue a detailed statement" about the Mayor's health. "The pressure" on him from newsmen was getting to be too much, Oldberg complained. He added that he had just talked with Art Snider, the science editor of the *Daily News*. (Within a few hours, the result of that conversation was to make headline news.) Dr. Oldberg said that Mrs. Daley had denounced the newspapers to him. "During our first years in office, the newspapers were good to Dick and me," Oldberg quoted her as saying, "but the way they have attacked my family these past three years, and especially my two youngest sons, I won't do anything to help them." A paraphrase of Dr. Oldberg's remarks to me regarding Mrs. Daley appeared in Mike Royko's column on the following day with no attribution. Dr. Oldberg, throughout this medical crisis, was a continuous mischief-maker, giving the media false medical information and half-truths.

I made no comment to the doctor regarding his statements, knowing his practice of repeating anybody's remarks to the media. At about 10:00 that morning, I had gone to the press room at City Hall to provide the beat reporters with information regarding letters the Mayor had been receiving while in the hospital. I was asked by the City News Bureau reporter whether the Mayor had suffered a stroke. Based on my conversation with two of his sons just two days before, I said no.

At about 3:30 in the afternoon, Walter Jacobson of WBBM-TV phoned to say that the *Daily News* was about to run a story that surgery was being considered for the Mayor "to prevent a stroke." Dr. Oldberg's interview had made print. I telephoned Michael Daley in his law office and repeated what Jacobson told me. Michael said we should both leave immediately for the hospital. When we arrived, William and John Daley said I should be ready to read to the newsmen a statement which finally had been prepared by Dr. Coogan. I told them I would have to see it before I could summon newsmen and that I would have to be able to talk to Dr. Coogan. I explained that I had to know exactly what was happening before meeting with reporters. John Daley said he did not understand why.

Minutes later, at about 5:10 p.m. on Monday, May 13, Mrs. Daley said the Mayor wanted to see me. He had been hospitalized for a week. I opened the door to his 10th floor room and walked in. It was the first time I had seen him since he was stricken. The mattress on his bed was raised so he was supported and sitting up. He had lost weight and looked sickly. It was disturbing to see someone who had been synonymous with active life now confined to a hospital bed. He wanted me to read Dr. Coogan's statement to newsmen and not to respond to any questions.

I then went to an adjoining room with William, Michael and John Daley and Dr. Robert Vanecko, their brother-in-law. They gave me Dr. Coogan's prepared statement. I read it and learned for the first time that the Mayor had suffered what was described as a "small stroke." I was saddened to think that he had been afflicted in this way. Dr. Coogan then joined us. I commented that the statement was an open and thorough one and commended those responsible for it. It told of how the Mayor on the preceding Monday had suffered a mild stroke which had temporarily caused a partial facial paralysis, a numbness in the left hand and a slurring of speech. These temporary disorders had ended, the statement said, but surgery would be necessary to prevent recurrence.

I went to a telephone at about 5:20 p.m. to summon newsmen for a 6:00 p.m. meeting at the hospital. At that time I stepped before the cameras and microphones and read the statement. Then I returned to the 10th floor of the hospital for several hours before going home.

The following day, the media wrath was unleashed. I was denounced in news stories and by Royko. As the week continued, the *Sun-Times* and the *Tribune* editorially joined the attack. I was accused of having deceived the media.

Thursday, plans were being made for the Mayor's departure from the hospital. I met with him on Friday to discuss the arrangements. Newsmen were notified that day that he was going to leave on Saturday morning.

On Saturday, the Mayor was ready early. He visited with the doctors and nurses who had attended him. Then, as he walked across the ground floor lobby, patients, visitors and staff called out, one after another, "God bless you, Mr. Mayor." He greeted the large crowd of newsmen which was waiting at the hospital's main entrance and climbed into his car for the trip to 3536 South Lowe Avenue. It was Saturday, May 18, 1974.

During the period from May 18 when he went home from the hospital until June 1 when he returned for surgery, I visited with Daley in his home on two occasions. On the first visit, he spoke with me at length about a variety of subjects. Sitting with me in his basement family room, he said that I was "a very decent person" and that I had "to start thinking" about my family and my future. The implication was that he would try to help me.

Looking back—on Saturday, April 26, Daley had learned that the federal government was investigating decades of his tax records. The long attack by the Nixon administration, its Attorney General, John Mitchell, and Nixon's politically ambitious appointee, James R. Thompson, had finally focused on its prime Chicago target. Ten days after receiving this news, the Mayor suffered a stroke. It happened less than three hours after private attorney John Coghlan, responding to an IRS subpoena, turned over to a federal grand jury the tax records pertaining to Daley's small real estate holdings.

Daley thanked me for everything I had done during the past year. "It was easy to be with me when things were going well," he said. He made it clear that it was not the way things had gone during the past year. He repeated that he had been betrayed by people close to him and he again named Matt Danaher and Earl Bush. Without giving details, Daley said that he had many opportunities to make large amounts of money even in his first few weeks as Mayor in 1955. One offer, he said, would have earned him more than $200,000 and another, more than a million dollars. "But I decided," he continued, "that the Office of Mayor was not going to be for sale." He said some people wanted to think he was going to seek profit from the office because he was an Irish-Catholic. That sort of thinking, Daley said, made him "all the more determined the office would not be for sale."

I met with him again in his home to work out the plans for media coverage of his return to the hospital. Bill Daley was present. An apprehensive Mayor spoke about his forthcoming operation. He was like a man on his deathbed, he said, who was asked by a priest if he renounced Satan. "No," said the man. "Why not?" asked the astonished priest. "Because," said the man, "in my condition I can't afford to make any enemies."

The Mayor also said he was reminded of the black minister who told his congregation, "We are all destined for heaven, and heaven is our home." The minister then leaned closer to his listeners and added —"but I want you all to know I don't feel the least bit homesick."

Daley, sitting alongside me in his pajamas and bathrobe, said he had asked his doctor what the percentage was that the surgery would turn out all right. The doctor replied such statistics were not kept. The Mayor said he then chided, "Come on, Doc. Do 75 percent come through all right? Is it 90 percent? You know what results you have." Daley said to me, "They keep trying to say there's nothing to it. But you know that some people don't come through, even if it's only two or three percent. Anytime you take a knife and cut into someone, it's a serious business."

On Saturday, June 1, he returned to the hospital in Mrs. Daley's blue Cadillac with license number RD 3536. The Mayor rode in the front seat with Commander Jack Townsend, who drove. Mrs. Daley and son John were in the back. At the hospital, the Mayor walked through the main entrance and took an elevator to the ninth floor. As he entered the hospital, I went to the telephone to notify the news media. I told newsmen the surgery was to be within a few days. It took place the following morning. I also told the media that the Mayor had instructed his doctors, as soon as reasonably possible following his operation, to issue a report on the surgery and his medical condition. Daley, however, did not want anyone to know in advance the time of his operation, just as he had not wanted anyone to know in advance the time of his return to the hospital. These matters, I thought, were within the prerogatives of any patient.

The Mayor was taken to surgery at 9:00 a.m. the following morning, Sunday, June 2. He was removed from surgery at 10:30 a.m. Moments afterwards Dr. Oldberg stopped by to visit Mrs. Daley. I knew that shortly after his departure the world would know about the surgery. The Mayor was then moved to intensive care. At 11:30 a.m., Dr. Hushang Javid, who had performed the operation, appeared on the ninth floor and said everything had gone well. The newsmen could have been told then that the operation had been completed. But the mayor, the doctors, the family and I had agreed that the statement of the Mayor's condition should come from doctors.

They began work on a statement at 12:30 p.m. At 1:15 p.m. it was ready. At 1:20 p.m. I took it to Mrs. Daley and members of the family for review. They agreed with every word Dr. Javid had written. At 1:45 p.m. I called the City News Bureau to report that there would be an announcement at 3:00 p.m. The media had been promised by me at least one hour advance notice.

At 3:00 p.m. I read the doctors' statement to the press in the hospital auditorium. The media, subsequently, was critical of what they called "secrecy."

As the week continued, the Mayor progressed. On Friday, I spoke with him about plans for his departure. During this conversation he spoke at length about former Chicago alderman and political opponent Seymour Simon. The Mayor described Simon as the most "corrupt man" he had ever known in politics. Simon, Daley said, had repeatedly used the Mayor's name and misstated his positions regarding zoning matters when Simon was president of the Cook County Board. On another occasion, according to Daley, Simon went to Frank

Whiston and announced that Whiston's property management company was going to have a partner in the operations of Chicago's Civic Center. Daley said he blocked that.

At 9:00 a.m. on Saturday, June 8, the Mayor left the hospital to recuperate from his surgery at his summer home in Grand Beach, Michigan.

Four days previously, from his hospital bed, Daley had given directions which helped shape a significant victory for the Regular Democratic Organization. Elections were held on June 4 to pick the men and women who would select delegates for Kansas City the following December. The regulars had elected 499 of the 500 persons who were to make the final delegate selection. Minimal news coverage was given this Daley victory.

The Mayor noted how pleased he was to have received a get-well letter from President Truman's widow, Bess. Senator Edward Kennedy's phone call to the hospital, however, had been declined. Daley did not forgive him for his refusal to support the seating of the elected Chicago delegation at the Miami convention.

By mid-June the Mayor's long recuperative period was well underway. The public was overwhelmingly sympathetic and pleased that he had come through his operation successfully. The media backed off somewhat in their criticisms. He had been unable to attend the annual Cook County Democratic dinner on May 22 at the Conrad Hilton Hotel but telephoned Jane Byrne in advance to have her relay his message to the attendees.

Throughout the summer, reporters, photographers, and camera crews sought glimpses of Daley in his Grand Beach retreat. Political opponents such as Alderman Leon Despres demanded that medical teams be dispatched to the Michigan hideaway to determine, for their satisfaction, the Mayor's condition. Most of the public, however, appeared to be happy with the assurances that Daley was recovering.

On Thursday, August 1, the Mayor telephoned and asked me to come to his Grand Beach home to discuss plans for his return to City Hall. My wife accompanied me on the ride and waited outside a friend's nearby house while I walked a short distance to visit with the Mayor.

It was my first trip to his Grand Beach residence. It was located north of the town at the end of a three mile dirt road. After walking past a small frame garage where one of the bodyguards was on duty, I went through the gate, past a swimming pool and ascended the wood steps that led to the kitchen door where Mrs. Daley greeted me.

The Mayor met me in the kitchen and escorted me to a closed porch overlooking Lake Michigan. Our meeting was to last two hours.

During the first half of it, the Mayor and I talked about his return to City Hall, about the media, and politics in general. As I started to leave, Mrs. Daley asked me to stay for lunch. When she insisted, I told her I had something "terrible to report." I left a girl outside waiting. "You left Sally in the car?" Mrs. Daley asked. When I said yes, she and the Mayor told me to get her right away. I ran the short distance to the friend's house and returned with Sally along the dirt road to be greeted by the recuperating Mayor who was standing just outside his property. "This is unforgivable," he said, referring to my keeping my wife waiting. He hugged Sally and we walked back to the house for a two hour lunch with Mrs. Daley. In the world of Richard J. Daley, a man's wife came first. He was not amused by someone who appeared to be placing his job ahead of his wife.

During our four hour conversation, the Mayor's remarks turned to "two of the biggest liars" he said he had ever known—the late Governor Adlai E. Stevenson and Senator Paul H. Douglas. Daley said that when he was State Director of Revenue he had complained to Stevenson that many of the top state officials had lied to him (Daley). Stevenson condoned this, the Mayor said, "saying it was the way things are in government." Douglas, according to Daley, on one occasion, years before, had told him he could not remember whether he authored a pro-communist letter.

The discussion was far-ranging and much of it dwelt on the imperfections of the news media. We also talked about what was certain to be a major topic of any press conference following his return to City Hall—the recent reports in the press pertaining to Elard Corporation, the company which he and his wife had established for ownership of their three small properties. I was told to meet with attorneys Harry Busch, Warren Wolfson and Michael Daley to work out a suggested statement which would explain Elard to the media. This was later done in Michael's office.

On the Saturday before Labor Day, I returned to Grand Beach to finalize arrangements for the Mayor's meeting with the press at City

Hall. On the morning after Labor Day, with the exception of one television reporter who wisely stationed himself outside the Mayor's South Side home, no newsmen were aware of Daley's return to City Hall until seconds after his arrival when I announced it in the City Hall press room. That was the way Daley liked to do things. Later that morning he held one of his most heavily attended news conferences. The subject of the Elard Corporation's holdings was overshadowed by the attention devoted to the Mayor's surprisingly strong physical appearance. The atmosphere was one of good fellowship and general satisfaction that he had returned to the job.

Again, events were to move rapidly. Eight weeks after Daley's return to City Hall there would be more elections. And the future called for another mayoral contest and a presidential campaign. My earlier intent to resign faded.

# His Comeback 33

*"Twenty years is long enough to be in any job."*

L ate in 1974, Daley was faced with the decision whether to seek a sixth term. Before the December filing deadline, however, the Democratic mini-convention in Kansas City was scheduled to take place. It proved to be a successful return for Daley to the national party scene. But the two day event pointed up his continuing poor relationship with the news media. His departure time from O'Hare Airport was kept secret. At his hotel in Kansas City, while newsmen waited at the front entrance, he secretly entered by a rear door. He then went immediately to his suite of rooms which was inaccessible to everyone except members of his entourage. Reporters were not even told the whereabouts of his rooms. Moreover, on the first night in Kansas City, Daley and a group of ten Chicagoans, including his bodyguards, attended a private dinner in the Crown Royal Hotel. Newsmen were not told about the event.

The following morning he left his hotel with Milwaukee Mayor Henry Maier to attend a news conference in a downtown hotel. There was no advance word to reporters. At the news conference Daley was the center of attention. He then returned to the Sheraton Hotel, where he was staying, for a meeting of the Illinois delegation. After being elected its chairman, he traveled to the convention hall where, at about 8:00 p.m., he delivered a short talk calling for support of Democratic moves in Congress to provide emergency public employment. It was his first speech to the national party since 1968 in Chicago.

During the mini-convention sessions on Saturday, he was widely credited with playing a major role in bringing an appearance of harmony to the party by concurring with the proposed requirement that there be affirmative action programs in all states to bring about political participation by minorities and women. The man who had been barred from the Miami convention two years before, had, of necessity, come into his party's current mainstream.

Two days before his departure for Kansas City, two delegations of citizens, encouraged by him, came to his office at City Hall to urge him to run for re-election. The press was speculating that he would make his announcement on the following Monday, the day after his scheduled return from Kansas City.

The day before we left for the mini-convention, I spoke with him at length in his office. He said he had made up his mind about running again. He had the blood pressure problem all over—just like he had before the stroke. Moreover, he said, he had been unable to sleep. His wife did not want him to run. She had wanted him to retire three months previously instead of returning to City Hall from Grand Beach after Labor Day. His family, he said, had left the decision to him, but his doctors were opposed to another campaign. They did not think he could take the strain.

"I'm being torn both ways," he said. "Some people have made very persuasive arguments about why I should run. But when I was a younger man, I was determined that I would not overstay my term. I never wanted anyone to say: 'Why doesn't that old SOB get out of there?' "

Now, he said, was a good time to leave. He could "leave them laughing." He chuckled because all the predictions were that he would run again, but now he could fool them all by not running.

I mentioned how both of us had admired Truman so much because he had been able to walk away from it all. The Mayor quoted Disraeli as having said something to the effect that it took real courage to walk away when you were up at the top. I said the important thing was his personal happiness. Would he be happy after April 1 if he were not Mayor? "Happiness is a frame of mind," the Mayor replied, "a state of mind." He and Mrs. Daley would travel but he would not be "completely retired." He would still remain as chairman of the Democratic Party of Cook County. He would help the candidates and the party.

He stated that he had offered to step down as Mayor in 1967 and that he had told his colleagues then that the party should always be open to younger men. (There was no mention of women.) He said he repeated this in 1971. Neither time, he maintained, was he "trying to play for a draft. I was simply offering to step down if the party felt a younger man was available to take the spot."

"Now, more than ever," he continued, "age should defer to youth." He said he almost came right out and announced this on election night the month before when he spoke publicly about passing the torch to the young.

"You know," he went on, "I was really never interested in power. They always talk about how Tom Keane wanted money and I wanted power. I never had any desire to have power—and I never made any money out of all this. In fact, if I went into retirement, it would happen without having made any money."

He said he was very grateful that he was not being shoved out. I told him that John Waner, his 1967 Republican opponent, had telephoned earlier in the day to state that, if the Mayor wanted it, he could have the Republican nomination as well as the Democratic.

Daley then asked me how I thought the announcement of his decision—either way—should be made the following Monday. I told him I thought it should take place at the luncheon scheduled for the Cook County Democratic Central Committee. "No," he said, with a chuckle, "we'll have the lunch and then, following it, we'll have the announcement."

I tried to list the pros and cons of another campaign and another term. I said the time period before the Feb. 25, 1975, primary was short. He disagreed. "There will be three long months," he said. "What it boils down to," I said again, "is how would you feel after April 1 if you didn't run again." "No," he replied, "the question is whether I will be alive on April 1." "Now," I said, "you're giving me a little of that Irish..."

"Fatalism," he injected, completing my sentence. "That's right," he went on, "twenty years is long enough to be in any job."

He said it was now actually hard for him to come down to work, "really hard." Several times he referred to his concern about what would happen if he decided to run and then got sick before the primary or before the election or even after he was sworn in again. He said people would say he knew he wasn't well. Why didn't he step aside? Why did he insist on running?

Then, suddenly, he reversed his field and exclaimed: "I also feel that sometimes you should have the courage to run and the courage to try."

"Ultimately," I observed, "this is a very personal thing, a very personal decision." Would he be happy after April? Would he go out of his mind with boredom? He replied, using my words, that he would not go out of his mind and he would not be bored.

If that is the case, I said, then there is no reason for you to run and subject yourself to all the work and pressures. There were the problems of the Board of Education and all the other troubles which loomed ahead. Why get into all of that? He had done enough. He had done everything. He'd be going out right at the top. His party had won the election on November 5. Everyone assumed he would be a shoe-in for a sixth term. I said: "Mr. Mayor, all the arguments, all the logic, are in favor of you not running again." He looked at me and there was a twinkle in his eye. "Don't go too far on that thought," he cautioned, "because we might decide the other way and announce on Monday that we are going to run." We laughed and shook hands. That was on Wednesday, December 4. On Monday, December 9, Richard J. Daley announced his candidacy for a sixth term as Mayor of Chicago.

His decision was made only an hour or so before the scheduled noon meeting of the Democratic Central Committee. On the previous day, Sunday, as he was returning from Kansas City, walking through the terminal at O'Hare Airport, he told me to prepare two statements —one announcing that he would run; the other, that he would not. I went to City Hall and wrote a statement that he would run. The opposite had been written before the Kansas City trip. The two statements were delivered to the Mayor's home that evening.

On the following morning, he conferred in his office with his sons. At 10:50 a.m. he told me to add some sentences to the conclusion of the "I will" run announcement and to be ready to distribute copies at the Democratic meeting at noon in the LaSalle Hotel. He then went to his office in the hotel and summoned two dozen of the Democratic organization's top leaders. He told them he had been considering stepping down. One by one they proclaimed their fealty and urged him to seek another term.

He then went into the Committee meeting and, before scores of newsmen and party leaders, announced his intention to seek re-election. It was a day of elation and excitement in anticipation of the race that was to come.

Mayor Daley was a master politician but his political campaigning was archaic. His final campaign for the Mayor's Office in 1975 was a good example. Between the day of the announcement of his candidacy on Dec. 9, 1974, and the primary election on Feb. 25, 1975, Daley did not hold a single news conference. He is probably the only major politician in a hotly contested election in the 1970s who could take that position and get away with it. During the course of the almost three month campaign he never granted a single newspaper or television interview. He declined all invitations to take part in television and radio programs except one. The only radio interview he granted was to WIND reporter Dick Stone. The interview took place in Daley's office at City Hall. During the course of it, to show his disdain for his critics, he quoted his mother as having said, if someone did not like his actions, they should note that there was always a mistletoe hanging from his coattails. I cringed.

Daley also refused to debate his three mayoral opponents, Alderman William Singer, State Senator Richard Newhouse and former State's Attorney Edward Hanrahan. Moreover, he rarely appeared before an audience which was not "controlled." Exceptions were the State Street Council and the City Club.

During these three months there was to be a major change in Daley's disposition and manner. The Democratic organization's long-time secretary, Mary Mullen, described him as being like a "wild man." He was always that way, Mullen said, during a campaign, but this time the result was that many of his employees, for the first time, expressed openly their disdain for his conduct. They included Mullen, secretary Kay Spear, bodyguards Graney and Vince Gavin and, in a very guarded way, Deputy Mayor Ken Sain. I agreed with all of them.

Daley's campaigns were not contemporary. There was no use of computers. There were no mass mailings. There was no bank of telephone callers to get out the vote. There was no professional polling.

His television commercials were produced by an independent film-maker, Hal Wallace, and me. In previous campaigns they had been done by Wallace and Earl Bush.

Daley acted as his own campaign manager. It was very difficult during this period for anyone to get an appointment with him. He had accepted an efficiency expert's recommendation that the Mayor's private secretary, Kay Spear, be moved from her desk immediately outside the door to the Mayor's inner office and that administrative assistant Tom Donovan be made the Mayoral appointment secretary, sitting at Spear's former desk. One of Daley's long-time strengths in administration was his practice of dealing directly with all city department heads and top appointees. Now, for the first time in his 20 years as Mayor, he began to delegate some of this responsibility, admittedly in very small doses, to Donovan. Daley had never authorized his female secretary to relay orders to top people, but Donovan was given this responsibility.

For more than a year before his illness, the Mayor had been planning to make an administrative change which would put Donovan in charge of appointments as well as patronage. The designation of a male appointment secretary had been recommended to Daley in an efficiency study. It was based on the sexist premise that a male secretary would be more efficient in restricting the number and duration of Daley appointments. No change was made, however, until the mayoral campaign got underway in January of 1975. The change was to be a significant factor in Daley's administrative practices. He had always avoided allowing someone else to speak for him to his key appointees. The contrary practice was a major factor in the destruction of the Nixon presidency. For 20 years there had never been a Halderman or an Erlichman in Daley's administration. There still was never to be such a person but, with Donovan, some mayoral orders, for the first time, began to be relayed through a middleman.

There was no doubt that this change was due to the need for relieving the Mayor of some of the pressures of his office and was brought on by his illness of the previous year.

Nevertheless, he waged an amazingly vigorous campaign. His schedule during the final two weeks before the primary was crowded. On Lincoln's birthday he held a formal luncheon honoring Lady Bird Johnson, followed in the evening by a large public ceremony at McCormick Place at which she received an award. In the days that followed, he held receptions for editors and publishers of foreign language newspapers, and for executives of community newspapers. There was a breakfast given for him by black clergymen, and a reception by lawyers. He was toasted by the Hellenic Bar Association. There was a Fiesta Party organized by *Hispanos Por Daley,* and the Chicago Alcoholic Treatment Center opened a new facility which he dedicated. Also dedicated was a new indoor sports complex named in honor of his late, long-time friend, labor leader William McFetridge. There was a rally at the Aragon Ballroom on the North Side organized by a handful of ward organizations. (It drew a small crowd which reflected the decreasing influence of those organizations.) A portrait of Madame Curie was presented during a high school dedication ceremony in a Polish area on the Southwest Side. The Kiwanis Club of the Roseland neighborhood was advised of his efforts to reclaim abandoned housing. Park field houses were dedicated. "For Chicago," the group organized by Lieutenant Governor Neil Hartigan and young business executives and their wives, held a series of breakfasts, lunches and receptions. There were senior citizens gatherings, businessmen's luncheons, an 11th Ward rally, a Chinese for Daley reception, a Swedish Club breakfast, a meeting with the City's sanitation workers, and an elegant fashion show in the Guild Hall of the Ambassador hotel organized by Jane Byrne.

Missing from his schedule, however, were many of the after-dark rallies, especially those held by ward organizations, which had been the standard fare of all earlier campaigns. Daley was an exceptionally vigorous 72 year old candidate. His stamina exceeded that of many, but it was not as much as he exhibited previously.

At a building trades council breakfast, scores of union leaders stepped forward to pledge their support. All labor in Chicago, except for the new leader of the steel workers, backed Daley. They showed this support at a huge luncheon in Plumbers Hall and by their votes on February 25.

Daley went to a rally on the University of Illinois Chicago Circle Campus, which he had helped build, to Democratic Party rallies in the Bismarck Theater, to the Svithoid Singing Club where the humor consisted of him being impersonated, and to senior citizens luncheons in the neighborhoods.

His opponent, Alderman William Singer, was campaigning even

harder. Also in the race were Senator Richard Newhouse, the first black to run for mayor in Chicago, and Edward Hanrahan, who was becoming the Harold Stassen of Chicago politics. Hanrahan had sought to recover from his November 1972 defeat in his bid for re-election as State's Attorney by running for Congress in the western suburbs in 1974. He was defeated, however, by Congressman Henry J. Hyde. In losing, Hanrahan had continued his proclivity for bad politics. Before all the returns were in, he claimed victory in his congressional race. When asked by a television reporter whether he had received campaign contributions from the Mayor, Hanrahan replied: "Mayor who?" His headquarters' workers laughed. The Mayor, who was watching on television, did not. A short time later, when all the votes in the congressional race were counted, Hanrahan had been defeated and Daley was pleased.

From the time he was dumped by Daley at the request of party leaders in December 1971, Hanrahan had harbored a smoldering grudge against the Mayor. This grew in intensity following Hanrahan's defeat in the November 1972 State's Attorney's race and his subsequent unsuccessful bid for Congress. Now, in the winter months of early 1975, the erratic, highly emotional Hanrahan was seeking to soothe his bruised ego. He retaliated for alleged wrongs by deciding to engage in a head on political collision with Daley. Senator Newhouse made a determined effort to siphon off the Mayor's black vote, but it was to be eight more years before Chicago was to have a black mayor. Daley disliked his main opponent, William Singer, because he had accused the Mayor of being personally responsible for corruption.

Daley controlled every aspect of his campaign. He chose the location for each billboard. He refused to place ads in the metropolitan daily newspapers. His advertising went to the more than 50 community papers which, with one or two exceptions, endorsed him. He was attacked on all sides. In addition to his three opponents, there were three opposing newspapers, an unfriendly federal bureaucracy and hostile federal courts. In the midst of the campaign, for example, a U.S. District Court Judge in Washington, D.C., ordered that all federal revenue sharing funds for the city of Chicago be withheld because of alleged racial and sex discrimination in the Police Department.

In the final weeks before the election, the Mayor talked about re-reading Merle Miller's book on Truman, *Plain Speaking*. Daley said he had been keeping it by his bedside and going over it. The book pointed up, the Mayor said, the problems since Truman of politicians being too concerned about their images and not concerned about the issues. He cited Nixon and Lindsay as examples. The "issues" which Daley emphasized in the primary campaign were unemployment, inflation, assistance for senior citizens, and better public health services. He had concrete suggestions for tackling the first—construction of the Governor Walker-blocked Crosstown Expressway, for example, would provide thousands of construction jobs right away and generate thousands of new jobs in the future. He also implied that he was in a better position than his opponents to bring about federal legislation providing more public service jobs.

Regarding inflation, however, no proposal was offered as to how it could be combated. He was also vague as to what could be done on a local level regarding senior citizens and health services. The implication was that, without federal funds, little could be accomplished.

The issues, in other words, to Daley, were mainly subjects about which he felt the voters had concern. But he offered little in the way of programs to correct problems.

It was also during the days before the election that the Mayor spoke privately about the Crosstown and Governor Walker. "He's a bad man," Daley said to me. "After the election, I am going to go away and think about how to handle that whole situation."

Daley also spoke of other frustrations. Returning from a "golden diners" club in the 41st Ward on the North Side, he talked in his car about how he had tried for years to get the Board of Education to utilize the talents of senior citizens by having them speak about their life experiences to high school students. The board never cooperated. He said how important it would be to have women talk about the joy and satisfaction of being a mother or a grandmother, and how "young girls rarely heard this nowadays with all the emphasis on working women."

Then he talked about St. Ignatius High School and what a rough time some of his sons had with their teachers. He recalled an instance where one teacher described the late Congressman William Dawson "as a big crook" and how one of the Mayor's sons defended Dawson in the classroom.

On the day before the primary, Daley told me to prepare a news release stating that Democratic committeemen had chosen State Representative John Fary as their candidate to run to succeed the late Congressman John Kluczynski. The order to prepare the news release preceded by several hours the committeemen's meeting to discuss who would be their choice.

In the days immediately before the primary, the three newspapers endorsed Singer. The *Tribune* said that the Mayor had been responsible for tarnishing Chicago's reputation more than any person since Al Capone. Daley had met separately with Marshall Field, publisher of the *Sun-Times,* and the *Tribune's* executives in unsuccessful efforts to obtain their endorsements.

He had support from a surprise source, however, former Republican State's Attorney Benjamin Adamowski, the man who had been his mayoral opponent in both 1955 and 1963. Adamowski now had a son who was an attorney for Daley ally Alderman Vito Marzullo. The latter arranged for the former G.O.P. prosecutor to attend a Democratic Party meeting at the LaSalle Hotel where he announced his Daley support. Republican mayoral candidate John Hoellen described ex-Democrat Adamowski as the "old wolf who was returning to his lair to die."

Primary day was cold and snowy. Daley with his wife and son, John, voted early in the fire house at 35th Street and Lowe Avenue. The Mayor then went to 11th Ward Democratic headquarters where he was advised that his friend, Elijah Muhammad, leader of the Black Muslims, had died. After authorizing the issuance of a statement of condolence, the Mayor went to party headquarters in the LaSalle Hotel.

Shortly after the polls closed, the results began to flow to the party workers in the LaSalle on the floor below the Mayor's office. He was going to win. His office began to fill with the usual election night crowd; Urban Renewal Commissioner Lewis Hill, private appraiser Miles Burger, William Lee, Charles Swibel, Representative John Touhy, Ray Simon, and Jane Byrne, among them.

Against three opponents, all the newspapers, the national media, and much outside money, Daley had won again. He received 58 percent of the vote. He turned to me and said: "I didn't think it would be that big."

He went down to the Chicago Room on the mezzanine level to

make his victory statement before the waiting newsmen. Accompanying him were his wife and family and Jane Byrne with her daughter. They then went to his primary headquarters in the Bismarck Theater for him to deliver his victory words before campaign workers. Five weeks later, on April 1, the scene was to be repeated after the mayoral election victory. It was then that Jane Byrne and her daughter were not permitted by Mrs. Daley to accompany the family in its moment of triumph.

On the Friday following the primary election, the Mayor asked me to come to his home. Mrs. Daley greeted me at the door and escorted me to the family room. She asked how my daughter Molly was doing and said what a beautiful girl she was. "These years go by so quickly," said Mrs. Daley, "and it is so wonderful to be close to your children during this period." Daley came down the steps a short time later, extended his hand and said, "Thank you for everything you have done for me. You did a great job." He gave me a check for a thousand dollars to enjoy a Florida vacation.

The Mayor left the next day for Palm Springs, California, and his friend Harry Chaddick's resort. Upon his return, the three week campaign against Republican Alderman John Hoellen preceding the April 1st election was low-keyed. Daley won a sixth term with 78 percent of the vote, his biggest mayoral victory. He also had a City Council where 45 of the 50 aldermen were in support of his administration. He had come back from his stroke with a political triumph which demoralized his opponents.

Previously, he had scored a resounding victory in the 1971 election, overcoming the intense opposition of many newsmen following the 1968 Democratic convention and the 1969 Black Panther controversy. His opponent, however, had been Richard Friedman, a colorless Democrat turned Republican, and the city administration was relatively free of public awareness of corruption. The Police Department had yet to come under federal attacks for corruption and brutality.

By 1975, however, much of this had changed. The newspaper editors had joined the reporters in opposition to continuation of the Daley regime, and there were three challenging candidates, each expected to chip away at part of the Mayor's traditional voting strength. Moreover, there had been an overwhelming amount of proven corruption, including the cases of Otto Kerner, Tom Keane, Paul Wigoda, Eddie

Barrett, Earl Bush, Chief Clarence Braasch, Commander Mark Thanasouras, more than 60 other police officers, additional aldermen, and others in the Daley administration. Matt Danaher had died before his indictment could be tried.

The Mayor himself had come under attack for his ownership of Elard Realty and his son's involvement in the city's insurance business. He had suffered a stroke and had been away from his office for four months. There had been difficult years as Mayor, with the Summerdale Police scandal in 1960 and the upheavals of 1968 and 1969, but these were nothing compared to the dark days of 1973 and 1974 which preceded his race for a sixth term.

But he was still the champion.

In July, the Mayor traveled to Boston for the U.S. Conference of Mayors. More time was spent sight-seeing and dining than attending meetings. At those he attended, however, he was not only the strongest exponent of urban America but probably the most liberal. He argued, unsuccessfully, for a resolution asking Congress to provide revenue sharing based on need. The federal money, he maintained, should be going to help children in the inner city and not to build unneeded village halls in well-to-do suburbs.

Daley arrived in Boston on Saturday, July 5. On Monday, he attended a talk by Senator Edward M. Kennedy. Then the Mayor returned to his hotel suite where I joined him for a bottle of beer. He tried unsuccessfully to persuade Mrs. Daley to accompany him to a Boston tavern called "The Last Hurrah" frequented by local politicians. The Mayor was well aware that the tavern was named after Edwin O'Connor's novel loosely based on the life of Boston's late mayor, James Michael Curley.

Curley and Daley were totally different types of Irish-American politicians—Daley had a reserved personality; Curley was gregarious —Daley was honest, Curley was not. Curley used muscle and intimidation to achieve his political goals; Daley did not. Curley was a rogue; Daley wasn't.

Chicago's Mayor, however, did not think unkindly of his former Boston counterpart. As we traveled about that city during the Conference of Mayors, Daley enjoyed pointing out the various public works improvements that had taken place in the Curley years.

There was not enough time, however, for a visit to "The Last Hurrah" before attending a luncheon where Daley was to be honored with an award from the Conference and would receive two standing ovations from his mayoral peers. Then it was time to return to Chicago for what might have been the best summer of his life.

# The Legend Grows:  *34*
# Summer and Fall of 1975

D aley's popularity was never more evident than in the summer of 1975. Yet he was pessimistic during those days about the state of the national Democratic Party. He maintained that if a convention were to be held then, it would probably renominate George McGovern. But as the summer progressed, the legend of Richard Daley continued to grow.

August 1975 was a time for hard work and a month of achievement. There also were changes in the Mayor himself. More and more he said exactly what he thought. Earlier in the year *Time* magazine had printed a Daley quote about the need for firearms control, referring to the Mayor as "blunt spoken." The opposite, of course, had been true during most of his public political discourse. He had been circumspect and guarded in his speech. But in the summer of 1975, changes were taking place. His guard was lowered. It was not that he was thinking of not running again so much as a confidence he could win without being as close-mouthed as in the past.

Some temporary changes also occurred in his relationship with the news media. Reporters began to recognize they were dealing with a legend, the likes of which they would never see again.

In the months that followed the February 25 primary, the number of petty attacks on the Mayor in the media was substantially reduced.

His journalistic opponents probably had been stunned into silence by his last mayoral election. The media had thought Singer would do better; not that they thought he would win, but they thought he would come much closer.

The year immediately following one of Daley's mayoral victories was a period of reduced warfare by his opponents. They always built up their hopes in the three years preceding these elections and usually required a 12 month period to recover from the shock of defeat.

An additional factor assisted the Mayor. That was the number of new city programs he instituted and new progressive ordinances he had the council enact. Harry Golden of the *Sun-Times* was later to describe the year following Singer's defeat as Daley's most productive.

In a 30 day period in August, newsmen watched him visit with the elderly in the Lincoln Park picnic for senior citizens, with black youths at Douglas Park, with boys and girls on the Park District fishing trip, in his congressional testimony on behalf of older workers, in an appearance before cheering conventions of Black Elks and Sons of Italy, before a friendly audience of West Side blacks at a dedication of a new police facility, with bankers at a news conference, with White Sox players at a baseball clinic, and with President Ford. Daley seemed to be everywhere, and his words were well received.

He attacked "the penny-pinching administration in Washington" which, he said, tried to "write off big city neighborhoods." He verbally went after bureaucrats on every level of government who, he said, interfere with the intent of Congress, especially regarding federal revenue sharing. He praised the Police Department for its integration policies. He explained the Lake Michigan fish were not biting because reporters were nearby. He told black audiences that black women could work together to deter crime and vandalism within the community. He told Italian-Americans he had closed the Loop theaters because of sex, crime and violent films. (This was contrary to an earlier explanation that the closings were because of fire code violations.)

He held the attention of every audience. People would rush to shake his hand upon the conclusion of his remarks. All this was observed by the local press. He said privately he did not have to do anything for a political reason because he had four more years in his term. More and more the reporters at his news conferences laughed with him and not at him. It took more than 20 years for the Mayor to achieve this degree of popularity. The legend was growing.

As fall approached, San Francisco had been shaken by police and fire strikes, New York City was on the brink of bankruptcy, and Daley was confronted with the threat of a strike by Chicago schoolteachers. The happy aura of August was about to end.

The teachers went out on strike and were brought back only after Daley's intervention and a 7-1/2 percent pay raise. Schools' Superintendent Joseph Hannon and a majority of the Board had been holding the line against what they believed were unreasonable demands by the teachers' union. In the midst of this controversy, the Board members met at the Conrad Hilton Hotel to hold a party. Daley summoned them to a hotel meeting room where he asked them to do what was necessary to bring the teachers back. Then, according to Chicago Budget Director Ed Bedore, the Mayor left the negotiating reigns in the hands of Bill Lee, president of the Chicago Federation of Labor. Lee was a good man but hardly neutral in labor disputes. Bedore was later to contend privately that the Board members went far beyond what Daley had intended as a reasonable settlement. The eventual contract was to result in a substantial educational deficit which was to plague the Mayor for months and all of Chicago for years. The press said Daley had dictated the amount of the settlement.

In October and November the Mayor sought unsuccessfully to override Governor Walker's veto of needed state educational funds. It was this veto which precipitated the entire school financial crisis. A dramatic moment in the override attempt came when the Mayor traveled to Springfield to address the Illinois General Assembly. He fell one vote short of overriding Walker's veto.

In November and December another political slate was assembled for another political campaign, with Secretary of State Michael Howlett chosen to oust Walker from the Governor's chair.

In a January 8 private talk with black committeemen, the Mayor admitted he had erred in 1972 when he backed Walker in the general election. The Mayor asked, however, how he was to know Walker would never attempt to reconcile their differences.

In the weeks before the March 16 primary, the Mayor called in former State Senator Bernard Neistein and told him that Iola McGowan, a protege of Jane Byrne, was to be the organization's candidate to succeed Neistein as committeeman of the all-black 29th Ward. Neistein, who was voluntarily stepping down from the post, agreed but later reversed himself when McGowan let it be known she intended, if elected, to fire all the ward's white precinct captains. Neistein felt an obligation to protect the captains. He withdrew his support for McGowan and entered his own candidate, Lester Flowers.

The lines were drawn. The Mayor, in support of Jane Byrne and Iola McGowan, was to pull out all the stops in an effort to crunch Neistein and his partially-Jewish, partially-black 29th Ward Organization. One day during the campaign, I was having coffee with Neistein in a restaurant across from City Hall when Senator Richard M. Daley walked by. The following day, in his limousine, the Mayor brought up Neistein's name. Daley and I had been talking about former Judge Edward J. Egan's primary campaign for State's Attorney when the Mayor suddenly warned me about the dangers of "the Heebs getting their hooks in you." Once this happens, he cautioned me, these Jewish politicians never relent in their pressures. It was his way of letting me know that I had been seen with Neistein who was not currently acceptable to the Mayor.

The stakes in the March 16 primary were high, among the highest in Daley's 23 years as party leader. A defeat for Howlett would be a great personal defeat for the Mayor. A victory would mean the removal of Walker as an obstacle for state programs benefiting Chicago and the end of the threat to the Mayor's dominant position in the Illinois Democratic Party.

Shortly after the returns began coming into the LaSalle Hotel on the night of the primary, it was apparent that Howlett was achieving such a victory margin in Chicago and Cook County that he would be unbeatable when the complete statewide results were in. Meanwhile, Daley's congressional candidate, Erwin France, was being overwhelmed by Congressman Ralph Metcalfe but the Mayor was later to describe that as "only a small ball game" when compared with the governor's race. Bernard Neistein's candidate defeated Jane Byrne's, and the Mayor's two handpicked choices for the Illinois Supreme Court lost. All this was obscured to a large degree, however, by the significance of Dan Walker's defeat. The Mayor had made one of the major gambles of his career and won. Even if Howlett were to lose in the

fall, it was unlikely the Mayor would ever again face such a total ob-
structionist opponent as Walker.

Daley was elated at the results. The next matter on the agenda was
the Democratic Convention in New York City in July and the nomination of a presidential candidate.

# Daley vs. the Media— 35
# Round 3

*"You've got to pay to get into bingo.*
*Everybody knows that."*

In Daley's early years as Mayor, local television news was
largely non-aggressive, with announcers (they were not
even called news anchors at the time) reading the news,
and a few reporters and crews out on the streets getting it. Then came
the Summerdale Police scandal in 1960 and television news began covering City Hall much more frequently.

Daley's press conferences were sit-down affairs in those days, with
the Mayor seated at a conference table across from the print reporters
regularly assigned to City Hall and an occasional visiting television or
radio news reporter.

This sit-down arrangement came to an end one day, however, after Daley started to get up from his chair and Ray McCarthy of the
*American* cried out: "Sit down, we're not through with you." Daley
saw to it that there would never be a repeat of that kind of incident. At
all future press conferences the Mayor would stand behind a lectern.
He would not be told again by some reporter to sit down and he could
exit swiftly from the conference room, especially when reporters began
to probe too hard on a sensitive issue.

The increased television coverage brought about by the police
scandal initially had Daley on the defensive when he appeared on the
evening news programs. Moreover, before the decade was to end, there

would be events in Chicago which would cause him to be viewed by a sizable segment of the population as a national villain because of what viewers saw on television. Nevertheless, television played a positive role in Daley's string of electoral successes throughout the 1960s and 1970s.

To some degree, politicians have always been at the mercy of the newspapers. But in Chicago, the impact of the local press had been minor for decades—certainly during the elections which sent Democrats to City Hall from 1931 on. Bad press accumulates though, and, prior to Daley, no mayor had ever been elected to more than three four year terms. Daley won in spite of the press in 1955 and with it in 1959. By April of 1963 stories about police and court corruption, however, were beginning to take a political toll. Daley defeated his opponent that year by a relatively close margin for a Chicago mayoral vote. The Mayor then went on to win elections in 1967, 1971 and 1975. Many factors were at work in these victories, but television was essential. If all that the voters had known about Daley was what they read in the newspapers during at least two of those elections, he might not have been as popular as he was. As it was, Chicagoans saw him on television almost every night of the week, and a substantial majority of them liked him. He was a father figure. He was strong. He had a great smile and infectious laugh. Among his immediate successors, only Harold Washington could do as well in front of the cameras.

An example of Daley's television style came while one of his strongest foes, Dan Walker, was seeking re-election as governor. Walker, in the hotly contested primary race, had been barred from a neighborhood bingo game while campaigning. The next morning, at his mayoral press conference, Daley feigned amazement that Walker would seek to campaign in a bingo hall without paying. "He doesn't know the rules of bingo," Daley solemnly told his television press conference. "You gotta pay to get into bingo. Everybody knows that."

During Daley's later years in office, his fellow politicians and the political job holders who continually curried the Mayor's favor never understood how essential television news was to his career. The most recurring example of their failure to appreciate television revolved around coverage of the City Council meetings.

Of the 50 aldermen, there were never more than four or five who would or could articulate opposition to Daley. The most effective of these was Alderman Leon Despres, a liberal attorney who long represented the ward in which the University of Chicago is located. Television reporters loved Despres, and Despres loved to needle Daley. The most commonly remembered Council film footage of the Daley years shows the Mayor, as presiding officer, repeatedly pounding the gavel in an unsuccessful effort to silence Despres by ruling him out of order or signaling a nearby technician to turn off the alderman's floor microphone. As this was happening, the Mayor's voice would grow louder and his face would become flushed and the anchormen on that night's news programs would routinely describe him as the "red-faced Mayor Daley."

This did not go well with his highest ranking political admirers. Consequently, they thought the television cameras should be barred from the Council Chamber and continuously urged Daley to take such action. These would-be advisors did not have the slightest idea how detrimental this would have been to the Mayor's effectiveness. Putting aside the fact that any such ban on freedom of press coverage of a public assembly would be swiftly overruled in court and that Daley would be justifiably viewed as an autocratic opponent of free speech, restrictions on television would have prevented the voters from enjoying and admiring the Mayor in the very personal way television makes possible. Television gave Chicago pure Daley.

He never spoke with me or anyone else about the value of television to his career. I do not believe he would have given it proper credit for his successes. But as a master politician, he certainly was at least subconsciously aware of the medium's value for conveying his message directly to the voters.

Despite his awareness that television was essential for communicating with the electorate, he never allowed it or any part of the news industry to venture into his private life and that of his family. After he was first elected Mayor in 1955, there was a memorable photo showing his family and him having breakfast in their home. In the years that immediately followed, however, there were only two or three newsmen who ever entered his house and, from 1960 on, there were none. They also were not permitted to ride with him in his city limousine and he did not meet with them away from his office at City Hall. Moreover, unlike the generations of politicians who have been shaped by the television age, he never physically went to the media. He did not go to television stations for participation in local news programs. From the very beginning, because of his pre-mayoral experience in Springfield, he could resist pressures from the media. Press conferences were fine. They were part of the job but additional pre-arranged contacts were not needed in his opinion. Then came 1968 and he was even tougher in resisting media demands. Despite this, or, perhaps to some degree because of it, his legend grew.

No politician since Daley, locally or nationally, has dared to be so resistant to the media. Nor should they be. It is in the public's interest and that of the politicians to show far greater flexibility. The art of the politician demands an attitude of continuous openness to the media and an absence of any display of hard feelings for past media injustices.

Daley understood how to use the media to communicate with his constituents. It is unlikely that any American politician held more press conferences than he. His 21 year tenure as mayor contributed to this. But so did the frequency with which he met with the press throughout most of his career. When I covered City Hall as a reporter, he held press conferences two or three times a week. After the 1968 Convention, the number tapered off. Nevertheless, there was at least one weekly conference during most of his remaining eight years in office.

Added to this, of course, were the countless contacts with the media as he left his home in the morning, arrived at City Hall, attended outside meetings and luncheons, and engaged in thousands of political activities. Daley was available to the media. But from the media's view, he was not available enough.

The media business has an insatiable appetite for newsmakers and, for more than two decades, everything Daley did and said made news in the city and, from 1968 on, in the country. To this day, the television networks and major newspapers across the country have on their staffs newsmen and newswomen who say that covering Daley at some point in their careers was the most interesting assignment they ever had. They may now occupy more visible or more influential news jobs in New York and Washington, but their days with the colorful and controversial mayor of Chicago continue to be their most memorable. The Daley news alumni include Carole Simpson and Chris Wallace of ABC, Bill Plante, Jack Smith and Bob Faw of CBS, John Palmer, Bob

Jamieson and John Dancy of NBC, and columnist Nicholas von Hoffman.

The media's demands on politicians for time grows each year. At the 1968 Democratic Convention, there were 6,000 news personnel. Twenty years later, the number covering the Republican Convention in New Orleans had jumped to 13,000. Each reporter covering Daley had one basic assignment each day—get some news about the Mayor. Meanwhile, the Mayor each day had dozens of governmental and political responsibilities to fulfill. The individual reporters at City Hall usually thought in terms of their own narrow interests. They did not think about the sizable number of reporters not assigned specifically to City Hall who also sought each day to obtain news about Daley. These included the representatives of at least four television stations, five daily newspapers, a half-dozen radio stations, three wire services and at least a dozen feature writers and representatives of miscellaneous news organizations. Each had questions, real or contrived, to ask. And that was on a quiet day.

When a heavy story broke—like Daley endorsing Carter for president—the media coverage would swell to include the three television networks, the Chicago bureaus of four out-of-town newspapers, correspondents for the news magazines, and dozens of additional journalists from the Chicago area and across the country.

In the aftermath of Woodward and Bernstein and a generation of advocacy journalists, news personnel want to leave a press conference with some negative story about someone. A person with a news background who becomes a politician's press secretary has a handicap in all this. Someone becomes a reporter because he views the job as an important public service, even an idealistic one. In my case, I never looked upon the role of a reporter covering government as being adversarial. I was there to be objective, to ferret out wrongdoing to be sure, but not to start with the assumption that all politicians are crooks. I viewed both government and the news business as two ways of serving the public interest. As Daley's press secretary, I found this view to be almost universally rejected by people in the news business. The most common question asked of me by reporters was "What's it like to be on the other side?" I never thought working for elected representatives of the people was being on the other side. I thought we were all on the same side, trying to work for the public interest. Like the reporters, Daley saw the politician-press relationship as a continuing clash. Unlike me, he never had any starry-eyed view of the media. Because I viewed the journalistic profession as one having high standards, I kept assuming, I guess foolishly, that most news people got up in the morning without the overpowering desire to do in Daley.

Gradually it dawned on me that I was mistaken.

One of the reasons a man like President Carter's press secretary, Jody Powell, was so good at his job was that he did not have the intrusive baggage of ever having been a newsman. He did not have to combat any personal idealistic view of the news business.

Daley's view of the media was capsulized in one incident. During the summer of 1965, an official of the U.S. Department of Health, Education and Welfare announced that $30 million in federal funds earmarked for the Chicago public schools was being withheld because of alleged segregation practices. City Hall reporters immediately sought, and the mayor provided, a news conference on the subject. At one point during the reporters' questioning, Dick Brasie of Westinghouse Broadcasting said to Daley, "You're a great friend of LBJ. Why don't you just call the White House and ask him to restore the money?" Said Daley: "Who are you to tell me what to do? You're nothing but a reporter."

Daley's style of press relations was dated for everyone except Daley. If he came on the scene today, he would have to make many changes in dealing with the press. He would have to make judgments as to when cameras might enter his home, when reporters might ride in his car, when he should go to television stations to answer questions on live news programs. He might still think, "You're nothing but a reporter," but this time around he should not say it.

# Right by the Door                    *36*

D aley's indifference to even the giants of the news media was best demonstrated on a single day early in 1976 during the presidential primary season. Within a three hour period, I received telephone calls from three journalists stating that they would fly to Chicago anytime if only they could interview the Mayor regarding whom he intended to support for the presidential nomination. The journalists were Harry Reasoner, James Reston and Theodore H. White, Jr.

When I relayed their requests to the Mayor, he rejected all three. He was especially down on Teddy White. "He lied about me, Frank," Daley said. The Mayor was referring to *The Making of the President, 1960* in which White wrote that, during the Democratic Convention in Los Angeles, the Mayor, hearing that Eleanor Roosevelt wanted to talk with him in a last-ditch effort to block the nomination of John F. Kennedy in favor of Adlai E. Stevenson, insisted that she walk across the convention floor to meet with him. "I never insisted on anything like that," Daley said, "I admired FDR. I would never have been rude to Mrs. Roosevelt. Teddy White lied."

One of Daley's weaknesses was that he was often influenced by rumors and gossip. During his era, the careers of many Chicagoans were greatly harmed by his vulnerability on this subject. On one occasion, for example, I told him that Alderman Robert J. O'Rourke, a Republican, had died earlier in the day from a heart attack. O'Rourke was one of the most decent people I knew in government. He was a bachelor, a man who engaged in athletic activities and took good care of himself. The Mayor, when he heard the news of O'Rourke's death, lifted his right arm as if he were about to take a drink. "Too much of this, too much of this," Daley said. As far as I knew, O'Rourke was a teetotaler. Someone apparently had given the Mayor erroneous information.

The Mayor also separated himself from colleagues who got in trouble with the law. What is overlooked, of course, was that these so-called colleagues most often were rival politicians. The fact that Daley supported them politically did not necessarily mean he liked them. An example of this was the way Daley was totally unsympathetic to the fate which befell Federal Judge Otto Kerner. When the former governor was on his way to prison, Daley told me that he, too, had been offered "the same racetrack stock deal" that Kerner accepted but that he, the Mayor, had turned it down. He had no patience for Kerner and his troubles with the federal government.

Another prominent person who was surprisingly rebuffed by the Mayor was the widow of the man he usually described as "our late, beloved, martyred President," John F. Kennedy. Three weeks before the Mayor's death, Jacqueline Kennedy telephoned him at City Hall. She was an editor for Viking Press in New York. The purpose of her call, she told the mayoral assistant, was to arrange an appointment with him for Eugene C. Kennedy who was writing a biography about the Mayor. Daley refused to take the telephone call. Showing how strong was his dislike for even the best intentioned of writers and editors, Daley snapped: "She's just trying to make money off of me. She's just trying to use me."

Throughout the late 1960s and early 1970s, Jesse Jackson was a formidable political foe of the Mayor. Daley respected him for his skill but disliked his objectives. Their rivalry reached its peak on that summer night in 1972 in Miami at the Convention when the delegates voted to seat the unelected group headed by Jackson and Alderman William Singer. Jackson dominated the television screens on that occasion, calling out repeatedly to his followers, "What time is it?" to which they replied in unison, "Nation time." Daley was not impressed.

The Jackson he knew was best exemplified during the hearings prior to the Convention before the Democratic Credentials Committee about which Chicagoans should be seated as delegates. It was disclosed by Jackson's own testimony that he had not been a registered voter for the 1968 Presidential election. Moreover, that year, he had endorsed a Republican candidate for governor of Illinois. In 1966, he endorsed the Republican candidate for the U.S. Senate and, in 1971, he backed the Republican candidate for Mayor of Chicago.

Alderman Edward Burke, questioning Jackson before the Credentials Committee, asked: "Can you tell us why you didn't vote in the election for the President of the United States in 1968?" Jackson replied: "I don't recall."

Daley had a facility for dismissing people. When reporters called me to see how the Mayor felt about Sargent Shriver's longing for the presidential nomination in 1976, I relayed the information to the Mayor. Daley said, "I told Shriver: 'No one wants you.'"

On the day that Daley was going to remove James B. Conlisk, Jr., as superintendent of the Chicago Police, he was reminiscing on how he had appointed Conlisk to the job in the first place. "I'll never understand it," Daley said. And he named a political ally who had told him that Conlisk was the bravest man he had ever seen in combat during World War II. I had written Conlisk's bio on many occasions. His military service was on the ground with the Air Force in England. Apparently, one of the reasons for Daley appointing him as police superintendent was based on misinformation.

When Police Superintendent James M. Rochford ordered his high command to take polygraph examinations to determine whether any had ties with the crime syndicate, the Mayor noted to me that Rochford had not consulted with him prior to the order. The newspapers had been running stories quoting Rochford as stating that it was he, not Daley, who was in charge of the Police Department. Said Daley to me: "Do you think he's starting to believe all that shit?"

After I had been working for the Mayor for a long period of time, I went in to ask him if I might take a week's vacation. I planned to go to Southwest Michigan with my wife and children. The Mayor said that I could and called in his secretary, Kay Spear, and directed her to draw up a check for me from one of the Democratic Party funds in the amount of $250. After she had done so and presented it to him, he handed it to me saying that I should use it to take my wife and children out to dinner. Then he proceeded to name the places from which I might choose. He said there was Skip's Other Place on the Red Arrow Highway or Skip's original place not too far away. There was Hymie and Maxine's in downtown Michigan City, The Red Lantern Inn in Beverly Shores, and Tosi's in Stevensville. He went on and on. He was a walking, talking glossary of Berrien County, Michigan restaurants. I thanked the Mayor for the check and his suggestions and shortly thereafter took my one week vacation.

Upon its conclusion, I returned to City Hall to find that the Reverend Jesse Jackson was conducting a demonstration in the fifth floor lobby at City Hall outside the Mayor's office. As I entered his office, I was aware of the demonstration and all of the problems the Mayor was facing, especially those of the Board of Education, but I knew that his first words would pertain to my vacation and whether I had followed his suggestion that I take my wife and family out to dinner. So I brought it up first. "I want to thank you very much, Mr. Mayor, for making possible the very nice dinner that my wife and children and I enjoyed the other night," I said. "Where did you go," the Mayor enquired. Now, the fact was that I had gone for six days without remembering the $250 check and the Mayor's dinner suggestion. On the final night of my vacation, I remembered and took my family out to dinner. But the easiest place to go was a nearby roadside inn called the "Blue Chip Lounge," where the dinner cost $16.50 for a party of five. I thereupon pocketed the remaining amount of the check. All this flashed through my mind when the Mayor asked his question. I knew he would think less of me if he heard that I had taken my family to such a relatively non-grandiose place for their meal so I decided to tell him that we had gone somewhere that he would approve. "I took them to Tosi's," I said.

"What night did you go," the Mayor asked. Now I could sense trouble approaching in the distance. I immediately decided to pick a night that I did not think he would be cruising about Southwest Michigan. "Wednesday," I said. "What time did you get there?" he asked. "About six o'clock," I replied, thinking that was too early for the Mayor to arrive for dinner.

I was sitting alongside the Mayor at his desk and with this answer he began to edge his chair a little closer to mine. "Where did you sit," he asked. I knew I had to pick a place that they were unlikely to have seated him so I said, "By the kitchen door."

"Didn't you see me?" he asked, drawing even closer. "No," I said. "If I had seen you I would have said 'hello'."

All the while Daley was asking these questions, he was concentrating on my face. I could tell he was wondering, "Why in the hell is Sullivan lying about something so unimportant as where he took his family for dinner?" Daley might also have been thinking, "I have sat here for almost 20 years lying to other men when I thought it was necessary. I never thought Sullivan had the guts to do the same thing." Suddenly, I sensed there was a touch of admiration in Daley's eyes.

The exchange continued. "Maybe you were there on Tuesday," he said, thinking that I might jump at the chance to switch dates. "No," I replied, "I know it was Wednesday." Then I was sure he was about to say: "Don't you remember when Mrs. Daley fainted in the baked Alaska and the fire broke out in the kitchen and all the firemen came running through the restaurant with hoses."

But, quickly, to change the subject before this happened, I told him that the Reverend Jackson was out in the corridor with demonstrators and asked what the Mayor would like to have me do about it. He responded and the subject of restauranting was dropped.

On the way out of his office, I asked one of his bodyguards what the Mayor had been doing the previous Wednesday night. "He and Mrs. Daley and another couple went to Tosi's in Stevensville for dinner," the bodyguard said. "What time did they get there," I asked. "About six o'clock," he replied.

And, my final question: "Where were they seated?" Said the bodyguard, "Right by the front door."

# Forgotten

*37*

*"He was a senior citizen being asked to take part in a press conference with the presidential nominee's mother."*

Jimmy Carter obtained the Democratic Party's presidential nomination without the Mayor's help. Daley's absence from the ranks of Carter's early supporters was not surprising. Few were in them. Carter had come to City Hall in 1975 to pay his respects and had remained in close telephone contact with Daley. As a rural, Southern, Protestant, non-office-holding candidate, however, Carter held little appeal to the Cook County Democratic organization.

Daley began making hints about Carter's acceptability in the spring of 1976 by stating that the party should not be expecting a perfect candidate. He cited Harry Truman as an example of a man who, in the presidential office, grew beyond the expectations of most of his fellow citizens, and he implied that the man chosen as the 1976 candidate would do the same.

Carter went all the way into June winning primary victories without Daley's support, even gaining a substantial number of delegates in the March 16th Illinois primary. Daley became convinced at the beginning of June that Carter was going to be the man. The timing of the mayoral announcement of support was an example of his political astuteness.

At a June 8th press conference, Daley stated, in a reference to Senator Hubert Humphrey, that anyone who had not entered the primaries should not be considered for the nomination, and that Carter, if he won in Ohio on the following day, had the nomination assured. That night Walter Cronkite reported Daley's comments. Humphrey's hopes of forming a stop-Carter coalition were doomed. One long-time admirer of both Humphrey and the Mayor, James A. Farley, immediately sent Daley a telegram accusing him of having "stabbed" Humphrey in the back. It was, perhaps, the former national chairman's last act. He was found dead of a heart attack in his apartment in New York the next morning, minutes before his telegram arrived at Chicago's City Hall.

The day after Carter won the Ohio primary, Daley again displayed good timing. As he was about to enter his office at 9:00 a.m., he was greeted by newsmen who questioned him about the Ohio results. After briefly responding, he started to walk away and, in reply to one more question, said he was going to vote at the New York convention for Carter. Newsmen showed disbelief at what they had heard. In contrast with his decades-old practice of remaining silent about his intentions before a national convention, Daley, more than a month before the Democrats convened in Madison Square Garden, had publicly announced his support for a candidate.

The news of Daley's decision preceded announcements of Carter support that were to come later that day from Governor Wallace and Senator Jackson. Before the day ended, Senator Humphrey made it final. He would not seek the nomination.

It was the final rush to the bandwagon, and the leader of the final rushers was Daley. He had urged all candidates to enter the primaries. He had waited and watched. It would have been unreasonable to have expected him as a big city leader to have been an early supporter of Carter. It was a tribute to the Mayor's political sense, however, that when the moment came he was convinced of Carter's national appeal and deservedness of the nomination, Daley moved quickly.

On July 1, he hosted a highly successful fundraising reception for Carter at the Blackstone Hotel preceding a dinner for the Illinois gubernatorial candidate, Michael Howlett. During the previous week, Daley had met briefly with Carter in Carter's hotel room in Milwaukee during the annual U.S. Conference of Mayors. At the July 1 reception, Carter told of how he had telephoned the Mayor on the morning following the Ohio primary and asked if he could relay any message to the press. Daley replied that the newsmen could be told the Mayor was going to vote for him at the convention, that he was going to ask all Illinois delegates to do the same, that he would do everything in his power to elect him, and he would go all out to help him to have a successful presidency. Is that all right, Carter quoted the Mayor as asking, and the candidate replied: "Yes, sir."

Daley's role in the primaries had been appropriate, considering his position as the last of the big city bosses. Carter was appreciative. But in New York, it was obvious that history was passing Daley by. The national media gave him attention but more as a curiosity from the past than as a mover of future events. The new powers of the Democratic Party were men whose ability to put together a political rally or organize a ward was questionable. Television attention was riveted on men of rhetoric rather than on those of organizational abilities, men who knew the first names of the Washington press corps, men like Senators Mondale, Muskie, Humphrey, Stevenson, and Church. The days of Governor David Lawrence of Pennsylvania, Carmine DeSapio of Tammany Hall, Governor Michael DiSalle of Ohio, and Speaker John McCormack of Massachusetts, along with political operators like Sam Rayburn and Lyndon Johnson, were over. So, too, was the day of Richard Daley as a power of the national scene.

Bob Greene, a newspaper columnist then with the *Chicago Sun-Times,* wrote an article in 1976 that gained wide circulation and also a good deal of praise. It was about Daley's triumphant return to the Democratic Convention.

Greene told how, on the convention floor, Daley was a prominent celebrity. Person after person, delegate after delegate, the reporter noted, made the long walk across the convention floor to shake the Mayor's hand. It was in stark contrast, Greene noted, to the 1968 convention and the emotions that had been engendered in Chicago, and the 1972 convention at which Daley was never even seated. But now it was 1976 and Richard J. Daley was back where he belonged, Greene said. He was once again the center of attention.

Greene meant well by the column and he also was accurately reporting what he saw on the convention floor. But what he was observing was misleading. The true story was much different—the truth was that Richard Daley's return to the 1976 Democratic Convention in New York City was a sad, lonely, even humbling experience.

The facts were that Mayor Daley and Mrs. Daley arrived in New York, went to their suite in the Waldorf Towers and, from the time of their arrival to the time of their departure several days later, not one major figure of the national Democratic Party came to see Daley. In fact, the only politician of note who made the trip to the Mayor's suite was Michael Howlett, the Democratic candidate for Governor of Illinois that year. The truth is that time and the politics of the Democratic Party had moved beyond Richard J. Daley. Politics had changed. The old guard was gone. Now it was a media spectacle with other types playing the role of king-maker. What Bob Greene saw were the rank and file, who, of course, were still there, greeting the Mayor with genuine affection and respect, but those acts were ultimately meaningless. Greene saw triumph where in reality there was only an anachronism.

Daley in the Waldorf Towers in 1976 was a lonely man. On the Sunday afternoon preceding the opening of the convention, the Illinois delegation met. He had tried earnestly to get the front-runner, Jimmy Carter, to come and appear before the Illinois delegation. Coming back from a meeting, Daley said to the Reverend Jim Wall, who was the Carter leader in Illinois, "I wish you would help try to get Carter to come." Daley told Wall that he (Wall) had much more influence with Carter. Wall thought the Mayor was joking. He could not believe that the legend, Richard J. Daley, could not personally get through to Jimmy Carter. But he couldn't, and Wall didn't, and Jimmy Carter did not appear before the Illinois delegation.

At the convention, Daley rarely left his suite in the Waldorf; he did not even take out to dinner his secretaries and staff who had come to New York with him. There was no camaraderie, no pleasantries were exchanged. He remained aloof and isolated with his wife; there were only visits from his sons who were ensconced in another suite across the hall. Daley was extended one small courtesy, however. Party Chairman Bob Strauss asked him if he would be one of the people to speak on behalf of the Democratic platform pertaining to the cities of America. Daley never liked being part of a crowd scene, and dozens of speakers had been asked to speak on behalf of the Democratic platform. At the last moment the Mayor had misgivings and wanted to back out and send Mike Howlett in his place. But he went through with it and delivered what one magazine later described as a lackluster speech. I had written it, and I was wrong. The convention staff had said that Daley should address himself to the actual planks in the platform and speak with reference to them. That is what I wrote, and that is what the Mayor did.

In retrospect, I wish that I had written what would have amounted to a short liberal plea on behalf of the cities which could have ultimately served as Daley's epitaph. (He was to die four months later.)

And it got worse. On the night of the presidential acceptance speech when Jimmy Carter went to Madison Square Garden, it was publicized that the presidential nominee was expected to walk near the Illinois delegation and shake hands with its chairman. When the moment actually came, Carter avoided going near the Illinois delegation and turned and walked toward the rostrum. It was a calculated gesture, just as everything Carter had done prior to that, to show that *he* was the wave of the future and was not to be associated with the Democratic bosses of the past.

The next morning a press conference had been scheduled at the Americana Hotel. The Mayor was invited by the presidential nominee's staff to hold a joint press conference with the president's mother, Lillian Carter. Daley was actually about to leave his suite in the Waldorf when it dawned on him what was happening. He was not being asked to take part in a press conference pertaining to whom would be vice president, or to join with the presidential nominee or advise him, or to have any role with the leaders of the Party. It was something very different. He was a senior citizen—a 74 year old man—being asked to take part in a press conference with the presidential nominee's mother. It was an extraordinary comedown for the man who had for so long been called king-maker. Daley changed his mind just as he was about to leave. He told one of his sons to call the Carter people and tell them he was going to be unable to join Miss Lillian. It was suddenly clear that the New York media, the networks media, and the people surrounding Jimmy Carter all viewed Richard J. Daley as something out of the distant past.

There really had been only one glorious convention for Daley, and that was Los Angeles in 1960—the convention that nominated John F. Kennedy as the Democratic candidate for president. Even that had not been solely Daley's show because he had assistance from other Democratic leaders such as Gov. David Lawrence of Pennsylvania. There were, however, many satisfying convention moments. One was in Chicago in 1952 when Daley's former boss, Gov. Adlai Stevenson, was nominated. Another was in 1956, again in Chicago, where Daley played a key role in the attempt to nominate Kennedy as vice president. He, of course, lost in the balloting to Estes Kefauver but it was the beginning of JFK's move toward the White House. In 1964 Daley had enjoyed the friendship of Lyndon Johnson when he was nominated for president. But 1960 was the highlight of Richard Daley's journey in national politics and prominence.

# November 1976                    *38*

*"Egan's down the drain."*

As the summer of 1976 drew to a close, polls showed
Michael Howlett trailing James Thompson for governor and the Cook County consensus was that the
Democratic State's Attorney candidate Edward Egan had not even begun his campaign. Egan's private grumblings about the Mayor's alleged failure to provide sufficient campaign funds got back to Daley
and the Mayor began lowering his enthusiasm for a defeat of the Republican incumbent. Ahead loomed another school crisis with a
school strike after Labor Day and local political defeat in November.

More and more, Nov. 2, 1976, appeared to be a highly significant
day in Chicago political history and in the life of Richard Joseph Daley. Still, in the summer of 1976 there was no open talk, only private
whisperings, that the Daley era was drawing to a close. After all, his
current term had more than two and one half years to run. But on the
morning of November 3, the day after the election, all this could be
different.

It was Daley who had urged Howlett, against his wishes, to seek
election as governor rather than a return to the office of secretary of
state. It was Daley who had slated Neil Hartigan for another term as
lieutenant governor. It was Daley who, without any consultation with
party leaders other than Assessor Thomas Tully, had selected Egan to

run for state's attorney. The defeat of the Democratic state and county tickets in November would be a Daley defeat and open the door to public talk of what, until then, had only been private conversations.

The door already was open a crack. On October 9 Edmund Kelly, one of the most aggressive ward committeemen, held a huge dinner to raise funds for himself. Alderman Edward Vrdolyak made no secret of his ambition. Assessor Tully was talking with friends about the end of Daley's power. Alderman Edward Burke, though loyal to the Mayor, was unhappy at the thought of remaining in the City Council. For more than 23 years Daley had run the Cook County organization. There was still no sign he had any intention of stepping down from his party post or the Mayor's office. Local defeat on November 2, however, would encourage others to force him to reflect on such possibilities.

The campaign entered its final days.

First there were only a small number of people in the building carrying the shopping bags. Then, as the crowd began to swell, it seemed that every other person had one. Before a half hour had passed, there were thousands of people carrying them—"William G. Scott for Illinois Attorney General" shopping bags with the words "Vote Republican" printed in large letters. It was the 17th Annual Holiday Folk Fair. The event had been arranged by the Mayor. It was held on the Saturday and Sunday prior to the November 1976 election. It was supposed to benefit Democratic candidates. Yet the entire length of Chicago's three quarters of a mile Navy Pier was filled with thousands of people carrying shopping bags that said "Vote Republican."

There had been a miscalculation. The orders had gone out to city personnel and Democratic politicians that no overt politicking should take place at the fair. Apparently, however, no one thought to tell this to the Republicans. One woman stood outside Navy Pier handing out the thousands of bags. Later that day Republican gubernatorial candidate James R. Thompson would visit the fair and be engulfed by admirers. The Daley event was being used to promote his political opponents.

None of the Daley lieutenants made a move to stop the woman with the shopping bags. Handing them out was lawful, they said. In past years surely one of Daley's people would have recalled some imaginary city ordinance prohibiting the passing out of campaign literature within 500 yards of an International Folk Fair. But there also was no imaginative spirit left in the Daley people to invent such a law.

So the tidal wave came on, the wave of opposition politicians about to engulf the Daley organization. Daley knew it. Weeks before, his son, the state senator, had talked privately about the problems a Howlett gubernatorial victory could bring. The old dislike by the Daley family of Howlett and his family was clear, as was the rationalization of the impending defeat.

Senator Daley talked about an "if." What would have happened, he said to me, if during the primary Governor Walker had come to the Mayor with an offer to fund millions of dollars' worth of road maintenance work in Chicago? If he had been the governor, the Senator said, that is what he would have done. Then, Richie Daley continued, the Mayor would have been faced with a dilemma. The implication, of course, was that Daley might have switched from organization man Howlett to independent Walker in the closing days of the primary. The hypothetical was an insight as to what Richie thought his father would have done if he were Walker.

National television networks agreed that the gubernatorial race was between Thompson and Daley, and that Daley was about to suffer a calamitous defeat. The *Chicago Tribune* already spoke in terms of the political demise of the Mayor.

The news industry knew it was coming. It did not take a straw poll to convince them, but the results of the one conducted by the *Sun-Times* in mid-October made it conclusive. Thompson would win the governor's race by a million votes. Egan, the head of the county ticket, would go down in defeat.

It could have been worse. Carter could have lost the presidency and key judicial candidates also could have been defeated. Carter lost Illinois but his national victory and that of all the judges who ran as Democrats in Cook County helped a little. The defeat of Howlett alone could have been rationalized, but the addition of the Egan loss gave the media what it needed—an argument that the Daley machine was through.

Michael Kilian of the *Tribune,* during the previous week, had written what many thought: Daley was on the verge of being viewed not as a political genius but as a tired, old politician who had stayed too long.

Running against the Mayor of Chicago had been the theme of Republicans in statewide races for more than two decades. Never had the theme been carried off as well as it was by Jim Thompson. But Richard Daley had given him a helping hand. Unlike 1972 when the organization initially backed downstater Paul Simon for governor and in 1968 when Kankakee resident Samuel Shapiro was slated, the 1976 Daley-picked candidates for governor and lieutenant governor were two Irish Catholics from Chicago. In 1960, and again in 1964, Otto Kerner had been successful statewide despite his Chicago organization-backing because of his decidedly non-machine image.

Daley's choice of two Irish Catholics from Chicago to head the state ticket contained the seeds of defeat. Added to this, he was compelled by the sluggishness of the Howlett campaign to inject himself into the race, making accusations and raising issues. A final factor in the Thompson victory was the organization's need to first wage the primary battle against Governor Walker. Walker partisans found it easy to transfer their support to the anti-machine campaign of Thompson.

The election results became known shortly after the polls closed on November 2. Despite the Howlett defeat, there was still hope that much could be salvaged by the Daley organization. The key was Egan's contest for state's attorney of Cook County. In the hours before midnight there was still hope at Democratic headquarters on the fifth floor of the Bismarck Hotel that Egan's lead in the early returns would hold up. Shortly after midnight, however, the lead began to evaporate. By 1:00 a.m., the room in which the Mayor sat, usually filled at that hour following elections with well-wishers seeking to share in a victory, was strangely quiet with few in attendance. Jane Byrne was there. So were Alderman Michael Bilandic and Judge Joseph Power.

With 8 percent of the suburban precincts and only 2 percent of those in the city yet to report, Egan had a lead of only 4,000 votes. Daley knew it was not enough. Then, as the clincher, he learned that a committeeman had made a 10,000 vote error in his computations. "Egan's down the drain," the Mayor said.

Earlier that day Daley had advised me of his post-election plan. He would leave Chicago by plane the morning after the election for a vacation in Florida, not to return until the eve of his annual city budget message on November 15. Later in the day, a City News Bureau reporter told me that he had learned of the Mayor's plans to leave.

Now with Egan's defeat apparent, the Mayor whispered to me that he would not meet with the press before going home, contrary to his custom following elections, but would have me issue a written statement to the press later that morning after his departure for Florida.

I told him that newsmen already knew of his plans and that he might want to change them. I added that he should not be definite about the written statement but should consider meeting with newsmen either then or after a few hours' sleep. "You have a tradition, Mr. Mayor," I said, "of always going right in and standing up no matter which way they [the elections] go." I told him what he already knew: that newsmen would be saying, "This is the end of the Daley organization." He bristled and said, "Not with 78 percent," a reference to his mayoral victory percentage over his Republican opponent the previous year. I went on. He should give them his account of what the election was all about and what its meaning was. After all, Carter had won and so had all the judges and Michael Bakalis for superintendent of state instruction, and Alan Dixon for secretary of state, and the whole county ticket except for Ed Egan. "You're right," said Daley. A few minutes later he told me he was going down "to say hello to the working men and women of the press." He was always good in situations like that. He smiled and told the newsmen no one should ever look back. There would be better days, he said. Then he went home. About five hours later, as he left his home en route to the airport, he was met by more newsmen. Then, in the terminal, an NBC television reporter questioned him. Unlike the Mayor's other vacations, this one was public knowledge even before his plane took off. Much was changing. And Richard Daley had only 48 days to live.

# The Last Day *39*

*"...he even beats us at basketball."*

Monday, Dec. 20, 1976, was the first work day of Christmas week. It began with a breakfast that the city department heads held in honor of the Mayor, a Christmas week tradition. It was arranged by Colonel Jack Reilly, the Mayor's director of special events, who this year asked the members of the Mayor's cabinet to donate $100 each to buy a special Christmas gift for the Mayor and Mrs. Daley—round-trip airplane tickets to Ireland.

The breakfast was held in the Medill Room on the third floor of the Bismarck Hotel, a room named in honor of the founder of the *Chicago Tribune,* a man who had been a staunch Republican and a major supporter of Abraham Lincoln. The department heads were already seated when the Daleys arrived, but rose to give the Mayor and his wife a standing ovation. The Daleys took their places at the head of the table with Police Superintendent Jim Rochford, Fire Commissioner Robert Quinn, and Deputy Mayor Ken Sain.

The brief speaking program began with remarks by Sain, who talked about the deep affection which the department heads had for the Mayor and his wife. Then Reilly stated that it had been difficult to decide upon "a gift for the man who had everything." He said he hoped that the Daleys would not think the department heads wanted them to leave town, but that two tickets were awaiting them at Aer Lingus for a trip to Ireland.

The Mayor thanked the Colonel. Daley repeated his frequent theme that no man walks through life alone and that whatever success there had been for the past 21 years was due to the work of the department heads. He added that he hoped everyone would be gathered again at a similar breakfast a year from then. As he said these words, I looked at his face, and his eyes indicated he knew exactly the message he was conveying—that he was living on borrowed time since the stroke of 1974 and there was no assurance of tomorrow.

At the conclusion of his remarks, Reilly noted that in the Chicago city government there is "always a day's work for a day's pay." The Mayor and his wife then stood up, signaling that the breakfast was over. There was another standing ovation and the Mayor and Mrs. Daley walked the length of the breakfast table to shake hands with each of the department heads. They then took the elevator to the ground level and parted in front of the hotel. Mrs. Daley got into the Mayor's limousine to be driven to some stores for Christmas shopping and the Mayor walked to City Hall for his first appointment.

At 9:30 a.m., as I approached the Mayor's office, Alderman Vrdolyak and he were laughing over some joke. When Vrdolyak left, I went in to check with the Mayor about which newsmen he wanted to receive ties for Christmas. It was his custom to provide such gifts for a dozen or so reporters. I always tried to expand the list because, I believed, it was important to reach out continuously to the people in the news business. On this particular morning, I presented to the Mayor a list with two new names: Marshall Field, the owner and publisher of the *Sun-Times*, and local CBS anchorman, Walter Jacobson. Daley took a pen and drew a line through their names. The list would not be expanded. He then asked me the status of a controversy from the previous week involving a land sale to the city near O'Hare Airport. I advised him that several department heads were waiting outside his office to discuss this particular matter with him. He told me to call them in.

A number of maps and aerial photographs of the O'Hare Airport area were placed on the Mayor's desk and he proceeded to question the department heads regarding the chronology of the land transaction. The owners, who were to be paid $600,000 for the property, included John Touhy, the Illinois Democratic Party chairman. The question raised by much of the news media was whether Touhy had advance knowledge that the City needed the land when he acquired it. The Mayor asked a series of probing questions and it became obvious he was not convinced as to whether or not Touhy had advance knowledge.

One of the minority aldermen had asked to see the airport plans and wanted to be accompanied in his viewing by newsmen. The Mayor said that anyone had the right to view the plans and that the Aviation Commissioner should cooperate. As we left the room the Mayor called to me: "You'll be with him, won't you, Frank?"

"Yes, sir," I replied, and left. That was the last time I saw Mayor Daley alive.

Shortly before noon, he left his office to walk across the street to the Civic Center Plaza to view some ice sculptures which were on display. Then he was driven to the dedication of a new park gymnasium on the far South Side. En route he told one of his bodyguards, Michael Morano, to telephone Dr. Thomas Coogan to request an appointment for early that afternoon. The Mayor said that he had felt a slight pain across his chest. The appointment was arranged.

Following the dedication ceremony at the park gymnasium, Daley was told by Parks Superintendent Edmund L. Kelly that the audience which had assembled wanted the 74-year-old Mayor to try to shoot a basket. Daley suggested that Alderman Vrdolyak, who also was on hand, take a shot. "He's supposed to be the athlete," the Mayor said, tossing the ball to the alderman. Vrdolyak took a long shot and missed. The ball then went back to the Mayor who tossed it to Kelly. The superintendent aimed for the hoop and missed. Then, according to Kelly, "I'll be damned if the Mayor didn't take a shot and make it. "You know," Kelly quoted Vrdolyak as saying, "he even beats us playing basketball."

The Mayor arrived in Dr. Coogan's office at 900 N. Michigan Avenue about 1:45 p.m. after the long drive from the far South Side. Coogan directed that an electrocardiogram be taken immediately. Following this, Daley went to an examining room. At the conclusion of the examination, Coogan was concerned and recommended that the Mayor enter Northwestern Memorial Hospital that afternoon for further examination. Daley agreed.

When Coogan left the room to make the arrangements, the Mayor made a telephone call to tell his son, Michael. When the doctor returned, he found Daley lying on the floor. Coogan called for his partner, Dr. Robert Reid, and the Fire Department paramedics were immediately summoned to the scene. A call went to Northwestern Memorial Hospital's cardiac unit for assistance. Specialists quickly left the hospital to race to Coogan's office three blocks away.

It was 2:20 p.m., approximately 20 minutes after the Mayor had been stricken when I received a call from his secretary, Kay Spear. Tom Donovan got on the phone and said the Mayor had suffered a heart attack and was about the be taken to Northwestern. I left City Hall and waved down a cab on Randolph Street. When I arrived outside the hospital about a mile away, the police were clearing the way to the hospital's emergency room. I ran inside. The hospital's public relations personnel said that the emergency room's staff was prepared for the Mayor's arrival but that he was still at Coogan's office.

I ran back outside. Police Commander Paul McLaughlin assigned a police car to take me to 900 N. Michigan. The car sped around the corner to Chicago Avenue, then to Michigan Avenue, and north in the southbound lanes to Delaware Place, stopping at the side entrance to the 900 N. Michigan building. All the streets in the immediate area had been blocked off by the police in anticipation of an ambulance carrying the Mayor. Spectators had gathered on the south side of Delaware, having seen all the commotion and hearing by word of mouth that the Mayor, the man who had dominated the life of the city for almost 22 years, was inside the building and that something critical was happening.

I jumped out of the police car and, along with the officer who had driven me, ran into the building and up the stairs to the second floor and Dr. Coogan's office. Several policemen and firemen had been positioned at the top of the stairs to keep out everyone except those who were performing emergency services for the Mayor.

At the end of the complex of examining rooms and doctors' offices was bodyguard Morano. The door to one of the examining rooms was partially open and I could hear the sounds of the paramedics working frantically to revive the Mayor's heart. It was futile. He was dead. They had cut into his chest in order to save him. I never looked into that room. I never wanted to have that memory.

His doctors later were to say that he had died instantly from a massive coronary attack just as he finished talking on the phone to his son, Michael.

Dr. Coogan's receptionist asked me if I would come to the office. Tom Donovan was calling. I told him that I thought he should come as quickly as possible, that this was going to be the end. Meanwhile, members of the Mayor's family had been arriving. Quietly they were escorted into a room which adjoined the one in which the Mayor lay on the floor. Mrs. Daley was there with her daughters, Mary Carol and Ellie, Bill Daley came and John. Dr. Robert Vanecko, Mary Carol's husband, came from Northwestern Memorial Hospital. Senator Richard M. Daley arrived. So did the Mayor's daughter, Patricia.

Then Reverend Timothy Lyne, the pastor of nearby Holy Name Cathedral, came to the second floor and went directly to administer the last rites to the Mayor. From the adjoining room, the voices of Mrs. Daley and her family could be heard praying a decade of the rosary.

Time passed and the doctors and paramedics continued to try to recover a heartbeat. Tom Donovan arrived. He was accompanied by Alderman Bilandic. Just a few hours before they had been at lunch together. Donovan was later to say that their discussion at that time had centered on what would happen if Daley were to die suddenly. Now, he and Bilandic, who was to succeed the Mayor, stood a few feet from the room in which Daley had, in fact, died suddenly. They were silent. No emotion was visible. A short time later, they left.

Then, the sounds of the family members praying stopped. And Bill Daley came out from their room. He was crying. So was his brother, John. And then, the commotion—all the activity in the room where the Mayor lay came to a halt and, one by one, the doctors began to emerge, Dr. Coogan and his partner and Dr. Vanecko and the others who had come from Northwestern's cardiac unit to do what they could do. It was over. Richard J. Daley was dead.

Now the family was being asked by the doctors and the police to remain in the adjoining room while the stretcher bearing the Mayor's body, which was covered with a blanket, was wheeled to an elevator. No one spoke. The firemen and policemen rolled the stretcher onto the elevator, the gates were closed and it descended. Then the Mayor's family was escorted from their room. When the elevator came up again without the Mayor's body, the family entered. Again no words were spoken. There was only quiet sobbing.

I had been asked by Bill Daley, speaking on behalf of his family, to wait until they had departed from the building before officially announcing the Mayor's death. After the family went down in the elevator, I walked down the steps to the building's Delaware Place entrance where there was a *Tribune* reporter and an NBC camera crew. I told them it was my sad duty to report to the people of Chicago that the Mayor was dead, that he had died from an apparent heart attack, that the doctors and paramedics had tried to save his life. And I added: "Let us all pray for the soul of this good man."

Then, as I walked into the adjacent alley, called Huguelet Place, behind the the 900 N. Michigan Building, I saw that fire department ambulance 42 was still parked there and that the Mayor's family was only then emerging from the building's alley exit and entering their cars. Then the procession moved slowly north toward Walton Street, and passed a group of approximately 50 media representatives. The procession turned east, carrying the Mayor's body on the final journey to Bridgeport.

As the cars disappeared from sight, I walked towards the reporters and cameras and repeated what I had said just a few moments before about the Mayor's death. Then I was assisted by police back down the alley to a waiting police car and was driven to McKeon's Funeral Home at 37th Street and Lowe Avenue.

The Mayor's death had come one day after he and his family had participated in their home in a Mass said by his close friend, Father Gilbert Graham. During the Mass, the Mayor read aloud a selection from the Scriptures.

In the 30 months following his May 6, 1974, stroke, he had exhibited a new peacefulness in his philosophy of life. He had come close to death on that Spring day, and ever since then he had treasured life. Newsmen would ask him at press conferences if something had caused him to be annoyed, if he were angered, if he were disturbed, if he were worried about this or that situation. Daley would always reply that he was just happy to be alive and that the good Lord had given him another day. He had continued his life almost completely immersed in activity and he had continued it with his firm belief that his wife and family came ahead of everything else.

The day after his death there would be a wake attended by an estimated 25,000 persons at Nativity of Our Lord Church. The funeral would be held on the day after that, attended by the president-elect of the United States, the vice president, the brother of a former president, and a man who had once been his party's candidate for president— Jimmy Carter, Nelson Rockefeller, Teddy Kennedy and George McGovern.

Richard Joseph Daley had been a self-disciplined man. He knew that some day a December 20 would come. And he probably was as ready for it as any man or woman could ever be.

# A Look Back                                    *40*

I t never seemed right—burying him in a suburb. It would
be like burying Thomas Jefferson in downtown Detroit.
Daley symbolized the city. But that was where his
mother had been buried 30 years before his death and nine years before
anyone knew he would be mayor. His father's grave was also there.

So that is where Daley was buried on that frigid morning three
days before Christmas—in Holy Sepulchre Cemetery in Worth, a
south suburb of Chicago. The grave site is dominated by an eight foot
high stone cross in front of a stand of trees. Over his grave is a granite
slab with the prayer of St. Francis of Assisi. That was the name of the
award Mayor Alioto had given him five years before in the shadow of
the bridge in San Francisco for helping poor people, not just in Chicago but in cities all over the country.

His life was one long success story. There were dark moments to
be sure, like the convention and shoot to kill and being barred from his
party's quadrennial meeting in Miami and the scandals in which others
were involved.

But these were only political moments. In what was most important to him, he was always a success—in his love affair with Sis Daley
and his relationship with his sons and daughters—as a son, as a husband and father, and as mayor. He always knew that some day every-

thing would change. There would be no office for him on the fifth floor. Someone else would preside over the City Council. Someone else would take his place at conventions. The parades would stop. The speech-making would end and all those plans for the future would not be needed. Everything would change—with one exception. Always, even in death, he would be the Mayor.

# Index